CW01326754

V&R

Forschungen zur systematischen
und ökumenischen Theologie

Herausgegeben von
Christine Axt-Piscalar und Gunther Wenz

Band 119

Vandenhoeck & Ruprecht

Kirsten Busch Nielsen
Ulrik Nissen / Christiane Tietz (ed.)

Mysteries in the Theology of Dietrich Bonhoeffer

A Copenhagen Bonhoeffer Symposium

Vandenhoeck & Ruprecht

Bibliografische Information der Deutschen Nationalbibliothek

Die Deutsche Nationalbibliothek verzeichnet diese Publikation in der Deutschen Nationalbibliografie; detaillierte bibliografische Daten sind im Internet über http://dnb.d-nb.de abrufbar.

ISBN 978-3-525-56347-2

Gedruckt mit Hilfe der Geschwister Boehringer Ingelheim Stiftung für Geisteswissenschaften in Ingelheim am Rhein.

© 2007, Vandenhoeck & Ruprecht GmbH & Co. KG, Göttingen
Alle Rechte vorbehalten. Das Werk und seine Teile sind urheberrechtlich geschützt. Jede Verwertung in anderen als den gesetzlich zugelassenen Fällen bedarf der vorherigen schriftlichen Einwilligung des Verlages. Hinweis zu § 52a UrhG: Weder das Werk noch seine Teile dürfen ohne vorherige schriftliche Einwilligung des Verlages öffentlich zugänglich gemacht werden. Dies gilt auch bei einer entsprechenden Nutzung für Lehr- und Unterrichtszwecke.
Printed in Germany.
Druck und Bindung: ⊕ Hubert & Co., Göttingen.

Gedruckt auf alterungsbeständigem Papier.

Preface

Half way between the sixtieth anniversary of Dietrich Bonhoeffer's death on April 9, 1945, and the centenary of his birth on February 4, 1906, the University of Copenhagen hosted a symposium on the theology of Bonhoeffer.

The symposium aimed at discussing some of the issues that have been dealt with in recent investigations into Bonhoeffer's writings: *cognition* (i.e., Bonhoeffer's understanding of theology as a science, especially in the early writings), *culture* (i.e., Bonhoeffer's understanding of art, music and the humanities, as well as his critique of the culture of his time, especially in the late writings) and *religion* (i.e., Bonhoeffer's critique of religion in his time, which seems to appear throughout all his writings). In relation to each of these issues, Bonhoeffer's insights seem worth dealing with not only for the sake of understanding Bonhoeffer better, but also as part of theology's dealing with these issues as such today – addressing Christian theology in the context of science, culture and religion. In Bonhoeffer's thinking, these issues secm to be kept together by the notion of mystery, *Geheimnis,* which holds a central position in Bonhoeffer's writings from the late 1920s to 1944, as in many parts of recent theology and philosophy. The concept of mystery sheds light on central ideas in Bonhoeffer's thought in relation to epistemology, culture, and religion.

As the title of this volume *Mysteries in the Theology of Dietrich Bonhoeffer. A Copenhagen Bonhoeffer Symposium* reflects, it contains papers from the symposium, most of them in a revised form. *Andreas Pangritz* lays the ground for the following contributions with an introduction to "mystery" in the writings of Bonhoeffer. Taking as their point of departure Bonhoeffer's notion of mystery, *Christiane Tietz* and *Peter Dabrock* both investigate aspects of Bonhoeffer's epistemology. *Barry Harvey* and *Peter Manley Scott* take up different questions related to mystery and culture. And *Niels Henrik Gregersen* and *Christoph Schwöbel* discuss Bonhoeffer's understanding of mystery in relation to his understanding of revelation and religion.

As the volume focuses on several aspects of Bonhoeffer's understanding of mystery, it shows new connections between his early and late writings and between christology, ontology and ethics. It also unfolds the complexity of "mystery" in Bonhoeffer's thinking; "mystery" has different meanings and functions in different parts of Bonhoeffer's theology. Hopefully, the volume will make new investigations into Bonhoeffer's writings possible, especially concerning (a) the connections between Bonhoeffer's theology of creation and his ethics, (b) the complexity of Bonhoeffer's understanding of mystery and (c) the possible tension between Christianity's arcane and its public character.

The Copenhagen symposium was organized by a small working group (Rev. Jacob Holm, Ph.D., Ass. Prof. Ulrik Nissen, Ph.D., and Ass. Prof. Kirsten Busch Nielsen, Ph.D.), and it was made possible by grants from the Danish Research Council for the Humanities and from the University of Copenhagen, for which the organizers want to express their gratitude. The preparations for this volume were undertaken by Ulrik Nissen, whereas PD Dr. theol. Christiane Tietz and Kirsten Busch Nielsen did the final work of bringing the papers into print, assisted by Lucas Ogden (who did the language revision) and Eva Heise (who assisted in establishing the print-ready version of the manuscript). We are grateful for the financial support of the publication provided by the *Geschwister Boehringer Ingelheim Stiftung für Geisteswissenschaften in Ingelheim am Rhein* and the *International Bonhoeffer Society, German Language Section*, and for the smooth cooperation with Vandenhoeck & Ruprecht. We are very pleased that the book has been accepted to be part of the *Forschungen zur systematischen und ökumenischen Theologie* series. Last but not least, we are grateful that the contributors were willing to make their papers available for publication.

Copenhagen,   Kirsten Busch Nielsen
Aarhus and Tuebingen, June 2007   Ulrik Nissen and Christiane Tietz

Contents

The Understanding of Mystery
   in the Theology of Dietrich Bonhoeffer
     Andreas Pangritz 9

The Mysteries of Knowledge, Sin, and Shame
     Christiane Tietz 27

Responding to "Wirklichkeit"
   Reclaiming Bonhoeffer's Approach to Theological Ethics
   between Mystery and the Formation of the World
     Peter Dabrock 49

Accounting for Difference
   Dietrich Bonhoeffer's Contribution
   to a Theological Critique of Culture
     Barry Harvey 81

Postnatural Humanity?
   Bonhoeffer, Creaturely Freedom
   and the Mystery of Reconciliation in Creation
     Peter Manley Scott 111

The Mysteries of Christ and Creation
   "Center" and "Limit" in Bonhoeffer's *Creation and Fall*
   and *Christology* Lectures
     Niels Henrik Gregersen 135

"Religion" and "Religionlessness" in *Letters and Papers from Prison*
   A Perspective for Religious Pluralism?
     Christoph Schwöbel 159

Contributors and Editors 185

Andreas Pangritz

The Understanding of Mystery in the Theology of Dietrich Bonhoeffer

It is generally accepted that the notion of "mystery" plays a crucial role in Bonhoeffer's theology. "'God revealed in the flesh,' the God-man Jesus Christ, is the holy mystery which theology is appointed to guard. What a mistake to think that it is the task of theology to unravel God's mystery, to bring it down to the flat, ordinary human wisdom of experience and reason! It is the task of theology solely to preserve God's wonder as wonder, to understand, to defend, to glorify God's mystery as mystery."[1] With these words Dietrich Bonhoeffer describes in a "Circular Letter" at Christmas 1939 to the brethren of the seminary and the pastors of the Confessing Church what should be the task of Christian theology in general and of christology in particular: to praise the glory of God in the wonder of his incarnation.

In what follows I will first treat the notion of "mystery" in Bonhoeffer's theological thinking in general. In a second section I will concentrate upon the specific way recommended by Bonhoeffer to deal with the mystery, i.e. the "arcane discipline". In a final chapter I will present some comparative reflexions referring to the relationship between "mystery" and "commandment" proposed by the German-Jewish thinker Leo Baeck.

1. The notion of "mystery" in Bonhoeffer's theology

It has become customary to regard christology as the center of Bonhoeffer's thought. And indeed, the question "Who is Jesus Christ?" forms the *cantus firmus* of Bonhoeffer's theological development from the beginning to the end.[2] This question, originally being latent in the interest for the sociology of the church, becomes explicit in Bonhoeffer's academic *Christology* lectures of 1933, the year when the Nazis came to power in Germany. And still in 1944, in his *Letters and Papers from Prison*, the programmatic question, "who Christ really is, for us today", forms the starting point of Bonhoeffer's

---

1 Kelly/Nelson, Testament, 472.
2 Cf. Pangritz, Jesus Christ, 134–153.

revolutionary theological reflections. However, the christological *cantus firmus* is continuously accompanied by "worldy" counterpoints, as Bonhoeffer phrases it in a draft for his *Ethics*: "The more exclusive, the more free and open. [...] The more exclusively we recognize and confess Christ as our Lord, the more will be disclosed to us the breadth of Christ's lordship."[3]

The *Christology* lectures have been handed down to us by notes from Bonhoeffer's students. According to Eberhard Bethge these lectures form "the high point of Bonhoeffer's academic career". At the same time, they can be read as a commentary on the socio-political context in Germany: Hitler had been Chancellor for three months when Bonhoeffer began his *Christology* lectures in summer 1933. As an academic teacher he attempted to speak strictly theologically, yet indirect reflections on the political context can be discovered in the text.

Bonhoeffer starts his lectures by emphasizing the "doxological" structure of the dogma:

Teaching about Christ begins in silence [...]. That has nothing to do with the silence of the mystics, who in their dumbness chatter away secretly in their soul by themselves. The silence of the Church is the silence before the Word. In so far as the Church proclaims the Word, it essentially falls down silently before the inexpressible [...].

The "study of this proclamation" is possible only on the condition of "the humble silence of the worshipping congregation [...]. To pray is to be silent and at the same time to cry out, before God and in the presence of his Word."[4]

It has often been observed that Bonhoeffer strongly supported the doctrine of the "two natures", divine and human, of Jesus Christ, which had found its "classical formulation" in the Chalcedonian Definition (451), according to which the person of Christ is perceived "in two natures, without confusion and without change [...], without separation and without division". Why is this formulation important in the year 1933? Obviously Bonhoeffer's support of the traditional christological dogma can be interpreted as an attempt at defending the doctrine of the church against the German Christian heresy which was en vogue at that time. On the other hand, Bonhoeffer in a kind of intensification of the traditional identification of Christ with the "logos" describes Christ as "the Counter-Logos".[5] Therefore, the creed of the fathers of the early church, according to which Christ is confessed as true God and true human being at the same time, should be interpreted in a critical way. In Bonhoeffer's words:

---

3   DBWE 6, 344.
4   Bonhoeffer, Christ, 27 (transl. altered).
5   Bonhoeffer, op. cit., 30.

What remains are simple negations. No positive form of thought remains to say what happens in the God-Man Jesus Christ. The mystery is left as a mystery and must be understood as such. The approach is reserved for faith only [...]. Since the Chalcedonian Definition, the theologian who is concerned with christology must keep within the boundaries drawn by the conceptual tension of this negative formula and preserve it [...]. It speaks about 'natures', but expresses the facts in such a way as to show that the concept of 'natures' is quite inappropriate for this use. It works with concepts which it declares to be heretical formulas unless they are used in contradiction and paradox.

According to Bonhoeffer it is just "in its negative formulations" that the Chalcedonian Definition is "the ideal conciliar theological statement".[6] It entails a "prohibition against using objectifying categories for the solution of the question of the God-Man relationship" in Jesus Christ. "By its insistence on the negative in contradictory opposites" the Chalcedonian Definition has, indeed, "superseded the doctrine of the two natures [...]. This critical significance of the Chalcedonian Definition is to be taken further."[7] In its negativity this definition provides a free space for the mystery of Christ.

Christology remains central in Bonhoeffer's further theological development. However, important shifts of accent can be observed within his dealing with the christological question. In the draft "Inheritance and Decay", which should form a part of his *Ethics*, Bonhoeffer notes in 1940 that "western history is, by God's will, indissolubly linked with the people of Israel". And in 1941, when the mass deportations of the Jews began, he emphasizes the christological consequences of this insight, inserting into his manuscript a prophetic clause, according to which western history is linked with Israel "not just genetically but in an honest, unceasing encounter. The Jews keep open the question of Christ [...]. Driving out the Jew(s) from the West must result in driving out Christ with them, for Jesus Christ was a Jew."[8]

In his prison correspondence with Eberhard Bethge Bonhoeffer discovers the significance of the mystery of God's name according to Jewish tradition and applies it to Christology: Already in the first smuggled letter to E. Bethge (November 18–21, 1943) Bonhoeffer notes that he now understands better than before "the fact that the Israelites *never* uttered the name of God".[9] One consequence of this observation is an important reservation with respect to all too direct christological thinking. In his letter of Advent 2 (December 5), 1943, Bonhoeffer is convinced that "it is only when one knows the unutterability of the name of God that one can utter the name of Jesus Christ". In Bonhoeffer's opinion

---

6   Bonhoeffer, op. cit., 87f (transl. altered).
7   Bonhoeffer, op. cit., 97f.
8   DBWE 6, 105.
9   LPP, 135.

it is not Christian to want to take our thoughts and feelings too quickly and too directly from the New Testament. [...] One cannot and must not speak the ultimate word before the penultimate.[10]

Again, at the end of the letter of April 30, 1944, Bonhoeffer emphasizes that the New Testament has to be read "in the light of the Old".[11]

Interesting enough, Bonhoeffer's new awareness of the "worldly" perspective of the Hebrew Bible leads him to a deeper understanding of the Chalcedonian Definition as well. Impressed by the erotic power of the Song of Songs he attempts to liberate the doctrine of the "two natures" in Christ from its dogmatic petrification by employing the musical imagery of polyphony:

Even in the Bible we have the Song of Songs; and really one can imagine no more ardent, passionate, sensual love than is portrayed there [...]. It's a good thing that the book is in the Bible, in face of all those who believe that the restraint of passion is Christian (where is such a restraint in the Old Testament?). Where the *cantus firmus* is clear and plain, the counterpoint can be developed to its limits. The two are 'undivided and yet distinct', in the words of the Chalcedonian Definition, like Christ in his divine and human natures. May not the attraction and importance of polyphony in music consist in its being a musical reflection of this Christological fact and therefore of our *vita christiana*?[12]

2. Aspects of Dietrich Bonhoeffer's "Arcane Discipline"

We turn now to Bonhoeffer's specific interest in "arcane discipline" as the way to deal appropriately with the mystery.[13]

2.1 The "arcane", "qualified silence" and the quest for a concrete commandment (1932/33)

Already in the published version of his doctoral dissertation on "The Communion of Saints" (1930), in the chapter dealing with "authority and freedom in the empirical church" inspired by Karl Barth's "Christian Dogmatics in Draft" (1927) Bonhoeffer recommends "qualified silence" instead of unqualified talk in order to prepare a qualified word of the church.[14] And again in the ecumenical address "On the Theological Basis of the Work of

---

10 LPP, 157 (transl. altered).
11 LPP, 282.
12 LPP, 303.
13 Cf. Pangritz, "Arkandisziplin", 755–768.
14 DBWE 1, 251.

the World Alliance" (for Promoting International Friendship through the Churches, July 26, 1932) Bonhoeffer reflects about the possibility of "qualified silence", this time within an ethical context: When the church does not have at her disposal a "concrete commandment" with respect to the problem of war and peace ("pacifism"!) or with respect to the urgent social problems ("socialism"!), "qualified silence may be more appropriate than unqualified talk" in hypocritical principles.[15]

Even more interesting is a place in Bonhoeffer's lecture on "Recent Publications in Systematic Theology" at Berlin university (winter term 1932/33), where he explicitly deals with the political events of the time. With Barth and against Gogarten Bonhoeffer insists on "the relative right of revolution" according to the "better justice" of the gospel,[16] whereas Brunner's Ethics seems him to lack political concreteness.[17] On February 21, 1933, in the days after the defeat of the Weimar republic, Bonhoeffer concludes his lecture with a comment on Hans Asmussen's *Altona Confession* ("Wort und Bekenntnis Altonaer Pastoren in der Not und Verwirrung des öffentlichen Lebens", December 19, 1932) on the occasion of a bloody Nazi riot in the communist dominated worker's district of Altona. In their "Confession" the Altona ministers, roused by the sight of shot workers in front of the church, had rejected the usual abuse of the church for military, state and party political purposes. Bonhoeffer appreciates this clarification. On the other hand he criticizes that "the conflict of the individual with the state is still looked upon too individualistically". He pleas for a distinction between confession, doctrine, and proclamation of the church: Whereas teaching and preaching should be directed towards the public, the confession of the church should be restricted to an event within the congregation. And in this context he recommends again "qualified silence".[18]

Trying to understand more precisely the content of this hardly disguised criticism of the public "Altona Confession" we have to consult Bonhoeffer's lecture on "The Nature of the Church" (summer term 1932), where he deals with the function of the confession of faith within the congregation. In this context we can read: "The confession of faith must be a wholly sincere response to God's Word of truth [...]. Confession of faith is a matter of our true, present stance before God."[19] And a few days later Bonhoeffer continues:

Confession of faith is not to be confused with professing a religion. Such profession uses the confession as propaganda and ammunition against the Godless. The confes-

---

15 Bonhoeffer, Weltbundarbeit, 330; cf. ibid. 332.
16 Bonhoeffer, Systematisch-theologische Neuerscheinungen, 167.
17 Bonhoeffer, op. cit., 176.
18 Bonhoeffer, op. cit., 177f.
19 Bonhoeffer, Kirche, 283.

sion of faith belongs rather to the Christian gathering of those who believe. Nowhere else is it tenable [...]. The primary confession of the Christian community before the world is the deed. (The confession belongs as arcanum to the worshipping service) [...]. The confession is not the same as loudly shrieking out propaganda, it must be preserved as the most sacred possession of the community. The deed alone is our confession before the world.[20]

From this unusual view of what should be the function of confession we can learn that Bonhoeffer already on the eve of the Nazi's access to power and two years before the Confessing Church was constituted in Barmen (1934) supported a position that was sceptical with respect to the possibility of a public confession of faith, as it was intended by the compromise found between Karl Barth and Hans Asmussen in Barmen. According to Barth, the "Barmen Declaration"[21] was primarily addressed to the church – "What we in Barmen wished to do was *gathering* of the dispersed (Lutheran, reformed, united, positive, liberal, pietist) Christian spirits"[22] – and in so far it would belong – in Bonhoeffer's words – to the "arcane" of the "Christian gathering of those who believe". According to Asmussen, on the other hand, the "Barmen Declaration" was addressed not at least to the public. Therefore he had to qualify the condemnation of the heresy with the political reservation: "[...] We are not protesting as members of the people against the recent history of the people, not as citizens against the new state, not as subjects against the authorities."[23]

Submitting the confession of faith to the "arcane", Bonhoeffer occupied a theological position which would lead him into continuous tension with the Confessing Church. The "arcane" confession of faith would lead him into a constantly deepening understanding of the passion of Christ as the "powerlessness of God in the World", whereas the quest for a "concrete commandment" would find its answer in his participation in the political conspiracy against Hitler as a "deed which interprets itself" as "the primary confession of the Christian before the world" in solidarity with the perpetrated.

---

20   Bonhoeffer, op. cit., 285; cf. Bonhoeffer, Church, 91 (transl. altered).
21   Cf. Burgsmüller/Weth (Ed.), Die Barmer Theologische Erklärung, 30–40. – English version: http://www.ucc.org/faith/barmen.htm (3/31/2007, 14:13 h).
22   Cf. Busch, Karl Barths Lebenslauf, 260.
23   Asmussen, Theologische Erklärung, 48.

2.2 The "arcane discipline" and the question of the boundaries of the church (1936/37)

It seems that in the Finkenwalde period Bonhoeffer for the first time explicitly used the term "arcane discipline". The students in Finkenwalde "were surprised when Bonhoeffer sought to revive this piece of early church history" of which they "had never taken any notice".[24] In at least three different Finkenwalde lectures Bonhoeffer used the term "arcane discipline" in order to recall a certain practice of the early church in her relation to the outsiders: in the lecture on "Catechetics" (winter term 1936/37), in the historical introduction to the lecture on "Homiletics" (summer 1937), and in the lecture on "New Testament" (1937) preparing the book on *Discipleship*.

The relevant paragraph in the Finkenwalde "Catechetics" is most detailed: Dealing with the structure of the "catechumenate" in the early church Bonhoeffer describes the "three-stage structure" of baptismal instruction. The third stage, when the symbol of faith, the creed, is expounded, is, according to Bonhoeffer, submitted to the "disciplina arcanorum". Bonhoeffer explains the function of this "arcane discipline" in the early church as follows: "During the period of persecution it held the congregation together and protected its services from the pagans. The situation of persecution by the state has caused this security measure."[25] It is immediately clear that this explanation intends to arouse associations with the situation of the Confessing Church in the Nazi state.

The common ground of the Finkenwalde allusions to the "arcane discipline" is the defensive attitude: Bonhoeffer characterizes the "arcane discipline" as a "protection measure" intended to underline the boundaries of the church.[26] In the book on *Discipleship* we can find another allusion with the same intention, when Bonhoeffer talks about the "costly grace" without, however, using the term "arcane discipline". But the allusion is quite clear when he asks:

What happened to the insights of the ancient church, which in the baptismal teaching watched so carefully over the boundary between the church and the world, over costly grace?[27]

However, the "arcane discipline" of the Finkenwalde period was a transition stage rather than Bonhoeffer's definitive position, protecting a "breath-

---

24 E. Bethge, Dietrich Bonhoeffer, 881.
25 Bonhoeffer, Katechetik, 549f, note 86; cf. ibid., 553; cf. also: ibid., 526 (Homiletik).
26 The most provocative expression of this attitude had been his essay on "The Question of the Boundaries of the Church and Church Union" (April/June 1936) with the phrase: "Whoever knowingly cuts himself off from the Confessing Church in Germany cuts himself off from salvation" (cf. Bonhoeffer, Testament, 173).
27 Cf. DBWE 4, 54.

ing space" for the "visible church" within a wicked world. After he had become involved with the military, Bonhoeffer questioned this conception of ethical

[t]hinking in terms of two realms [which] understands the paired concepts worldly-Christian, natural-supernatural, profane-sacred, rational-revelational, as ultimate static opposites that designate certain given entities that are mutually exclusive.[28]

And looking back from the "Outline for a book" conceived during his imprisonment in Tegel in August 1944, we may ask if Bonhoeffer's own understanding of the "arcane discipline" during the Finkenwalde period is not part of what he later criticized as "the church on the defensive. No taking risks for others".[29]

2.3 The "arcane discipline" and the "theology of powerlessness" in a "world come of age" (1944)

We have now to consider Bonhoeffer's references to the "arcane discipline" in his prison correspondence with Eberhard Bethge. The main theological question of Bonhoeffer's *Letters and Papers from Prison* is a new formulation of the Christological problem. As Bonhoeffer writes programmatically in his famous letter to E. Bethge on April 30, 1944: "What is bothering me incessantly is the question what Christianity really is, or indeed who Christ really is, for us today".[30] As already in his *Christology* lectures of 1933, Bonhoeffer obviously "does not consider from a distance how much of tradition can be retained, but [...] inquires into the person of Christ and into the way in which he encounters and defines us today". To put it more precisely, Bonhoeffer "inquired into the way in which Christ is Lord" in a world come of age.[31] Or, in Bonhoeffer's own words (June 30, 1944): "Let me just summarize briefly what I am concerned about – the claim of a world that has come of age by Jesus Christ."[32]

It is striking that the first reference to the "arcane discipline" occurs right in the first "theological letter" on April 30, 1944, where Bonhoeffer raises the question "who Christ really is, for us today".[33] After asking how Christ can become "the Lord of the religionless as well" Bonhoeffer goes on praising Karl Barth, "who is the only one to have started along this line of

---

28 DBWE 6, 58f.
29 LPP, 381.
30 LPP, 279.
31 E. Bethge, Dietrich Bonhoeffer, 864.
32 LPP, 342.
33 LPP, 279.

thought", but "did not carry it to completion".[34] But at this point another series of questions follows: "What do a church, a community, a sermon, a liturgy, a Christian life mean in a religionless world? How do we speak of God – without religion [...]?"[35] Bonhoeffer does not yet propose any answer, but rather he concludes as a kind of postscript with a new series of questions:

> What is the place of worship and prayer in a religionless situation? Does the arcane discipline, or alternatively the difference (which I have suggested to you before) between penultimate and ultimate, take on a new importance here?[36]

Immediately in the following letter to Bethge on May 5, 1944, Bonhoeffer takes up the theme again, announcing "a few more words about 'religionlessness'". Again Bonhoeffer admits that "Barth was the first theologian to begin the criticism of religion", which "remains his really great merit".[37] However, according to Bonhoeffer, Barth's approach "makes it too easy for itself, by setting up [...] in the last analysis a law of faith", where each dogma of the church, whether it be "virgin birth, Trinity, or anything else" is "an equally significant and necessary part of the whole, which must simply be swallowed as whole or not at all".[38] In contrast, Bonhoeffer affirms: "There are degrees of knowledge and degrees of significance; that means that an arcane discipline must be restored whereby the *mysteries* of the Christian faith are protected against profanation."[39]

It seems that the function of the "arcane discipline" has changed in these notes compared with the Finkenwalde period: Still there is something to be protected. But it is no longer the boundaries of the church which should be defended against the attack by a wicked world, now "the *mysteries* of the Christian faith" are in danger. And these mysteries are threatened not by the world outside, but by "profanation" through the church itself. The danger comes from within. Therefore Bonhoeffer contrasts his quest for a restored "arcane discipline" with Barth's alleged "positivism of revelation", which would convert faith into a "law". Independently of whether Bonhoeffer's characterization of Barth is fair or not,[40] it is clear that the problem with "positivism of revelation" is – in Bonhoeffer's view – that "virgin birth, Trinity etc.", i.e. the mysteries which form the very content of the Christian

---

[34] Here we hear for the first time the infamous remark on Barth's alleged "positivism of revelation".
[35] LPP, 280. – Cf. ibid., 280f: "In what way are we [...] the 'ek-klesia', those who are called forth, not regarding ourselves from a religious point of view as specially favoured, but rather as belonging wholly to the world?".
[36] LPP, 281 (transl. altered). – Cf. DBWE 6, 146ff: "Ultimate and Penultimate Things".
[37] LPP, 286.
[38] Here Bonhoeffer again criticizes Barth's "positivist doctrine of revelation", which "isn't biblical".
[39] LPP, 286 (transl. altered).
[40] The purported quotation "Like it, or lump it" (LPP, 286) is certainly unfair.

creed, would be used as a means of religious propaganda if they were cried out into the world untimely.

Bonhoeffer makes this very clear in his "Thoughts on the Day of Baptism of Dietrich Wilhelm Rüdiger Bethge" (May 1944). Though he does not refer explicitly to the notion of "arcane discipline" there, the occasion itself – baptism! – makes the allusion clear enough. The situation of the child that is baptized without knowing anything about it is interpreted by Bonhoeffer as an example for the situation of all Christians in "the revolutionary times ahead".[41] Not only the child but all Christians "are once again being driven right back to the beginnings of our understanding. Reconciliation and redemption, regeneration and the Holy Spirit, love of our enemies, cross and resurrection, life in Christ and Christian discipleship – all these things are so difficult and so remote that we hardly venture any more to speak of them. In the traditional words and acts we suspect something quite new and revolutionary, though we cannot as yet grasp or express it." Bonhoeffer emphasizes that this situation is

our own fault. Our church, which has been fighting in these years only for its self-preservation, as though that were an end in itself, is incapable of taking the word of reconciliation and redemption to humanity and the world. Our earlier words are therefore bound to lose their force and cease, and our being Christians today will be limited to two things: prayer and righteous action among the people. All Christian thinking, speaking, and organizing must be born anew out of this prayer and action.

Therefore "the Christian cause will be a silent and hidden affair, but there will be those who pray and do right and wait for God's own time."[42]

"Ultimate and penultimate" are to be distinguished. Prayer – this is the dimension of "mystery" in faith corresponding to the ultimate, which is not addressed to the public and therefore has to be submitted to the "arcane discipline". Righteous action – this is the dimension of "obedience" in faith corresponding to the penultimate, the dimension of "the deed which interprets itself", the dimension of political commitment within the "world come of age". Therefore, non-religious Christianity or "profound this-worldliness"[43] as the dialectical counterpoint correlated to the "arcane discipline" is the act of interpreting the traditional terms preserved in the "arcane" – "reconciliation and redemption" etc. – by the means of "righteous action", i.e. doing justice, suffering for righteousness' sake and sharing "the sufferings of God in the secular life".[44]

---

41   LPP, 295.
42   LPP, 299f.
43   Bonhoeffer, Letter to E. Bethge, July 21, 1944, LPP, 369.
44   Bonhoeffer, Letter to E. Bethge, July 18, 1944, LPP, 361.

2.4 Non-theological dimensions of the "arcane discipline"

In his biography of Bonhoeffer Eberhard Bethge observes that the term "arcane discipline" "occurs only twice in the prison letters". But he emphasizes that

> the question of arcane discipline was not as peripheral for him as the infrequency of the phrase might suggest. His whole personality led him to put a protective screen around the central events of life.[45]

It seems that we can speak of a kind of emotional or psychological "arcane discipline" in Bonhoeffer's personal life, which may have formed the background for his theological interest in "mystery". Renate Bethge reports that

> Bonhoeffer found in his family a reticence which he himself employed, too, but which was not common practice. This stimulated him again and again to reflect upon the function of silence.[46]

"In Bonhoeffer's family it was the general expectation that there were things about which one did not talk and feelings which one did not show." However "emotions were not weak but strong in the family. By hardly talking about them their value was raised."[47] We may recall in this context Bonhoeffer's prison letter to his fiancée Maria von Wedemeyer (August 1944), where he warns:

> It happens to be that certain things remain unsaid in my family [...] I can imagine that at first it will be hard for you that many things, especially in religious matters, remain unexpressed at home.[48]

Renate Bethge adds a comment to this "reticence" in Bonhoeffer's family: "Without practice in such secrecy it would have been impossible to get involved with conspiracy."[49] It seems to be legitimate, therefore, to speak of "a kind of 'political arcane discipline'" with respect to Bonhoeffer's participation in military conspiracy against Hitler and the Nazi government. The term "political arcane discipline" is used by the Bethges[50] with respect to a passage in Bonhoeffer's *Drama* fragment written in prison, where dramatis persona Christoph notes:

---

45 E. Bethge, Dietrich Bonhoeffer, 881.
46 R. Bethge, "Elite" und "Schweigen", 125. – Cf. also: R. Bethge, Bonhoeffers Familie.
47 R. Bethge, op. cit., 127; cf. also ibid.: "In this family you learned to talk about things silently or indirectly and to understand things said this way."
48 Von Wedemeyer-Weller, The Other Letters, 25. – Cf. also: Bonhoeffer/von Wedemeyer, Brautbriefe, 203.
49 R. Bethge, "Elite" und "Schweigen", 126.
50 R. and E. Bethge, Introduction, 11; cf. ibid., 180, note 32: "a kind of secular, political dimension of the 'arcane discipline'".

I speak to you to protect from abusing the great words that have been given to humanity. [...] What well-meaning person today can still utter the besmirched words freedom, brotherhood, or even the word Germany? [...] Let us honor the highest values by silence for a while. Let us learn to do what is the right without words for a while.[51]

In contrast to the theological "arcane discipline" the subject matter of the "political arcane discipline" would not be the "mysteries of faith" but political values like freedom, solidarity or nation. These values should no longer be used in terms of political propaganda, but they should be fought for without words.

It seems to be likely that Bonhoeffer's involvement with conspiracy – a type of political commitment which cannot adequately be understood without the specific background of the virtues and traditions of his middle-class family – had reinforced his theological quest for a renewed arcane discipline in the prison correspondence with Eberhard Bethge. The theological interest in the "arcane" had been there already at the begin of the thirties.[52] But the urgency by which Bonhoeffer finally writes to Eberhard Bethge that "an arcane discipline must be restored whereby the *mysteries* of the Christian faith are protected against profanation",[53] is due to the dramatic turns of his life which let him experience the value of family traditions like reticence and secrecy in situations, when he was forced to learn "to see the great events of world history from below".[54]

3. "Mystery" and "Commandment" in Leo Baeck and Dietrich Bonhoeffer

Finally, let's have a comparative look upon Leo Baeck's way of dealing with the notion of "mystery".[55] It was the late Albert H. Friedlander, who pointed out a certain affinity between Bonhoeffer's thinking and the polarity of "mystery and commandment" in Leo Baeck, the famous liberal rabbi of Berlin during the Weimar period and "teacher of Theresienstadt" in the times of the Holocaust.[56]

---

51   DBWE 7, 50.
52   It can also be found in Bonhoeffer's theological reflexions on "shame" (cf. DBWE 4, 113–118; cf. also: DBWE 6, 299ff ["God's Love and the Disintegration of the World"]; cf. also the letter to E. Bethge, November 27, 1943, LPP, 146).
53   LPP, 286.
54   LPP, 17.
55   Cf. Pangritz, 'Mystery and Commandment', 44–57.
56   Friedlander, Israel and Europe, 117: "Baeck's teaching of classical religion against romantic religion, his vision of the commandment which leads to the mystery, of the mystery out of

Baeck had established a reputation before Bonhoeffer was born, especially with his book *Das Wesen des Judentums* (*The Essence of Judaism*, 1905, 2nd revised edition 1922). This work was the most prominent Jewish response to the famous series of lectures *Das Wesen des Christentums* (*The Essence of Christianity*), held by Bonhoeffer's later teacher Adolf von Harnack in the winter semester of 1899/1900. Baeck contrasted Judaism as the "classical religion of the act" with Christianity as the "romantic religion of emotion".[57] Whereas Christianity yearns for redemption, Judaism endeavours to improve the world. Baeck's book could have interested Bonhoeffer, who, especially after the fateful year of 1933, was more and more concerned with the "concreteness of the commandment" and was unable to find satisfaction in the conclusion that "We don't know what we should do". But, as Bethge observes:

> In contrast to the fame of Harnack's *Das Wesen des Christentums* [...] was the neglect accorded to Leo Baeck's special way of joining the debate with his *Wesen des Judentums*.[58]

Later, under the influence of his study of Jewish mysticism, Baeck was to see the essence of Judaism "in a dialectical confrontation of mystery and commandment", as he expounded it in an essay entitled "Mystery and Commandment" in 1922.[59] In a sense this anticipates the dialectic of "arcane" and "this-worldliness" in Bonhoeffer's prison theology. In his essay Baeck assumes "two experiences of the human soul in which the meaning of his life takes on for a man a vital significance: the experience of mystery and the experience of commandment".[60] Baeck quotes a pivotal sentence in Deuteronomy in support of this polarity: "That which is concealed belongs unto the Lord our God, but that which is revealed belongs unto us and our children for ever, that we may do all the words of this Torah" (Dtn 29,29). We could also describe this duality as that of humanity's relationship with God and with the world, of faith and ethics. Now, according to Baeck, the peculiarity of Judaism is "that these two experiences have here become one, and are experienced as one, in a perfect unity". For: "from the one God come both mystery and commandment, as one from the One, and the soul experiences both as one", so that "all faith" means and suggests also "the

---

which the commandment must emerge, parallels the vision of Bonhoeffer." – In his biography of Leo Baeck, Friedlander mentions Bonhoeffer at one juncture as evidence that the theological tradition of Lutheranism must be seen in a more differentiated light than in Baeck's polemic (cf. Friedlander, Leo Baeck, 271).
57 Cf. Baeck, Romantische Religion, 42–120.
58 E. Bethge, Dietrich Bonhoeffer and the Jews, 52.
59 Baeck, Geheimnis und Gebot; cited according to the English version: Mystery and Commandment, 171–185.
60 Baeck, op. cit., 171.

law, and all law, faith".[61] The consequence for Baeck is that "Judaism lacks any foundation for the conflict between transcendence and immanence". For Jewish piety "there is no such thing as this world without any beyond, nor a beyond without this world; no world to come without the present world, and no human world without that which transcends it".[62]

This calls to mind similar formulations by Bonhoeffer in his *Letters and Papers from Prison*: "God is beyond in the midst of our life [...]. That is how it is in the Old Testament, and in this sense we still read the New Testament far too little in the light of the Old", he writes to Eberhard Bethge (April 30, 1944).[63] And again: "What is above this world is, in the gospel, intended to exist *for* this world" (May 5, 1944).[64] A day after the failed coup d'état against Hitler, he writes of "the profound this-worldliness of Christianity":

> I don't mean the shallow and banal this-worldliness of the enlightened, the busy, the comfortable, or the lascivious, but the profound this-worldliness, characterised by discipline and the constant knowledge of death and resurrection.[65]

The structural affinity of Bonhoeffer's "profound this-worldliness" with Baeck's concept of Judaism is striking. Leo Baeck stresses that

> the religion of mere activity without devotion – this religion which becomes an ethic of the surface, or no more than the custom of the day – is not Judaism. The world of Judaism is to be found only where faith has its commandment, and the commandment its faith.[66]

Again one can find structurally related thoughts in Bonhoeffer when he demands the restoration of an "arcane discipline", a commitment of divine mystery that makes "true worldliness" possible, or when he writes, in the "Thoughts on the Day of the Baptism" of his grand-nephew (May 1944): "Our being Christians today will be limited to two things: prayer and righteous action among human beings."[67] Baeck expresses a similar view with regard to Judaism, when he writes of "the unity of devotion and deed": "The commandment is a true commandment only because it is rooted in

---

61 Baeck, op. cit., 173. – In Judaism "any opposition between mysticism and ethics has no place [...]. All ethics has its mysticism and all mysticism its ethics [...]. All absorption in the profundity of God is always also an absorption in the will of God and His commandment. And all Jewish ethics is distinguished by being an ethic of revelation [...] it is the tidings of the divine" (ibid., 175).
62 Baeck, op. cit., 174.
63 LPP, 282.
64 LPP, 286.
65 July 21, 1944, LPP, 369.
66 Baeck, Mystery and Commandment, 176. – Cf. ibid.: "The religion of mere passivity, devoid of commandments, is no longer Judaism. Nor is Judaism to be found where the commandment is content with itself and is nothing but commandment."
67 LPP, 300 (transl. altered).

mystery, and the mystery is a true mystery because the commandment always speaks out of it."[68]

Furthermore, Baeck sees the "commandment of God" as one "that leads into the future […]. It contains a promise, it has a life that continually comes to life, it has a messianic aspect."[69] Here again one is reminded of Bonhoeffer's "Thoughts on the Day of Baptism", where he adds a "waiting for God's own time" to the polarity of "prayer and righteous action".[70] The promissory nature of the commandment should not be confused with withdrawal from the world or from the present. Baeck specifies the messianic element in the commandment as God's "lasting covenant with man": "Religion is not, in our case, a faith in redemption from the world and its demands, but rather – and this has often been called the realism of Judaism – trust in the world or, to be more precise, the assurance of reconciliation." "Redemption here is not redemption from the world, but in the world, consecration of the world, realisation of the kingdom of God."[71]

Here, too, we find an exact parallel in Bonhoeffer. On June 27, 1944, he writes to Eberhard Bethge about his reading of the Old Testament:

Unlike the other oriental religions, the faith of the Old Testament isn't a religion of redemption. It's true that Christianity has always been regarded as a religion of redemption. But isn't this a cardinal error, which separates Christ from the Old Testament […]? […] The redemptions referred to here are *historical*, i.e. on *this* side of death, whereas everywhere else the myths about redemption are concerned to overcome the barrier of death. Israel is delivered out of Egypt so that it may live before God as God's people on earth.

According to Bonhoeffer even the proclamation of "the hope of resurrection" does not mean "the emergence of a genuine religion of redemption". As he writes:

The difference between the Christian hope of resurrection and the mythological hope is that the former sends a man back to his life on earth in a wholly new way […]. This world must not be prematurely written off; in this the Old and New Testament are one.[72]

This is the background to Bonhoeffer's notorious critique of religion: "Faith" for Bonhoeffer is "something whole, involving the whole of one's life", whereas the "religious act" seems to him to be "something partial". However, Jesus "calls people, not to a new religion, but to life". "To be a Christian", therefore, "does not mean to be religious in a particular way

---

68 Baeck, Mystery and Commandment, 178.
69 Baeck, op. cit., 179f.
70 LPP, 300.
71 Baeck, Mystery and Commandment, 180f.
72 LPP, 336f (June 24, 1944).

[…], but to be a human being."[73] Thus he writes in the last letter to Eberhard Bethge before the failed coup d'état on July 18, 1944.

In contrast to Bonhoeffer, Leo Baeck was not influenced by the new approach of "dialectical theology" after World War I. In the tradition of liberal theology he did not hesitate to use the term "religion" for his understanding of Judaism. But this understanding of it is in accord with what Bonhoeffer referred to as "non-religious Christianity". Baeck writes:

> Thus religion is everything here. It permeates the whole of life […]. Religion here is nothing isolated, nothing that is shut off; it does not exist only alongside our life or only under or above our life. There is no mystery outside of life and no life outside the commandment.

The other side of the coin is the sanctification of the everyday world: "There is nothing left that could be called mere 'world', and nothing set aside as basically merely 'everyday'; there is no mere prose of existence." Judaism "does not lead man out of his everyday world, but relates him to God within it".[74]

Baeck makes this clear with reference to the Sabbath:

> It is […] the recreation in which the soul, as it were, creates itself again and catches its breath of life […]. The Sabbath is the image of the messianic; it proclaims the creation and the future […]. A life without Sabbath would lack the spring of renewal.

The Sabbath renders people "different" among human beings:

> Whoever experiences mystery and commandment becomes unique among men, different, an individual within the world […]. Whoever experiences both, both in unity, lives in the world and yet is different.[75]

A Christianity that was once again to take cognisance of its Jewish roots would have a lesson to learn from such messianic non-conformity in the world. It seems that Bonhoeffer with his concentration upon the "mystery" was a pioneer of such non-conformity for humanity's sake. "Mystery stands in relation to the 'Word' like the rest to the music out of which it is born or at least: breathes" (F.-W. Marquardt, 1987).

---

73 LPP, 361f (transl. altered).
74 Baeck, Mystery and Commandment, 181f.
75 Baeck, op. cit., 184. – Cf. ibid., 185: It is perhaps for this reason the "historic task" of Judaism, "to offer this image of the dissenter, who dissents for humanity's sake".

Bibliography

Primary Sources

ASMUSSEN, H., Vortrag über die *Theologische Erklärung* zur gegenwärtigen Lage der Deutschen Evangelischen Kirche, in: A. Burgsmüller/R. Weth (Ed.), Die Barmer Theologische Erklärung, 41–58.

BAECK, L., *Romantische Religion*, in: Baeck, Aus drei Jahrtausenden. Wissenschaftliche Untersuchungen und Abhandlungen zur Geschichte des jüdischen Glaubens, Tübingen 1958, 42–120.

–, *Geheimnis und Gebot*, in: C.H. von Keyerling (Ed.), Der Leuchter: Weltanschauung und Lebensgestaltung. Jahrbuch der Schule der Weisheit, Vol. 3, Darmstadt 1921–1922.

–, *Mystery and Commandment*, in: Baeck, Judaism and Christianity, transl. with an introduction by W. Kaufmann, Philadelphia 1960, 171–185.

BONHOEFFER, D., Sanctorum Communio: A Theological Study of the Sociology of the Church, ed. by C.J. Green, Minneapolis 1998 (= DBWE 1).

–, Discipleship, ed. by G.B. Kelly/J.D. Godsey, Minneapolis 2001 (= DBWE 4).

–, Ethics, ed. by C.J. Green, Minneapolis 2005 (= DBWE 6).

–, Fiction from Tegel Prison, ed. by C.J. Green, Minneapolis 1999 (= DBWE 7).

–, Zur theologischen Begründung der *Weltbundarbeit* [On the Theological Basis of the Work of the World Alliance], in: Bonhoeffer, Ökumene, Universität, Pfarramt 1931–1932, Dietrich Bonhoeffer Werke, Vol. 11, ed. by E. Amelung/Ch. Strohm, Gütersloh 1994 (= DBW 11), 327–344.

–, Das Wesen der *Kirche*, in: DBW 11, 239–303.

–, Besprechung und Diskussion *systematisch-theologischer Neuerscheinungen*, in: Bonhoeffer, Berlin 1932–1933, Dietrich Bonhoeffer Werke, Vol. 12, ed. by C. Nicolaisen/E.-A. Scharffenorth, Gütersloh 1997 (= DBW 12), 153–178.

–, *Katechetik*, in: Bonhoeffer, Illegale Theologenausbildung: Finkenwalde 1935–1937, Dietrich Bonhoeffer Werke, Vol. 14, ed. by O. Dudzus/J. Henkys et al., Gütersloh 1996 (= DBW 14), 530–554.

–, The Nature of the *Church*, in: G. Kelly/F.B. Nelson (Ed.), A Testament to Freedom: The Essential Writings of Dietrich Bonhoeffer, San Francisco 1990, 87–92.

–, *Christ* the Centre, transl. by E.H. Robertson, New York 1978.

–, Letters and Papers from Prison. The Enlarged Edition, ed. by E. Bethge, New York 1972 (= LPP).

–/ VON WEDEMEYER, M., *Brautbriefe* Zelle 92: 1943–1945, ed. by R.-A. von Bismarck/U. Kabitz, München 1992.

BURGSMÜLLER, A./WETH, R. (Ed.), *Die Barmer Theologische Erklärung*, Neukirchen-Vluyn 1984.

KELLY, G./NELSON, F.B. (Ed.), A *Testament* to Freedom: The Essential Writings of Dietrich Bonhoeffer, San Francisco 1990.

VON WEDEMEYER-WELLER, M., *The Other Letters* from Prison, USQR 23, 1967, 23–29.

Secondary Sources

BETHGE, E., *Dietrich Bonhoeffer and the Jews*, in: J.D. Godsey/G.B. Kelly (Ed.), Ethical Responsibility. Bonhoeffer's Legacy to the Churches, New York/Toronto 1981.

–, *Dietrich Bonhoeffer*. A Biography, überarbeitete Ausgabe, revised and edited by V.J. Barnett, Minneapolis 1999.

BETHGE, R./BETHGE, E., *Introduction*, in: D. Bonhoeffer, Fiction from Prison. Gathering Up the Past, transl. by U. Hoffmann, Philadelphia 1981, 1–12.

BETHGE, R., *"Elite" und "Schweigen"* in Bonhoeffers Denken und Persönlichkeit ["Elite" and "Silence" in Bonhoeffer's Thought and Personality], epd-Dokumentation 2/3, 1981, 123−127.

−, *Bonhoeffers Familie* und ihre Bedeutung für seine Theologie. Beiträge zum Widerstand 1933– 1945, ed. by Gedenkstätte Deutscher Widerstand, no. 30, Berlin 1987.

BUSCH, E., *Karl Barths Lebenslauf.* Nach seinen Briefen und autobiographischen Texten, München 1975.

FRIEDLANDER, A.H., *Leo Baeck*: Teacher of Theresienstadt, New York/Chicago/San Francisco 1968.

−, *Israel and Europe*, in: Bonhoeffer's Ethics. Old Europe and New Frontiers, ed. by G. Carter et al., Kampen 1991, 112−120.

PANGRITZ, A., "Who is *Jesus Christ*, for us, today?", in: The Cambridge Companion to Dietrich Bonhoeffer, ed. by J.W. de Gruchy, Cambridge/New York/Melbourne 1999, 134–153.

−, Aspekte der *"Arkandisziplin"* bei Dietrich Bonhoeffer, Theologische Literaturzeitung 119, 1994, 755–768.

−, *'Mystery and Commandment'* in Leo Baeck and Dietrich Bonhoeffer, European Judaism. A Journal for the New Europe, Vol. 30, No. 2, Fall 1997, Issue No. 59, 44–57.

Christiane Tietz

The Mysteries of Knowledge, Sin, and Shame

To talk about knowledge, about sin and about shame, means to talk about relations. We can say in a first definition: *Knowledge* is a person's recognition of somebody or something; and *shame* is an affect of wishing to hide something from somebody. Bonhoeffer discusses knowledge and shame both between two human beings and between human beings and God. And he sees the relation between two human beings and the relation between human beings and God from a theological standpoint as qualified by *sin*. As taking place in those relations knowledge and shame are also qualified by sin.[1] Or, to say it differently – the mystery of knowledge and the mystery of shame are rooted in the mystery of sin.

In the following reflections on knowledge, sin and shame I'll concentrate on Bonhoeffer. His reflections on these topics are so deep that analyzing them should be interesting as such.

Because knowledge and shame are qualified by sin I have to begin with Bonhoeffer's concept *of sin*.

1. Sin

It is the signature of the creature that it exists in relation: in relation to God and in relation to the other creatures. The existence of creature is qualified through having to rely on somebody else.[2] In Bonhoeffer's eyes, this "dependence on the other" is what makes a creature:

> The creatureliness of human beings […] can be defined in simply no other way than in terms of the existence of human beings over-against-one-another, with-one-another, and in-dependence-upon-one-another.[3]

In his book *Creation and Fall*, Bonhoeffer states that in the beginning those relations are an unbroken unity. This includes that human beings live in

---

1   Cf. DBWE 3, 116: "From now on no human assertion can be made about human beings that fails to bear in mind, and to take into specific account, their being sicut deus." Cf. DBWE 1, 63: "The Christian concept of person should be thought of historically, i.e., in the state after the fall".
2   Cf. DBWE 3, 64.
3   DBWE 3, 64.

"unbroken unity of obedience" to God.[4] God commands and human beings simply and immediately obey.[5] They obediently respect the given limits and boundaries. But, soon, the problems begin:

1.1 Asking a question

Sin starts with the temptation to question God's word. "Did God really say?" – this question goes behind God's word. To ask this question includes the intention to judge God's word from an external standpoint. From his own understanding of who God is, man wants to define what God's word could be. He wants to use his own idea of God, his own concept of God as the criterion of whether some word can be God's word.[6]

From this first train of thoughts we can follow that sin starts with the wish to gain an autonomous knowledge about God. Through this wish man steps out of the unbroken unity with God. In that the immediate obedience to God ends.[7]

1.2 Eating the fruit

In then eating the fruit man goes beyond God's command, beyond the given limits. Stepping beyond a limit for the first time changes the human existence fundamentally. Now, human beings are aware of the possibility to go beyond the boundaries and therefore are aware of the boundaries as boundaries. Thus, they exist without *any* limit.[8]

Bonhoeffer identifies this existing without any limit with "being alone".[9] This identification is so important that we should dwell on it for a while. Existing without limits, says Bonhoeffer, means living alone. So, being *not* alone, being in *community* with others means existing *with* limits! And this is what Bonhoeffer in fact is convinced of: Being in community with others means that I respect a space where the other is and not me. Being in com-

---

4 DBWE 3, 84. Cf. DBWE 1, 62f: in "unbroken community with God" and in "unbroken social community".

5 The well-known example for this is: God tells Adam not to eat from the tree of knowledge about good and evil. Bonhoeffer states that obeying this command is possible very easily. For, obedience to this command is possible without any knowledge about good and evil (DBWE 3, 87). It is a plain and straight obedience.

6 Cf. DBWE 3, 107f.

7 Cf. DBWE 6, 311: "The question 'did God really say …?' […] is the question that conceals all the disunion".

8 Cf. DBWE 3, 115.

9 DBWE 3, 115.

munity means to allow the other to set a limit for me. I do accept that he is a boundary to me because I love him.[10] We will come to that point later. For now it might be sufficient to note that even in the origin, in the immediate unity, the other limits my existence.

In the origin, human beings are not aware of these boundaries as boundaries which can be crossed.[11] They respect them without any question. In the origin, the boundary isn't seen negative because it isn't understood as restriction and as taking away that which lies beyond.[12]

Bonhoeffer recognizes that after having eaten the fruit, the boundary becomes negative. It is now seen as a boundary that is rooted in God's hate and jealousy. The God-given boundary is becoming something threatening.[13]

Man now is no longer simply obeying God;[14] he is independently judging what is right, what is good and what is evil.[15] Now human beings live in "Entzweiung"[16] from God, in disunion and estrangement.[17] From this "Entzweiung" from God follows an "Entzweiung", an estrangement also from each other, the world of things and from oneself.[18]

Especially the other human being as the concrete given boundary[19] is now threatening. To overcome the threat of those boundaries human beings want to possess each other and thus to destroy the others' freedom as creatures.[20] Man now wants to live on his own. Egocentricity becomes the characteristic of every human behavior.[21] Thus "the relation among human beings [...] is purely demanding".[22]

---

10 Cf. DBWE 3, 98.
11 Cf. DBWE 3, 87.
12 Cf. DBWE 3, 122.
13 Cf. DBWE 3, 122.
14 Jesus shows such behavior: "The freedom of Jesus is not the arbitrary choice of one among countless possibilities. Instead, it consists precisely in the complete simplicity of his action, for which there are never several possibilities, conflicts, or alternatives, but always only one. Jesus calls this one option the will of God." Jesus "lives and acts not out of knowledge of good and evil, but out of the will of God. There is only *one* will of God. In it, the origin has been regained. It is the source of freedom and simplicity in everything that is done." (DBWE 6, 313).
15 This knowledge about good and evil is identical with the fundamental division of human life, for the term good is only possible when we also have the opposite: evil. Thus knowledge about good and evil is a sign of sin.
16 DBW 6, 302.
17 The German word "Entzweiung" means "in zwei Teile teilen" – split into two parts. Cf. Grimm, Art. Entzweien together with Art. Zweien.
18 Cf. DBWE 6, 303.
19 Cf. DBWE 3, 99.
20 Cf. DBWE 3, 123.
21 Cf. to the power of the ego in Bonhoeffer's writings Green, Sociality, 109.
22 DBWE 1, 108. Bonhoeffer sees sexuality as the original expression of this addiction. "The sexuality of the human being who transgresses his or her boundary is a refusal to recognize any limit at all; it is a boundless obsessive desire to be without any limits. Sexuality is a *passionate*

From this follows that through sin a "rupture has come into the unbroken community. Losing direct community with God, [human beings ...] also lose [...] unmediated human community. A third power, sin, has stepped between human beings and God".[23] From this disunion arises shame.

2. Shame

2.1 The essence of shame

Shame[24] starts with knowledge. Shame starts with recognizing the result of sin. It starts with the recognition of being "in [...] disunion from God and one another".[25] What does this recognition of disunion include?

In *Creation and Fall*, Bonhoeffer argues that in the beginning human beings weren't covered at all;[26] they lived in nakedness, one revealed to the other without being aware of their nakedness.[27] In his *Ethics*, Bonhoeffer says that in the beginning God and the other were a cover for man.[28] However one might value this difference, in both cases the recognition of the *disunion* includes the recognition of oneself "as naked",[29] as without coverage and as being exposed to the other.

This is the moment when shame appears. Shame is "a cover in which I hide myself from the other because of [...] evil".[30] Shame hides something from the other; shame causes secrets.

---

hatred of any limit. It is extreme lack of respect for things-as-they-are [Unsachlichkeit]; it is self-will, an obsessive but powerless will for unity in a divided [entzweiten] world." (DBWE 3, 123) The astonishing thing in sexuality is that one is searching for unity but unable to reach the original unity. Cf. Claß, Zugriff, 149. Claß criticizes Bonhoeffer's understanding of sexuality for good reasons (ibid., 150).

23 DBWE 1, 63.
24 Cf. to the whole topic Bammel, Augen, 264–272. 276–281.
25 DBWE 6, 303.
26 Cf. DBWE 3, 101.
27 Cf. DBWE 3, 124.
28 Cf. DBWE 6, 303.
29 DBWE 6, 303. Hartenstein argues that the Hebrew text uses "naked" in a twofold sense: ᶜarummim Gen 2,25: nakedness without shame, and ᶜerummim Gen 3,7a: nakedness as result of sin (cf. Hartenstein, Anthropologie, 278). Gen 2,25 should be translated with "they did not shame each other" (J.M. Sasson; quoted from Hartenstein, ibid., 286) to make clear that the reciprocity of the relation is important. That "they did not shame each other" is not the feeling of each of them but the expression of their undisturbed community (Hartenstein, ibid.).
30 DBWE 3, 101. But shame doesn't only arise from the evil of disunion; man also is ashamed because he himself causes the lost of the original unity. Cf. DBW 6, 304f: "Der Mensch schämt sich [...] der verlorenen Einheit", means: is ashamed that he lost it.

Human beings now recognize their relation to each other as qualified by sin. They are now aware of the fact that the other wants to do evil to them, that the other wants to possess or to destroy them.[31] This is why they are covering themselves from the other.[32] Shame is a protection against the evil-doing of the other. It is the "natural defense against outside invasion"[33] and thus the protection of one's own freedom "against any form of rape".[34]

But shame isn't only a covering because of the evil of the other. It is also a covering because of *my own* evil.[35] For: In sin, I want to live on my own. This has severe consequences. While in the origin I understand myself out of the relation to the other[36] I now interrupt this relational self-understanding. I no longer want to understand myself outside of the relation to the other. Therefore I cut this relation through hiding something from the other in shame.[37] As a sinner, I want to understand myself only out of myself; this is why I hide myself in shame.

And, there is another aspect why shame is rooted in *my own* evil: My evil deeds cause me to hide them from the other who would dislike and despise me for that.

In that manifold way resulting from the evil and the disunion of sin, shame is "the irrepressible memory of disunion from the [...] origin. It is the pain of this disunion".[38]

But shame isn't only the memory of disunion, it also is "the helpless desire to reverse"[39] the lost unity. How does shame try to regain the lost unity? To attempt to regain and to overcome the estrangement[40] takes place precisely *in* the covering. Bonhoeffer doesn't explain how this covering tries to

---

31   Cf. DBWE 3, 99.

32   Cf. DBWE 3, 101. Hartenstein shows that clothing constitutes social location whereas nakedness means having no social status (Hartenstein, Anthropologie, 279). In the biblical story, God makes clothes for human beings and in this "accepts human beings for what they are, as fallen creatures. [...] God does not expose them to one another in their nakedness" (DBWE 3, 139).

33   DBWE 6, 214. Cf. Claß, Zugriff, 150ff.

34   DBWE 6, 214.

35   Cf. DBWE 3, 101.

36   Cf. DBWE 3, 101.

37   Cf. DBWE 3, 123f: "Human beings with no limits, in their hatred and in their obsessive desire, do not show themselves in their nakedness."

38   DBWE 6, 303. Even if Bonhoeffer in his later writings, e.g. in his *Ethics*, has a different understanding of sin (cf. Busch Nielsen, Sünden, 37ff) and no longer focuses on the disunion and estrangement but on the reconciliation in Christ that has changed the reality of the world as a whole (cf. DBWE 6, 83: "Now there is no more godlessness, hate, or sin that God has not taken upon himself, suffered, and atoned"), and understands men now as fundamentally distinguished from their sin (Krötke, Weltlichkeit, 157), shame still remains important for him.

39   DBWE 6, 303. Cf. ibid.: "[...] human beings are ashamed because of the lost unity with God and one another". Shame is the sign of "missing something". It is not the sign of having done something wrong.

40   Cf. DBWE 6, 304.

overcome the estrangement. But I guess it is correct to assume the following: On the one hand, a cover is the attempt to hinder the other from abusing me and in this to overcome a result of the estrangement. And on the other hand, a cover is the attempt to hide my evil from the other; it hinders the other from withdrawing from my evil through which our estrangement would become even bigger.

2.2 The dialectic of covering and uncovering

Shame is not static but dynamic: It reminds human beings of the loss of the original unity and the fundamental estrangement; but it also aims at overcoming the estrangement; thus it keeps a person in a continuous dynamical tension to origin and estrangement. To this dynamic belong several aspects:

First of all, from the necessity of shame and covering arises the *right* of every human being to keep things unsaid. Everybody has the right to have secrets! Bonhoeffer writes in *Life Together*: "Who is allowed to force one's way into one's neighbor?"[41] "[...] others have their own right [...] to defend themselves against unauthorized intrusions. Other persons have their own secrets that may not be violated without the infliction of great harm."[42]

But it's even more: Human beings also have the *duty* to keep things unsaid: If people don't keep their own secrets they are "destroying themselves".[43] Bonhoeffer talks about this duty impressively in *Letters and Papers from Prison*. He expresses his astonishment about how freely the other prisoners talk about their fright. Bonhoeffer writes to Eberhard Bethge: "[...] fright is surely something to be ashamed of. I have a feeling that it shouldn't be talked about". He calls frankly talking about fright "ungodly".[44] And he argues: "God himself made clothes for men; and that means that *in statu corruptionis* many things in human life ought to remain covered". "[...] since the fall there must be [...] secrecy".[45]

But, and this is the *second* aspect, human beings do not always respect the secrets of the other. They ignore the other's shame and that the other wants to cover things; they want to know things which the other himself wants to hide. This is the reason why Bonhoeffer in *Letters and Papers*

---

41   I'm translating the German version here, DBW 5, 88: "Wer darf in den Nächsten eindringen?" DBWE 5, 103 has: "Who has permission to force oneself on one's neighbor?".
42   DBWE 5, 104.
43   DBWE 5, 104.
44   LPP, 146.
45   LPP, 158.

from Prison criticizes a searching for the "secrets known to a man's valet – that is […] the range of his intimate life, from prayer to his sexual life", the "sniffing-around-after-people's-sins".[46] Such a sniffing is disrespecting the other's freedom.

In a London sermon, Bonhoeffer describes vividly what happens if one inquisitively exposes another person's secret. If the secret comes to light he is outraged at how immoral that person is. But, says Bonhoeffer, everybody has secrets. And he remarks astutely that the difference between the so called immoral and the so called moral persons is only a minimal one: We call immoral those persons, whose secrets have come to light; and we call moral those persons, whose secrets just still are hidden.[47]

Instead of trying to expose the secret of another person, human beings should – and this is the *third* aspect – respect the "secrecy, intimacy, and concealment" of the others.[48] Bonhoeffer argues in *Fiction from Tegel Prison* in the words of Renate that it is not necessary to perceive the other like a camera which registers every single detail of the other; it is better to perceive the other with the eyes of love which concentrate on the essentials of the other and let the other have his secret.[49]

Letting the other have his secret means nothing else than respecting the freedom of the other and understanding him as a God-given boundary. Then the words in which the other is telling his secret become free gifts to me. Then I'm not forcing the other to tell everything but am respecting the will of the other to have secrets. I'm just waiting for if a time will come when he might tell his secret.[50]

But, *fourthly*, even if the other might some time tell his secret and lift his cover, the cover between two persons never should be lifted totally. "[…] human beings live *between* concealment and disclosure, *between* hiding and revealing themselves".[51] There is no need to reveal every secret.

And whenever a secret is uncovered between two persons there is the need of a new cover. More precisely: Situations in which the cover is lifted have to be under a new cover in regard to a third party. Bonhoeffer gives an example: When two human beings become one flesh a cover between them is lifted. But: they should use a new cover in not speaking about their sexual relationship publicly.

---

46 LPP, 344f.
47 Cf. DBW 13, 320.
48 LPP, 159. In Bonhoeffer's eyes this respect is fundamental for the question what it means to speak the truth: "'Speaking the truth' […] means […] saying how something really is – that is, showing respect for secrecy, intimacy, and concealment." (Ibid.). Cf. ibid., 163.
49 Cf. DBW 7, 47.
50 Cf. DBW 7, 136f.
51 DBWE 6, 305 (emphasis added).

Why is this new cover necessary? I think we can distinguish two aspects: First, it is totally inadequate and a breach of confidence to tell the secrets of the other to somebody else.

Second, when somebody freely lifts his secret this is nothing other than a new quality of relationship. The relation between the one who tells his secret and the one who does deserve to be trusted is not the former relation of disunion and estrangement; rather it is a relation of confidence and respect. That this is possible between two sinners, this in fact is a *miracle* or – a *mystery*. "*That* the other is so closed to me, this is the biggest mystery".[52] And Bonhoeffer thinks that talking about this mystery would destroy it: "It can be felt as an injuring of shame if a relationship that one has with another person is expressed in words, thereby revealing and exposing oneself."[53] In these insights, we've reached an important point which I would like to explain a little bit further. I think there is a difference between *secret* and *mystery* in Bonhoeffer's theology. In the German text, Bonhoeffer uses only a single term for both: "Geheimnis". But in my eyes, it's important to mark a difference between Geheimnis as secret and Geheimnis as mystery. What is the difference?

I'm using distinctions of the German theologian Gerhard Ebeling to explain what I mean: "Geheimnis" as "secret" is a human *product*; it results from the event that a human being is covering him- or herself; it means secrecy, "Geheimhaltung". However, "Geheimnis" as "mystery" is something that is not produced by human beings; it is something in which a human being rather finds him- or herself. Ebeling gives an example in which we can find both aspects: homicide. On the one hand a homicide can remain unsolved; then it remains a secret. On the other hand homicide refers to the mystery of evil and the mystery of death; both mysteries aren't human products but describe the character of human existence.[54]

As far as I see the same difference can be found in Bonhoeffer's texts. On the one hand, Bonhoeffer talks about secrets; people have to cover things, stories, feelings because of their own and the other's evil. Those secrets produced by human beings have their right to be kept. But from time to time a person lets somebody into his or her own secrets. On the other hand, Bonhoeffer talks about mysteries; they are not something produced by human beings but something that is a fundamental miracle of human existence[55] in which one finds oneself.[56]

---

52 DBW 13, 361 (my translation).
53 DBWE 6, 305 (translation altered).
54 Ebeling, Profanität, 197f.
55 Cf. Bethge, Biographie, 988.
56 Cf. e.g. DBW 5, 88: "Der Andere hat sein eigenes Geheimnis [...] Es ist nicht ein Geheimnis des Wissens oder Fühlens, sondern das Geheimnis seiner Freiheit, seiner Erlösung, seines

The difference becomes clear in the fragment "What Is Meant by 'Telling the Truth'?" There Bonhoeffer speaks about "the cynic who claims 'to speak the truth' at all times and in all places to all men in the same way". The cynic doesn't respect the hidden secret of the other. His behavior means that he "desecrates mystery".[57] The German text here has "*entheiligt das Geheimnis*"[58] and thus shows that "Geheimnis" here not only refers to a hidden secret but to something existentially fundamental. This insight is confirmed by the context: The cynic "desecrates mystery, breaks confidence, betrays the community in which he lives".[59] Obviously, mystery here refers to the reliable, confidential character of the community. Thus it follows: Someone who is forcibly revealing the *secret* of the other is destroying the *mystery* of their relationship.

In Bonhoeffer's texts, shame has to do with both types of "Geheimnis", with secret and with mystery. Bonhoeffer seems to be of the opinion that it is necessary to cover and to hide both. We will come back to this point.

After this clarification on the character of mystery, we can ask a question in regard to the first part of this article: What does *sin* have to do with mystery? First: Questioning God's word – which happens in sin – means to not adore God's wisdom but to ask "why?" and to question God's goodness.[60] It is the attempt to go beyond God's commandment. In Bonhoeffer's view, God's commandment is nothing to discuss about from an external standpoint[61] or to integrate into one's own system of values. Or, to say it shortly: God's commandment is a mystery.[62] In questioning God's word sin is destroying this mystery. And second: The *fact* of sin is a mystery itself. That Adam did evil is the incomprehensible; it doesn't follow from anything.[63]

There is one aspect of shame that still needs to be considered. Bonhoeffer not only speaks about shame in human relations. Bonhoeffer also speaks

---

Seins." DBWE 5, 104 translates "Geheimnis" with „secret", but it should be translated better with "mystery".

57 E-NY 360f.
58 DBW 16, 623.
59 E-NY, 361.
60 Cf. DBWE 3, 122. Cf. ibid., 120: "The question why there is evil is not [!] a theological question, for it presupposes that it is possible to go back behind the existence that is laid upon us as sinners."
61 Cf. DBWE 3, 111.
62 God's *love* is a mystery as well (cf. DBWE 6, 84).
63 Otherwise the responsibility of Adam – and of ourselves – would be denied (cf. DBWE 3, 120). Cf. DBW 10, 373f (translation from the forthcoming translation in DBWE 10, translated by Douglass Stott, edited by Clifford Green): "If sin and faith are among the possibilities of human beings, then the complete incomprehensibility, inexcusability, and infinity of the Fall is rationalized into a comprehensible actualization of immanent possibilities." Then forgiveness as well is understood as (God given) realization of human possibilities.

about shame between a human being and God:[64] Human beings are ashamed before God; they try to hide from God, and this takes place in *conscience*. Bonhoeffer writes in *Creation and Fall*: conscience is shame before God.[65] What does this mean? Bonhoeffer understands the conscience not as God's voice but as man being his own judge.[66] This includes a basic fault: through judging himself, man escapes from God's judgment. In conscience, humankind "lives truly out of the resources of its own good and evil".[67] Thus, conscience is the "final grasp" at oneself. It is the "confirmation and justification of [one's ...] self-glorifying solitude" because it appeals to a person's better self.[68] This appeal is possible only because conscience interprets sin in the category of act, not in the category of being.[69] It understands sin as something done from time to time. In that, conscience is wrong.

And besides, conscience shows the dominance of the relation to oneself over the relation to the others. For conscience makes people assume that through "relating properly to themselves" they could also "regain the proper relationship to God and to others";[70] conscience makes people assume that if they live in accordance to themselves they automatically will be in adequate relations to the others.

We said: Conscience causes man to hide from God (this is its character of shame). Paradoxically, in this it admits that God is right.[71]

---

64 Shame is also something that takes place between human beings and the world of things. A "union of human beings with the world of things" happens in works of art, in scientific discovery and every other creative work. In this union, the division is overcome. But the process, the emergence of the work of art or of scientific discovery should be covered and respected as a mystery; this process belongs to the area of shame (cf. DBWE 6, 306).

65 Cf. DBW 3, 120: "Das Gewissen ist die Scham vor Gott". The English translation has: "Conscience means feeling shame before God" (DBWE 3, 128). – In his *Ethics*, Bonhoeffer distinguishes between shame and conscience. While shame "reminds human beings of their disunion with God and one another" conscience "is the sign of human beings' disunion within themselves". That it is possible to disconnect the relation to God and to the other human beings from the relation to oneself, this in itself is a sign for the fall (DBWE 6, 307).

66 Cf. DBWE 3, 128.

67 DBWE 2, 139.

68 DBWE 2, 139. Cf. DBWE 6, 307: Conscience is the call "to preserve the unity of the self".

69 Cf. DBWE 2, 144. – In his *Ethics*, Bonhoeffer sees this as the difference between "shame" and "conscience". Instead of obeying a commandment, conscience "divides life into permitted and prohibited". Conscience "is satisfied when the prohibition is not defied". It doesn't register that human beings are still in disunion with the origin even when they only do permitted things. Thus, "unlike shame, conscience does not encompass the whole of life, but only reacts to a specific action" (DBWE 6, 307). Bonhoeffer is convinced that this is not enough: "If sin were no more than a free act of the particular moment [freier Akt je und je], a retreat to sinless being would in principle be possible" (DBWE 2, 145). The severity of sin and the necessity of Christ's death would be ignored. Recognition of sin is adequate only if I understand the single sinful act as the estrangement of my *whole existence* from God (cf. DBW 12, 196).

70 DBWE 6, 308.

71 Cf. DBWE 3, 128.

The Mysteries of Knowledge, Sin, and Shame 37

But finally "God slays the conscience".[72] Thus, shame is overcome. It is important to note that shame is *not overcome* by the "dialectic of covering and uncovering". "Shame can be overcome only where the original unity is restored".[73] This takes place in an "inevitable exposure before God"[74] – which happens in confession.[75] In confession man stands naked and revealed before God. In this an "act of ultimate shaming"[76] takes place. This ultimate shaming overcomes the former shame. But it is not the exposure before God that causes this ultimate shame. It is God's forgiveness.[77] This forgiveness causes a shaming not because the other is evil but because the other, i.e. God, is so good. This forgiveness restores the community with God.[78]

Bonhoeffer seems to be convinced that man should not speak to others about this religious experience.[79] Even if man lost his shame in regard to God, shame still "safeguards against any display of the relationship to God".[80] Here we have the same mechanism as we had before: The secret is lifted between the two; but this lifting and the new encounter are a mystery which should not be talked about publicly.

Let me summarize what shame has to do with mystery and secret: Shame causes secrets. And shame hides the mystery of deep personal encounter. Because shame and the covering of shame are rooted in a person's freedom shame is nothing one can reckon with. Thus shame itself is a mystery as well.

The important thing about a mystery is that it occurs unpredictably; you cannot anticipate it beforehand, it is something you cannot reckon with. For that very reason it isn't astonishing that human *knowledge* has difficulties with the category of mystery.

---

72 DBWE 3, 129.
73 DBWE 6, 306.
74 DBWE 6, 306.
75 Cf. LPP, 146 and 159. Cf. Bammel, Ende, 158.
76 DBWE 6, 306.
77 Cf. DBW 6, 308: "Überwindung der Scham gibt es nur in der Beschämung durch die Vergebung der Sünde".
78 God's forgiveness is the new clothing of man. Man no longer feels ashamed because of who he is. Cf. DBWE 6, 306.
79 Cf. DBWE 6, 304f.
80 Cf. DBWE 6, 305. And the same is true about a person's relation to himself: "[…] human beings also preserve an ultimate concealment with respect to themselves, they protect their own [mystery …] from themselves, by refusing, for example, to become consciously aware of everything that is germinating within them." (Ibid.; I'm translating "Geheimnis" with mystery, not with secret here.) That Bonhoeffer speaks about "everything that is germinating within them" shows that he isn't speaking about everything that somebody doesn't want to be aware of but of something that is slowly growing in him and still fragile.

3. Knowledge

3.1 The disunity of knowledge

In the beginning, there is a special kind of knowledge.[81] Adam only knew himself in relation to the other; he knew himself as derived from and destined for the other.[82] He immediately understood himself out of the other.

But since the fall, as already mentioned, man lives in "Entzweiung", in disunion and estrangement. From this arises the fundamental characteristic of human thinking and knowledge. Bonhoeffer writes in *Creation and Fall*: "Because we do not exist in a state of unity, our thinking is torn apart as well."[83] Human reason now no longer knows God alone, but *good and evil*. Man is no longer obeying the good God but becoming himself the "origin of good and evil".[84] Good now doesn't refer to God anymore but to the human possibility of being good – and bad.[85]

Knowing about good and evil includes the possibility to judge, yes even more: "Knowing about good and evil, human beings are *essentially* judges."[86] This judgment is passed on the other human being. That again shows the reality of sin: Judging presupposes disunion with the other.[87]

And – as was already mentioned – judgment also takes place in one's own conscience where a human being becomes his own judge: In that, a human being is divided within himself.[88] Now, man becomes "self-reflective".[89] Without his knowledge about good and evil man was simply obeying, not asking why or what for. Now this immediate and simple obedience is destroyed. Man is no longer orientated to God but to himself. In his deeds, he "seeks to be seen, judged, and acknowledged as good, even if only before one's own ego".[90] Consistently, conscience becomes the guiding principle in ethics.

And in the epistemological perspective, self-knowledge becomes most important.[91]

---

[81] "Living in the origin, human beings know nothing but God alone." (DBWE 6, 300) They also know other human beings, themselves and the world of things, but only *in* knowing God.
[82] DBWE 3, 101.
[83] DBWE 3, 92.
[84] DBWE 6, 302.
[85] Cf. DBWE 6, 300. Thus, the knowledge about good and evil is knowledge "in opposition to God" (ibid.).
[86] DBWE 6, 314 (emphasis added).
[87] Cf. DBWE 6, 314.
[88] Cf. DBWE 3, 128.
[89] DBWE 6, 308.
[90] DBWE 6, 314.
[91] Cf. DBWE 6, 308.

3.2 The circular structure of knowledge

Bonhoeffer argues in his *Ethics* that in *self-knowledge* human beings try "to overcome their disunion with themselves through thought".[92] Therefore self-knowledge becomes the most important issue of human beings. And every other knowledge is used for self-knowledge: "Knowing now means establishing the relation to oneself, recognizing oneself in everything and everything in oneself."[93] This is a "sacrilegious grasping"[94] of the world; God, human beings and things are no longer seen as themselves but misused for the self.

As Bonhoeffer argues in *Act and Being*, thinking always means a "system confined in the I [...] in which the I understands itself through itself", in which "the I understands itself from itself within a closed system".[95] Bonhoeffer assumes that this is true for every kind of thinking. For, to think something means to take hold of it: "Through the act of knowing, the known is put at the disposition of the I." What is at the disposition of the I, "can be classified within the system of knowledge. As something known, it 'is' only in this system." But a system is a real system only as a closed system. Thus, the "aim of cognition is to close this system. If this happens, the I has become lord of the world".[96]

In 1932, Bonhoeffer describes this "inevitable autocracy and self-glorification" of thinking as "the corruption of the mind, which is caused by the first fall". Since the first fall, man misuses everything for himself. This sinful structure becomes concrete in his thinking: "Man 'in' and 'after' the fall refer[s] everything to himself, puts himself in the center of the world, does violence to reality, makes himself God, and God and the other man his creatures."[97] In his thinking he pulls reality "into the circle of the ego, taking away from it is original 'objectivity'."[98] Thus, the structure of sin is repeated in the structure of knowledge. Or, as Bonhoeffer says in *Act and Being*:

---

92   DBWE 6, 308.
93   DBWE 6, 308. In Bonhoeffer's eyes, this is true for every philosophical knowledge; in every philosophical concept self-understanding means "to understand oneself [...] out of oneself" (DBWE 2, 45).
94   DBWE 6, 308.
95   DBWE 2, 76. Cf. DBW 10, 444: "At the basis of all thinking lies the necessity of a system. Thinking is essentially systematic thinking, because it rests upon itself, it is the last ground and criterion of itself." Cf. to Bonhoeffer's concept of knowledge in his early writings as a whole Tietz-Steiding, Kritik.
96   DBWE 2, 94. Cf. DBWE 2, 67: "In the system lies the mastery of being by the knowing I".
97   DBW 10, 425.
98   DBW 10, 424.

Human beings have torn themselves loose from community with God and, therefore, also from that with other human beings, and now they stand alone [...] Because human beings are alone, the world is 'their' world, and other human beings have sunk into the world of things [...] God has become a religious object, and human beings themselves have become their own creator and lord, belonging to themselves. It is only to be expected that they should now begin and end with themselves in their knowing, for they are only and utterly 'with themselves' in the falsehood of naked self-glory.[99]

The thinking of a man outside revelation is – as man himself – self-encapsulated. "Godless thought [...] remains self-enclosed."[100]

That thinking puts the known at the disposition of the I, is true also if thinking tries to think something beyond the I. The early Bonhoeffer is convinced that thinking never reaches reality. Reality isn't at the disposition of the I but resists this seizing hold of it. This is why philosophical thinking remains only "within the category of possibility. Philosophical thinking can never extend beyond this category – it can never be a thinking in reality. It can form a conception of reality, but conceived reality is not reality any longer."[101] Philosophical thinking cannot reach that form of reality which is fundamentally important: the reality of the other person.

In Bonhoeffer's eyes philosophical thinking is not able to be aware of the other as a free, real subject. Through reason we destroy the mystery that the other is a person. We do so because we see in the mystery of the other a limitation of ourselves. But we want to have everything to our disposal. We want to reckon with the world. Mysteries don't fit with this desire to reckon. If reason meets a mystery it always tries to dissect it.[102]

From these insights about the character of reason Bonhoeffer concludes in *Sanctorum Communio*: "There is no cognitive way to reach" "the other as independent subject".[103] But the fact that the other *is* a free subject is of fundamental importance for Bonhoeffer as we've seen in the discussion of shame where we mentioned that shame protects the freedom of the subject, and that the shameful cover should only be lifted by the subject itself. Recognizing the other as a free subject is the fundamental event of *Christian knowledge*.[104]

---

99 DBWE 2, 137.
100 DBWE 2, 89. This self-encapsulation of thinking is a total one. This includes that thinking isn't able to recognize its own corruptness. For, if it would be able to do so, it would be able to recognize truth. And "such knowledge would already signify a placing of oneself into truth" and a certain freeing from self-encapsulation. But "[t]hinking is as little able as good works to deliver the *cor corvum in se* from itself" (DBWE 2, 80).
101 DBW 10, 424.
102 Cf. DBW 13, 360.
103 DBWE 1, 45. Cf. ibid.: "I bear within me the forms of the mind to grasp this object that, for precisely that reason, remains a mere object and never becomes a subject, or 'alien I'."
104 Cf. to the following Tietz-Steiding, Redlichkeit, 295ff.

3.3 Acknowledgement

The young Bonhoeffer studied Eberhard Grisebach's philosophy[105] and took from it the basic insight: The concrete You is a real barrier for the I. It is because it evades our grabbing. Therefore the You is a *mystery*.[106]

The encounter with the You takes place in the so called "ethical or social sphere" "when my spirit[107] is confronted by some fundamental barrier".[108] In the encounter with another person the claim of the other is a real barrier which forces me to decide if I want to answer this claim or not. In this situation of being asked to respond to a claim human beings become responsible. And, Bonhoeffer says, they become persons.

> It is a Christian insight that the person as conscious being is created [...] in the situation of responsibility, passionate ethical struggle, confrontation by an overwhelming claim; [...] the real person grows out of the concrete situation.[109]

It is only through the encounter with another human being that man finds himself.[110]

Let me mention that in Bonhoeffer's opinion the You has this significance only because it is *God's* You that encounters me in that human You.[111]

It might be astonishing that Bonhoeffer is not of the opinion that man also finds the *I* of the other through that encounter. But that the other is an I, a person, means that one can only find the other if he shows himself, if he reveals himself.[112] Only if a person chooses freely to be at our disposal is there then the possibility that we no longer forcibly dominate the other.[113]

---

105 Cf. Grisebach, Gegenwart, 480f: In der ethischen Begegnung begrenzt ein anderer Mensch, "ohne Voraussetzung der Gleichheit und Selbigkeit, [...] den Erkennenden deutlich vernehmbar von außen gegen alle und jede Berechnung, so daß diese 'Erfahrung' als dringlich und unausweichlich bezeichnet werden muß". "So geschieht eine *Begrenzung* jeder Entfaltungstendenz durch ein Transzendentes, d.h. eben durch ein den Zirkel des Ich von außen störendes und widersprechendes Wort".

106 Cf. DBW 13, 360: "Das Geheimnis [...] entzieht sich unserem Zugriff".

107 The German text has "Geist" which should be translated with spirit not with intellect as in DBWE 1 because Bonhoeffer is not only talking about intellectual barriers.

108 DBWE 1, 45.

109 DBWE 1, 49.

110 This encounter is where human beings meet the reality. "[...] reality must be given before and beyond all thinking. Reality is consequently beyond my own self, transcendent – but, again, not logically transcendent, but really transcendent." (DBW 10, 425).

111 Cf. DBWE 1, 54f. Bonhoeffer is convinced that it is possible to evade the claim of another human being, but that it is impossible to evade God's claim; thus "the human person originates only in relation to the divine", be it in resistance, be it in being overwhelmed (ibid., 49). Cf. DBWE 2, 127: "Only through Christ does my neighbor meet me as one who claims me in an absolute way from a position outside my existence."

112 Cf. DBWE 1, 56 and 213.

113 For example this takes places when a person freely lifts his or her secret.

We in fact don't dominate the other when *faith* appears.[114] Faith doesn't destroy the transcendence and freedom of the other. Faith accepts the freedom of the other and understands him as a God-given boundary (which includes letting the other have his secret).

And faith acknowledges the claim of the other. Faith doesn't try to deduce the claim of the other and in this to see it in relative terms; faith submits to the claim of the other.[115] To quote *Sanctorum Communio*: "[…] one person cannot know the other, but can only acknowledge and 'believe' in the other".[116] In faith, a human being breaks out of the closed circle of thinking and of his self-encapsulation. In faith and in being obedient to the claim of the other, he acknowledges the other as something beyond his own thinking and being. Faith is "an act which makes me transcend the limits of myself, which carries me out of the circle of my selfhood in order to acknowledge the transcendent God"[117] and the transcendent other human being.[118]

Let's concentrate for a moment on the Christian knowledge of God. For Bonhoeffer, God's revelation in the person Jesus Christ is the source of the Christian knowledge of God.[119] In Christ, "God himself speaks his word"[120] freely. God's revelation is nothing that can be calculated beforehand and reckoned with. It's a mystery.[121] The recognition of this mystery is possible only by faith.[122] Faith is that special kind of knowledge (the "believing way of knowing") which corresponds to the revelation. Bonhoeffer stresses that the "object of faith is the person of Christ *preached* in the community of faith".[123] Thus the "believing way of knowing" starts with *listening*.

In his *Ethics*, Bonhoeffer emphasizes that in Christ one knows the reconciliation or "God as the annulment of all disunion". This is "a new knowledge in which the knowledge of good and evil has been overcome".[124] This

---

114 "The […] idea of self-revelation has as its counterpart the idea of faith" (DBW 10, 431). Cf. ibid., 425: "Reality limits my boundlessness from outside, and this outside is no more intellectually conceivable but only believable."

115 Cf. DBWE 1, 202 and DBWE 2, 126.

116 DBWE 1, 54.

117 DBW 10, 431.

118 Bonhoeffer calls this faith *actus directus* because in faith one is directed only towards the other.

119 Cf. DBW 10, 460.

120 DBW 10, 428.

121 Cf. DBW 13, 362. Cf. Krötke, Bedeutung, 15ff.

122 When Bonhoeffer talks about God's "revelation in hiddenness" (DBW 10, 429) he talks about a presence of God which can only be seen by faith.

123 DBWE 2, 126.

124 DBWE 6, 317. The overcoming of the knowledge of good and evil is not a "psychologically observable fact" (ibid., 319). There can still be "an equally legitimate and necessary self-examination". But this self-examination is concentrated on the question of being elected to do the

knowledge means not knowing one's own good doing.[125] It is a knowledge that "consists entirely in doing the will of God". "The knowledge of Jesus is translated entirely into doing, without any self-reflection whatsoever."[126] A new obedience takes place. It is "self-evident, joyous, certain, and clear",[127] spontaneous and non-reflexive.[128]

3.4 Theology

Theology is the reflection of this immediate Christian knowledge. In Bonhoeffer's eyes, there is a basic difference between *philosophical* and *theological* knowledge. In 1932, he writes:

Philosophical thinking attempts to be free from premises […]; Christian thinking has to be conscious of its particular premise, that is, of the premise of the reality of God, before and beyond all thinking.[129]

Theology isn't possible without faith: "The basis of all theology is the fact of faith. Only in the act of faith as a direct act is God recognized as the reality which is beyond and outside of our thinking". Theology is, as Bonhoeffer states in accordance with Karl Barth, "a construction […] a posteriori".[130] Thus theology is possible only "by holding fast in humility to the word that has been heard".[131] It is the obedience of thinking that makes the difference between theological and philosophical reason. This obedience and humility not only stands at the beginning of theology. It also has to be its constant companion. For, theological thinking also tries to make a system out of the revelation.[132] There is always the danger that theology tries to

---

will of God, not of choosing between several possibilities (ibid., 320). This new knowledge is self-understanding *through* Christ (cf. DBWE 2, 141. Cf. ibid., 143f: "self-understanding is possible only where the living Christ approaches us"). Only through Christ can one's own sin be recognized (cf. Busch Nielsen, Sünden, 33). The recognition of one's own sin is not possible directly. Being a sinner is an "existential designation"; the sinner is totally qualified by "not being in the truth" (DBWE 2, 136). Thus, recognition of sin is possible only through revelation.

125 Cf. DBWE 6, 317.
126 DBWE 6, 318.
127 DBWE 6, 309.
128 This is why Bonhoeffer can say that the basis of Christian ethics is "to supersede" the knowledge of good and evil (DBWE 6, 299).
129 DBW 10, 424. Nevertheless theology needs philosophy because theology uses philosophical terms (cf. Bonhoeffer's own enterprise in *Act and Being*).
130 DBW 10, 425f.
131 DBWE 2, 131.
132 Cf. DBW 10, 426. This characteristic has its roots not in the sinfulness of the theologian but in the fact that thinking in its essential meaning, that is in the origin and in the eschaton, develops a system because it doesn't need to interrupt itself: "That thought tends toward system, unable to disrupt itself, containing itself within itself – this is its designation by virtue of creation

reckon with God's revelation and to destroy the mystery. Therefore it is important that theology is "in immediate reference to preaching"[133] that is in reference to the place where a new encounter with the mystery is possible.

For Bonhoeffer, the main duty of theological knowledge is to deal adequately with the mystery. God's revelation in flesh is the crucial mystery theology has to keep. It is not the task of theological knowledge to abolish this mystery. It's the duty of theology to keep God's miracle as miracle. But how is this possible?

Of course we could argue that theology should *hide* the mysteries of God and no longer speak about God publicly. At first glance this seems to follow from Bonhoeffer's own explanations. Hanfried Müller for example argues that Bonhoeffer wanted the abolition of public Christian religiosity and that this is the core of his non-religious interpretation.[134] Bonhoeffer's texts seem to support this interpretation. His idea of arcane discipline seems to point in that direction.[135]

In his *Ethics* Bonhoeffer writes that he often,

precisely in completely serious situations – for instance, when facing someone grieving deeply over a death – [...] decide[s] on a 'penultimate' response, such as a kind of helpless solidarity in the face of so terrible an event, expressed through silence, instead of speaking the words of biblical comfort.[136]

And in *Letters and Papers from Prison* he argues that "a secret discipline must be restored whereby the *mysteries* of the Christian faith are protected against profanation".[137]

I want to shed a different light on that matter in asking: What is meant by "profanation"? In *Act and Being*, Bonhoeffer uses the expression "profane" to describe the character of *philosophical* thinking which – as we have seen – takes hold of the thought thing and puts it at the disposition of the I. From this we can follow: The profanation of mystery that Bonhoeffer is talking about in *Letters and Papers from Prison* could mean: to reckon with it, to seize hold of it and no longer letting it take hold of me.[138] This in fact is the

---

and eschata [...] in which thought no longer needs to disrupt itself because it is in reality, placed by God eternally into the truth, because it sees." (DBWE 2, 89).

133 "[...] helping its preparation, all the while humbly submitting to its 'judgment'" (DBWE 2, 131).

134 Müller, Kirche, 400.

135 Cf. Pangritz, Forderung, and his contribution in this volume.

136 DBWE 6, 152.

137 LPP, 286.

138 Cf. DBWE 4, 45: "Costly grace is grace as God's holy treasure which must be protected from the world and which must not be thrown to the dogs. [The editors here refer to his idea of arcane discipline.]" The context makes clear what Bonhoeffer means with the concept of arcane discipline here: The problem of costly grace thrown to the dogs is that it is a grace that doesn't take hold of our whole life, that isn't realized in discipleship.

mistake of the religious: The religious allocate God to a special place when they *reckon* with God at the boundaries of life. Bonhoeffer himself wants to restore the mystery of Christ in the centre of life. In this he wants to restore that Christ "claims for himself and the Kingdom of God the whole human life",[139] a claim which takes hold of me.

This interpretation matches with how Bonhoeffer continues the quoted passage from the *Ethics* where he talks about "someone grieving deeply over a death": Speaking Christian words in such a serious situation would probably mean "having it [sc. the word of God] at one's disposal".[140]

If this is correct then our dealing with mystery is problematic *if* our thinking and speaking forces the mystery under our disposal and in this destroys its character of mystery.[141]

In a London sermon from 1934, Bonhoeffer admits that *thinking* does not *necessarily* do so. He admits that our thinking about God could also make *God's mystery visible*. And he argues: *The better* we know something, the more mysterious it becomes for us. If our knowledge is a believing and loving knowledge which acknowledges the freedom of the other then the mystery of the other is not decreasing if we know more and more about him. It's the other way around: The more we know about him the more mysterious he becomes.[142]

Is *talking* about the Christian mystery then also permissible? Here again the distinction between secret and mystery might become helpful. Of course, one should not talk about the *secrets* that somebody told him. But a mystery – and especially the mystery of God – is something different. Ebeling writes that mystery *doesn't want* to be hidden; a mystery wants to be told.[143] Of course it should not be told as something to reckon with or to solve. And it should not be told via an exposure of one's personal experience with God.[144] But language that doesn't announce a mystery becomes empty. And a mystery that isn't told by words vanishes.[145] Ebeling argues that telling a mystery lets the mystery be seen as something that gives us reason to think and to believe, to hope and to love.[146] My question is if it's

---

139 LPP, 342.
140 DBWE 6, 152.
141 Cf. also Krötke, Bedeutung, 17f.
142 Cf. DBW 13, 361.
143 Cf. Ebeling, Profanität, 197f.
144 Cf. DBWE 6, 304f.
145 Ebeling, Profanität, 200: "[...] Sprache [dient] dem Wahrnehmen und Wahren von Geheimnis. Sprache, die es nicht mehr mit dem Ansagen von Geheimnis zu tun hat, wird leer. Geheimnis, das nicht mehr durch das Wort vorgebracht wird, entschwindet." Cf. Ebeling, Gott, 398: "Wir dürfen das Reden von Gott nicht unverantwortet fortsetzen, aber auch nicht unverantwortet unterlassen."
146 Ebeling, Gott, 413.

possible to interpret Bonhoeffer's theory of mystery in this perspective. Or, if that's impossible then I would like to ask if it isn't necessary to criticize Bonhoeffer's emphasis on silence and on not speaking about mysteries.[147] Of course, we should not talk about secrets. But we could talk about mysteries if we speak about them without reckoning with them.

Let me conclude with two paragraphs in Bonhoeffer's later texts which point in that direction. First: In a "Theological Letter" in December 1939, Bonhoeffer explains that theology arises from kneeling in front of the mystery of incarnation. God in flesh, that's where theology begins. He stresses that through the christological paradoxes of the Old Church the character of this mystery is shown.[148] And then he says that the Old Church dared to *pronounce* these paradoxes. In the Chalcedonense, without destroying the mystery the Old Church is *pronouncing* it.[149] Why? Bonhoeffer says: They were unable *not* to speak about it.[150]

Second: In the quoted paragraph of his *Ethics*, Bonhoeffer emphasizes that "God will speak [his word] in God's own time". But, and this is important: God can speak "only through a human mouth".[151] Would somebody totally refuse to speak about God and his mystery publicly then he in a certain sense would *take hold* of God's word. And this would mean to destroy the Christian mystery as well.

Bibliography

Primary Sources

BONHOEFFER, D., Sanctorum Communio: A Theological Study of the Sociology of the Church, Dietrich Bonhoeffer Works, Vol. 1, ed. by C.J. Green, transl. by R. Krauss/N. Lukens, Minneapolis 1998 (= DBWE 1).

–, Act and Being: Transcendental Philosophy and Ontology in Systematic Theology, Dietrich Bonhoeffer Works, Vol. 2, ed. by W.W. Floyd, Jr., transl. by H.M. Rumscheidt, Minneapolis 1996 (= DBWE 2).

–, Schöpfung und Fall, Dietrich Bonhoeffer Werke, Vol. 3, ed. by M. Rüter/I. Tödt, München 1989 (= DBW 3).

---

147 I guess it's questionable that Bonhoeffer advises not to talk about feelings (cf. Bethge, Biographie, 941 and 948). Is it really a helpful advice? What for example about all the love songs and love poems?

148 Cf. DBW 15, 538f.

149 Cf. DBW 15, 542.

150 Cf. DBW 15, 541. In the same letter Bonhoeffer asks in a normative sense where in the faculties the mystery of God in flesh was *taught* as mystery and where we *heard* it *preached* (DBW 15, 538).

151 DBWE 6, 152f.

–, Creation and Fall: A Theological Exposition of Genesis 1–3, Dietrich Bonhoeffer Works, Vol. 3, ed. by J.W. de Gruchy, transl. by D.S. Bax, Minneapolis 1997 (= DBWE 3).
–, Discipleship, Dietrich Bonhoeffer Works, Vol. 4, ed. by G.B. Kelly/J.D. Godsey, transl. by B. Green/R. Krauss, Minneapolis 2001 (= DBWE 4).
–, Gemeinsames Leben. Das Gebetbuch der Bibel, Dietrich Bonhoeffer Werke, Vol. 5, ed. by G.L. Müller/A. Schönherr, München 1987 (= DBW 5).
–, Life Together. Prayerbook of the Bible, Dietrich Bonhoeffer Works, Vol. 5, ed. by G.B. Kelly, transl. by D.W. Bloesch/J.H. Burtness, Minneapolis 1996 (= DBWE 5).
–, Ethik, Dietrich Bonhoeffer Werke, Vol. 6, ed. by I. Tödt/H.E. Tödt/E. Feil/C. Green, München 1992 (= DBW 6).
–, Ethics, Dietrich Bonhoeffer Works, Vol. 6, ed. by C. Green, transl. by R. Krauss/Ch.C. West/ D.W. Stott, Minneapolis 2005 (= DBWE 6).
–, Fragmente aus Tegel, Dietrich Bonhoeffer Werke, Vol. 7, ed. by R. Bethge/I. Tödt, Gütersloh 1994 (= DBW 7).
–, Barcelona, Berlin, Amerika 1928–1931, Dietrich Bonhoeffer Werke, Vol. 10, ed. by. R. Staats/ H.Ch. von Hase together with H. Roggelin/M. Wünsche, München 1991 (= DBW 10).
–, Berlin 1932–1933, Dietrich Bonhoeffer Werke, Vol. 12, ed. by C. Nicolaisen/E.-A. Scharffenorth, Gütersloh 1997 (= DBW 12).
–, London 1933–1935, Dietrich Bonhoeffer Werke, Vol. 13, ed. by H. Goedeking/M. Heimbucher/ H.-W. Schleicher, Gütersloh 1994 (= DBW 13).
–, Illegale Theologenausbildung: Sammelvikariate 1937–1940, Dietrich Bonhoeffer Werke, Vol. 15, ed. by D. Schulz, Gütersloh 1998 (= DBW 15).
–, Konspiration und Haft 1940–1945, Dietrich Bonhoeffer Werke, Vol. 16, ed. by J. Glenthøj/ U. Kabitz/W. Krötke, Gütersloh 1996 (= DBW 16).
–, Ethics, transl. by N.H. Smith, New York et al. 1995 (= E-NY).
–, Letter and Papers from Prison. The Enlarged Edition, ed. by E. Bethge, transl. by R. Fuller/ F. Clark et al., New York et al. 1997 (= LPP).

Secondary Sources

BAMMEL, CH.-M., Aufgetane *Augen* – Aufgedecktes Angesicht. Theologische Studien zur Scham im interdisziplinären Gespräch, ÖTh 19, Gütersloh 2005.
–, Das *Ende* der "gottlosen Offenheit". Die Frage nach dem Menschen in einer "Kultur wechselseitiger Anerkennung". Momentaufnahmen im Gespräch mit Dietrich Bonhoeffer, Dietrich Bonhoeffer Yearbook 2, 2005, 146–169.
BETHGE, E., Dietrich Bonhoeffer. Eine *Biographie*, Gütersloh [8]2004.
CLASS, G., Der verzweifelte *Zugriff* auf das Leben. Dietrich Bonhoeffers Sündenverständnis in "Schöpfung und Fall", NBSTh 15, Neukirchen-Vluyn 1994.
EBELING, G., *Gott* und Wort, in: Ebeling, Wort und Glaube, Vol. 2, Tübingen 1969, 396–432.
–, *Profanität* und Geheimnis, in: Ebeling, Wort und Glaube, Vol. 2, 184–208.
GREEN, C.J., Bonhoeffer. A Theology of *Sociality*. Revised Edition, Grand Rapids/Cambridge 1999.
GRIMM, J. AND W., Deutsches Wörterbuch, Vol. 3 and Vol. 32, München 1984.
GRISEBACH, E., *Gegenwart*. Eine kritische Ethik, Halle an der Saale 1928.
HARTENSTEIN, F., "Und sie erkannten, dass sie nackt waren ..." (Gen 3,7). Beobachtungen zur *Anthropologie* der Paradieserzählung, EvTh 65, 2005, 277–293.
KRÖTKE, W., Die *Bedeutung* von "Gottes Geheimnis" für Dietrich Bonhoeffers Verständnis der Religionen und der Religionslosigkeit, in: Krötke, Gottes Kommen und menschliches Verhalten. Aufsätze und Vorträge zum Problem des theologischen Verständnisses von "Religion" und "Religionslosigkeit", Stuttgart 1984, 9–23.

–, *Weltlichkeit* und Sünde. Zur Auseinandersetzung mit Denkformen Martin Luthers in der Theologie D. Bonhoeffers, in: Krötke, Die Universalität des offenbaren Gottes. Gesammelte Aufsätze, München 1985, 152–164.

MÜLLER, H., Von der *Kirche* zur Welt. Ein Beitrag zu der Beziehung des Wortes Gottes auf die societas in Dietrich Bonhoeffers theologischer Entwicklung, Leipzig ²1966.

NIELSEN, K.B., Starke und schwache *Sünden*. Zum Sündenverständnis Dietrich Bonhoeffers, KuD 47, 2001, 30–41.

PANGRITZ, A., Dietrich Bonhoeffers *Forderung* einer Arkandisziplin – eine unerledigte Anfrage an Kirche und Theologie, Köln 1988.

TIETZ-STEIDING, CH., Bonhoeffers *Kritik* der verkrümmten Vernunft. Eine erkenntnistheoretische Untersuchung, BHTh 112, Tübingen 1999.

–, Verkrümmte Vernunft und intellektuelle *Redlichkeit*. Dietrich Bonhoeffers Erkenntnistheorie, in: Ch. Gremmels/W. Huber (Ed.), Religion im Erbe. Dietrich Bonhoeffer und die Zukunftsfähigkeit des Christentums, Gütersloh 2002, 293–307.

Peter Dabrock

Responding to "Wirklichkeit"

Reclaiming Bonhoeffer's Approach to Theological Ethics between Mystery and the Formation of the World

1. Why look back to Bonhoeffer's *Ethics*?

1.1 Recent expectations and disappointments concerning theological ethics

Theological ethics from a Protestant perspective appear subject to various critiques. From a non-theological perspective, it has been accused of being irrational or having been rendered redundant in light of philosophy. Since it seeks to play a part in forming the overlapping consensus of liberal societies, it is argued that theological ethics should reduce its convictions to the level of public reason – i.e. to abandon its comprehensive doctrines. From a dogmatic-theological perspective – depending on the respective denominational background – it might be critiqued on the basis of an (allegedly) overly-strong focus on God's demand, instead of God's promise. In effect, this point of view sees theological ethics as being in danger of thoughtlessly shifting the co-ordinates of good Protestant theology.

These constellations between the fictions of identity search and outcome accountability are confusing. Not only do they raise expectations, but the "expectation of expectations" (as Luhmann observed). In such a situation, it is worthwhile to look back on similar historical constellations. Of course, the idea here is not simply to repeat the past but to develop new perspectives in order to cope with the present: to widen one's own horizon by engaging with a strange past. The following remarks seek to address this basic concern.

1.2 Disagreements in the response to Bonhoeffer's *Ethics*

Although Bonhoeffer lived in a political and societal situation quite different from ours, his reflections on ethics still impact upon us. The reason lies in the fact that, despite the dramatic circumstances in which he lived, Bonhoeffer struggled in both practical and theoretical ways with the same tension we currently deal with, namely: how can theological ethics be founded and justified so that it opens up new vistas on the formation of the world, on the one hand, and yet not surrender its own Christian (or, respectively, Protestant) authenticity on the other hand? Can theological ethics be conceived in such a way that it does not degenerate into a civil-societal function for stabilisation, but rather effectuates societal relevance as an intrinsic aim?

Bonhoeffer was concerned with this task all his life, up to his martyrdom, though his thorough fascination with the theoretical conceptions of ethics extended beyond the testimony of his death. As Bethge noted, finding an adequate approach here seemed to be a "life duty" for Bonhoeffer,[1] reminding us of one of his well-known statements: "I sometimes feel as if my life were more or less over, and as if all I had to do now were to finish my *Ethics*" ("manchmal denke [ich], ich hätte nun eigentlich mein Leben mehr oder weniger hinter mir und müßte nur noch meine Ethik fertigmachen").[2]

However, it is no secret that the history of responses to Bonhoeffer's *Ethics* has been one of irritation. Reactions have ranged from pitiful sneers, indifferent nodding and suspicion, to somewhat benevolent and somewhat old-fashioned admissions that the volume lacks originality or is simply an unfinished, non-adapted fragment and that most of the inconsistencies and insufficiencies would have been eliminated by the author.[3] Other recipients enthusiastically celebrate the *Ethics*:

These fragments contain such a new, even revolutionary approach of theological ethics that you may confidently speak of a self-sufficient, although unfinished ethic. Its impact on resolving recent key problems is obvious.[4]

Nevertheless, despite the different assessments, there has been a general agreement in principle throughout the long history of interpretation surrounding Bonhoeffer's *Ethics* that the response has fallen short of the respective researcher's expectations.[5] Kinder evaluations often predict that the *Ethics* will become more important in future times[6] – unfortunately, this prediction has been made throughout the entire history of responses to the *Ethics*.[7]

---

1 Bethge, Bonhoeffer, 801.
2 LPP, 163. DBW 8, 237. Cf. DBW 8, 188.
3 Cf. Krause, Bonhoeffer, 61f; Honecker, Christologie; Slenczka, Schuld, 106.
4 Mokrosch et al., Bonhoeffers Ethik, 13.
5 This complaint arose soon after the publication of the *Ethics* fragments, notably first by editor Eberhard Bethge himself (cf. DBW 6, 11), and has continued to the present day; cf. e.g. Wannenwetsch, Gestaltwerdung, 64; Green, Introduction, 1.
6 Cf. Wannenwetsch, Gestaltwerdung, 64.
7 Cf. Moltmann, Herrschaft, 6.

Apart from taking an interest in such speculation, one should not pass over the doubtlessly irritating discrepancy between the often-claimed (yet rarely demonstrated) importance of the text. The peculiar reception-history may serve to warn us away from particular responses: to avoid hagiolatries, eisegeses, interest-driven manipulations, improper modernisations as well as alleged historical-critical summaries. One must simply read the original! The first group overemphasises their own interests, thereby destroying the strangeness of the literal and biographical texts; the second group denies any engagement with the text and thus misses the challenges posed by the strange words and peculiar times.

1.3 How Bonhoeffer's *Ethics* can pose a challenge for today

How can one escape this dilemma, which the interpretation of Bonhoeffer shares with responses to other significant texts? In his early 1959 study on Bonhoeffer, Jürgen Moltmann already picked up on this odd situation and declared:

Recent Bonhoeffer interpretation suffers from the fact that several ideas of the *Ethics*, or of the last letters and papers from prison, were considered in an isolated way. Their original rootedness in his early systematic writings concerning the sociology of the church (*Communio Sanctorum*, written 1927, published 1930, republished 1954) and concerning the issue of a theological ontology (*Akt und Sein*, 1931, ²1956) were not sufficiently taken into account.[8]

In my opinion, it is unfortunate that Moltmann overstresses his (otherwise helpful) advice to pay attention to Bonhoeffer's early writings. Although his study is an excellent reconstruction and contextualisation of Bonhoeffer's theological ideas, Moltmann could have done more than merely present a (more-or-less) differentiated report. (Admittedly, this observation is written 46 years after the fact – with the hindsight of 46 years of reception-history.)

Calling attention to Bonhoeffer's *Ethics* as an adaptable *and* irritating challenge for us today, I would like to follow Moltmann's approach in respect to content – in other words, to pay attention to Bonhoeffer's early systematic writings while reading his ethical works. It is not sufficient to interpret the fragments of the *Ethics* simply with or from the perspective of the letters and papers from prison.[9]

---

8   Moltmann, Herrschaft, 5 (my translation).
9   In my opinion, the question of the continuity or discontinuity in Bonhoeffer's theology (which has fascinated the Bonhoeffer research community for so long) is of little importance. Each of the different assessments depends on the particular presuppositions regarding the meaning of "continuity", and when such continuity ends, despite the legitimate transformations evident in

Putting Moltmann's suggestion into practice, I will not focus primarily on Bonhoeffer's terminological and conceptual solutions but rather on his sensitivity for particular problems. This highly-developed capacity is echoed in Bonhoeffer's tendency to provide various delimitations,[10] though these did not always lead to the presentation of constructive alternatives for the points he was critiquing.

When dealing with Bonhoeffer's considerations, one could be content with a precise examination of the positions and sources disapproved of by Bonhoeffer himself. This method may appear fruitful – and some progress might even be made (simply due to the insights gained by a process of dismissing various alternatives) – but such an approach will not produce a high yield from a systematic perspective since one never risks engaging with one's own convictions. A further alternative might be to examine the distinctions put forward by Bonhoeffer himself, and then to try and discover new challenges for our time "between the lines", using our terms and reflecting on our own problems. If one asks in this way, and listens carefully to the possible responses of the text (beyond the limits of our former questions), then this may actually broaden our horizons.

This alternate type of response – a transforming listening – was previously proposed by Heinrich Ott and Oswald Bayer, among others. Yet their own implementation of this hermeneutical idea met with a great deal of criticism.[11] In order to counter the suspicion that this approach provides nothing but badly-packed eisegesis, it is worth pointing out that in some cases (indeed exactly in those cases we are interested in) our own analytical methods now far exceed those available to Bonhoeffer in his time. Making such a contextual jump by no means implies any disregard for Bonhoeffer, rather it takes into account our own insights and progress in methodology. Indeed, this hermeneutical approach might gain additional acceptance by applying such a method (which Bonhoeffer himself used, though at an earlier stage of development). Using such a method provides one (but by no means the only) bridge between historic sources and systematic applications. In the following sections, my aim is to cross such a bridge by using the phenomenological method to interpret one of the key concepts of Bonhoeffer's *Ethics* – namely "Wirklichkeit".[12] It is important to note here that since the term "Wirklichkeit" has more connotations in German than pro-

---

every approach. Since these presuppositions cannot be standardised – how (and why) should they? – this debate remains futile. At most it provides deeper insights into a researcher's own methodological assumptions.

10 Cf. Tödt et al., Afterword, 439.
11 Cf. Ott, Wirklichkeit, 65; Bayer, Mitte, 276. For a critique of Ott cf. Mayer, Christuswirklichkeit, 31-33.
12 Cf. e.g. Ott; Mayer; Abromeit.

vided by the simple English translation "reality", I will leave it untranslated in this paper. This will also serve to highlight the strangeness of the concept.

The phenomenological method is able to act as such a bridge since, from the beginning, Bonhoeffer's thinking was both in critical dialogue with phenomenology and also influenced by it. This has been noted by several commentators.[13] When speaking of phenomenology, I will concentrate primarily on Bernhard Waldenfels – since Waldenfels has established an ingenious synthesis of the dramatically different works by Merleau-Ponty, Lévinas, Derridas, Nietzsche and Foucault.[14] When interpreting the *Ethics* with this new phenomenology, three intermediary results and one challenge quickly become apparent. First, as Bonhoeffer himself noted: "Wirklichkeit" cannot be interpreted adequately in essentialist or idealistic terms.[15] Second, "Wirklichkeit" will not be found in isolation from so called significative differences (addressed in more detail below). Third, using "Wirklichkeit" requires a bond or connection to our external world and experiences, though that does not mean identification with that world or those experiences. At the same time, theology faces the challenge of bearing in mind the sensitivity concerning "distorted" reason.[16]

Within the internal language of theology, these three intermediary results, and final challenge, concerning this single, qualified term "Wirklichkeit" might easily be addressed. There is no doubt that the fragments of Bonhoeffer's *Ethics* prefer such an internal language. But if one attaches any importance to the demand expressed in 1 Peter 3,15 – "Always be ready to make your defence to anyone who demands from you an accounting for the hope that is in you"[17] – then one must allow for a communicative option, in order to justify the theological understanding of "Wirklichkeit" in extra-theological context.[18] I am sure that this communicative challenge will also result in noteworthy, inner-theological insights.

---

13 Cf. v. Soosten, Nachwort, 314f; Boomgaarden, Wirklichkeit, 203–299; Tietz-Steiding, Kritik, 40–88; Wannenwetsch, Gestaltwerdung, 59; Reuter, Nachwort, 175.

14 For a deeper understanding not only of Waldenfels' phenomenology, but of its sources as well as the options and limitations for its applicability in theological contexts, cf. Dabrock, Glaube.

15 Cf. Tietz-Steiding, Kritik; Tietz-Steiding, Redlichkeit.

16 Bonhoeffer criticised phenomenology in *Act and Being* mostly due to its inability to adequately pay tribute to this state of human nature. Apart from (justifiably) doubting that it must be a duty of philosophy to transcend the human sphere, it could be sufficient that it reconstructs the openness and infinitude of human 'world interpretations'. No more is required of a realistic philosophy, and theology – for which God is more than necessary (cf. Jüngel, Geheimnis, 30f. 35. 37) – should not expect any more from an honest philosophy.

17 This verse has been called the "Magna Charta of fundamental theology". Cf. Seckler, Fundamentaltheologie, 468.

18 "Extra-theological" here does not mean "non-theological" – as a sweeping prejudice in Protestant theology concerning fundamental theology suggests. "Extra-theological" merely desig-

By using Waldenfels' phenomenology, it can be shown that the significative difference Bonhoeffer introduces between "Christuswirklichkeit" as "Wirklichkeit" expresses a so-called responsive difference between the (believed) Word of God (in Jesus Christ) and the response (as formation of the world). Bearing this difference in mind does not only reclaim the mystery of "Wirklichkeit", but also represents a challenge by theological ethics to other ethics that do not attend to the "polyphony of life"[19] – because they do not begin with this responsive difference, but rather overemphasise structural or intentional orders. Contrary to those approaches, it should be asked how (according to Bonhoeffer) responsiveness to the mystery of "Christuswirklichkeit" is to be expressed as "formation" ("Gestaltung") and as "preparing the way" ("Wegbereitung").

Dealing with a new phenomenology will also produce more insights beyond those inner-theological intermediary results already mentioned. Bonhoeffer's understanding of "Wirklichkeit" as a responsive difference can serve to mediate between three topics which were often seen to exist in tension: (1) the identification of "Wirklichkeit" with the one and only "Christuswirklichkeit",[20] (2) the simultaneously asserted differentiation between the Ultimate and the Penultimate, and (3) the discrepancy in ethical options between situation ethics, normative ethics and the ethics of responsibility caused by this tension.

In short, by conceptualising theological ethics as responsive ethics the way Bonhoeffer did (not primarily by his concepts, but by his intention), not only can theological ethics defend a believer's hope, it can also shape public reason. In any case, it will pursue the mystery which, as Eberhard Jüngel notes, becomes more mysterious the closer one comes to it.[21]

---

nates the location or topos of theological arguments, not their method. Several Catholic and Protestant approaches to fundamental theology have demonstrated convincingly that it is possible and necessary (if one takes one's dialogue partner seriously) to justify and reformulate intrinsic religious convictions in the language of public reason. Furthermore, in this sphere they give rise to new perspectives on old questions and thus challenge other "Weltanschauungen" in this way. Of course, in so doing, the theological message will be changed from the dictum of the gospel to the dictum of law (cf. Jüngel, Entsprechungen, 292).

19 LPP, 303.
20 This assumed thesis led to the allegation of christomonism. Cf. Mayer, Christuswirklichkeit.
21 Cf. Jüngel, Entsprechungen, 330 (Jüngel distinguishes between "mystery" and "puzzle" in that the latter can and should be solved. Cf. Jüngel, Gott als Geheimnis, 304–347).

2. Responding to the mystery of "Wirklichkeit"

2.1 The legitimacy of delimiting Hume's law

Before we can focus on our analysis of Bonhoeffer's conception of "Wirklichkeit", one further incidental remark is necessary if we wish to be taken seriously in the field of general ethics. It is by no means a given to concede a central place in moral discourse to a term with ontological connotations, viz., "Wirklichkeit". Such an immediate sharing of terms conflicts with one of the most fundamental axioms of modern ethics which has come to be known as Hume's law with its short formula "You cannot go from is to ought".[22] But questioning this axiom itself does not only correspond to Hume's original idea but is also consistent with many other older, as well as more recent, ethical theories. To mention just one: we have seen the idea that obligation is based on corresponding capabilities (*nulla obligatio sine posse*), which is an old ethical principle bequeathed to us from the Scholastics. Reformulated in the language of system-theory, it means that "communication depends on appropriate codes and programmes". These approaches insist that being must be taken into account at least indirectly within the moral sphere.

Most descriptions of society take a lot of implicit evaluations and crypto-normative claims for granted. The socio-psychological awareness of this fact inversely alludes to a contamination of being with norms and values. Moreover, it denies and rejects any such strict separation as a methodological coercion disconnected from the real life-world. Approving so-called bridge principles[23] seeks to undermine such a rigorous separation. In analytical ethics, especially analytical bioethics, these bridge principles propose the idea that some being does have an ought-character in itself or, put more carefully, that ignoring such a recognition bears the burden of proof. Our intention here is not to discuss deconstructive or Protestant-theological approaches which cast doubt on ethics in general, since this causes all inner ethical differentiations to lose ground.[24] Ultimately, it might be asked how one deals with a "moral primal scene".[25] This expression comes from Bern-

---

22 Cf. Hume, Natur, 469. However it is generally overlooked that Hume merely cautioned against this crossover from is to ought, never declaring it to be an outright impossibility. This cannot be pursued here.

23 Cf. Ruß, Wissen.

24 Cf. Caputo, Sketch; Maurer, Gerechtigkeit.

25 The moral primal scene finds its most radical articulation in the following formulation which Lévinas reminds us of: "The face of the Other means: 'You shall not murder/you will not murder!'" Not recognising this call effectuates not only a moral lapse, but also a so-called performative contradiction. That is, by the mentioned meaning of the face, an "ethical" chasm opens up in the

hard Waldenfels, who uses it to describe a situation where we are confronted with a claim we seemingly cannot withdraw from. I will expand on this special topic below.

Enumerating these very different pieces of theory (even without being able to develop them here) aims to underline the fact that while we will not follow Hume's law, we do not hold an irrational view of ethics and are indeed aware of a crossover from is to ought. This also means that when Bonhoeffer grants a central place in his *Ethics* to the conception of "Wirklichkeit", he should not be reproached for a lack of complexity. Far from it. Rather, we can learn from those for whom ethics was a "life duty" that ethics is a bold venture inasmuch as we must face both the moral and transmoral reasons for our actions.[26] This may produce an "outrageous demand"[27] for other ethics because it "supersede[s]" their

> presuppositions [...] that it is questionable whether it even makes sense to speak at all of Christian ethics. If we do it nevertheless,[28] then this can only mean that Christian ethics claims to articulate the origin of the whole ethical enterprise, and thus to be considered an ethic only as the critique of all ethics.[29]

How this works in Bonhoeffer's approach is the issue we will now explore.

2.2 "Christuswirklichkeit" as the responsive difference of the reality of the world

When experts on Bonhoeffer consider "Wirklichkeit" as the (or at least one) crucial conception of the *Ethics*,[30] they refer to the following passage:

> In Christ we are invited to participate in the reality of God and the reality of the world at the same time, the one not without the other. The reality of God is disclosed only as it

---

direction of all metaphysical and moral orders. It precedes the separation of being and ought. The formula "You shall not murder/you will not murder!" not only expresses an imperative, but also forms the first condition of all communication. Either one has always recognised this claim of the Other or – heaven forbid! – she will be murdered, thus ignoring this condition. Beyond the second "alternative" one always moves in the trace of the (transcendental) recognition of the Other. This insight has a high impact on bioethical questions today; cf. Dabrock/Klinnert/Schardien, Menschenwürde, 117–147.

26 Cf. for this expression Fischer, Gründe.
27 DBWE 6, 47.
28 And it is done throughout the whole text of the *Ethics*!
29 Cf. DBWE 6, 299f. Note that three different text-components – each probably intended as the opening passage of the envisioned book – each convey the same message of attacking other ethics; cf. DBW 6, 435. DBWE 6, 429.
30 Cf. Tödt, Perspektiven, 36; Abromeit, Geheimnis, 122.

places me completely into the reality of the world. But I find the reality of the world always already borne, accepted, and reconciled in the reality of God. That is the mystery of the revelation of God in the human being Jesus Christ. The Christian ethic asks, then, how this reality of God and of the world that is given in Christ becomes real in our word.[31]

In fact, we encounter here terms which are most important for Bonhoeffer (as we know from other contexts), terms like "mystery" (the main theme of this volume), but also: "reality", "reality of the world", "Jesus Christ", and "revelation". Trying to understand the text, and ourselves in view of the text, requires us to take note and be aware not only of the meanings of the terms but also of their interrelations. For example, each gradient of validity depends on the specific position which each term holds only in relation to the systematic positions of the other terms. For this reason, let us start by looking at a single section of this passage, which Heinz-Eduard Tödt – one of the best experts on, and interpreters of, Bonhoeffer – considered to be the key for any understanding of Bonhoeffer's entire *Ethics*:[32]

The reality of God is disclosed only as it places me completely into the reality of the world. But I find the reality of the world always already borne, accepted, and reconciled in the reality of God.

In this passage we find a double, asymmetrically disposed relationship between "the reality of God" and "the reality of the world". The conceptual distinction between "the reality of God" and "the reality of the world" raises a mutual challenge.[33] This polemic occurs concurrently, in the same extensionality: i.e. the *one* reality we live in. It is nothing other than the "one realm of the Christ-reality [...] in which the reality of God and the reality of the world are united".[34] Since "thinking in terms of two realms" appears to be a static and (theologically speaking) legalistic way of thinking, Bonhoeffer argues unambiguously against it.

Seeing that Bonhoeffer considers many points of access to the one reality through different accounts to be possible, his method (intentionally or unintentionally) shares the phenomenological interpretation of reality and ex-

---

[31] DBWE 6, 55. Cf. DBW 6, 40: "In Christus begegnet uns das Angebot, an der Gotteswirklichkeit und an der Weltwirklichkeit zugleich teil zu bekommen, eines nicht ohne das andere. Die Wirklichkeit Gottes erschließt sich nicht anders als indem sie mich ganz in die Weltwirklichkeit hineinstellt, die Weltwirklichkeit aber finde ich immer schon getragen, angenommen, versöhnt in der Wirklichkeit Gottes vor. Das ist das Geheimnis der Offenbarung Gottes in dem Menschen Jesus Christus. Die christliche Ethik fragt nun nach dem Wirklichwerden dieser Gottes- und Weltwirklichkeit, die in Christus gegeben ist, in unserer Welt".

[32] Cf. Tödt, Perspektiven, 36.

[33] Bonhoeffer even speaks of a "polemic unity" of the worldly and the Christian (cf. DBWE 6, 60. DBW 6, 45).

[34] DBWE 6, 58. DBW 6, 44.

perience. Phenomenology argues that reality (or the way we access it) does not occur as raw data or *facta bruta*. Rather, it appears (or, correspondingly, we receive it) in the manner of "something *as* something".[35] Thus we have experience by interpretation and, at the same time, interpretation by experience – a modus Waldenfels calls "significative difference".[36] In using this idiom, Waldenfels underlines that all our descriptions of reality are "interpreted and treated experience[s]".[37] Since the significative difference marks the constitution of reality for us, Waldenfels characterises it as the "fundamental difference"[38] by which phenomenology passes or fails.[39] He characterises it as the eye of a needle[40] – as its true, irreducible beginning.[41] Many reasons may underlie that tiny divider "*as*", "which functions as a sort of joint, connecting the disconnected",[42] such as "special shadings, the temporal aspect, the modality [...], the cognitive [...] or practical character".[43] Therefore, reality neither runs out into the unrelated, unstructured plenitude of data nor exists as a descending function of an *a priori ideatum*.

Because of this constitutional interrelation between experiences and interpretation, phenomenology has to inquire into these interpretative schemes as conditions of possibility or impossibility for accessing reality. Traditional phenomenology treats these fields of meaning with two queries: the eidetic reduction and the transcendental reduction. Waldenfels explains their specific functions as follows:

> The *eidetic* reduction answers the question, how the 'as something' should be considered, while the *transcendental* reduction explains, how the difference between 'something' and 'as something', between What and How should be conceived.[44]

If one applies these methods when interpreting Bonhoeffer's understanding of "Wirklichkeit", one can state, at first, that although faith recognises only one "Wirklichkeit", there are descriptions of reality which are in part far removed from theology with regard to their own self-image. Bonhoeffer calls these "the world, the natural, the profane, and reason".[45] Theology must also deal with these. Bonhoeffer goes to great lengths to look for Christian reasons for such immense conceptions like reason, justice, cul-

---

35 Waldenfels, Spielraum, 129.
36 Waldenfels, op. cit., 129f; Phänomenologie, 15f; Topographie, 19.
37 Waldenfels, Spielraum, 130.
38 Waldenfels, op. cit., 129: "Grunddifferenz".
39 Waldenfels, Normalisierung, 21.
40 Waldenfels, Phänomenologie, 15.
41 Cf. Waldenfels, Spielraum, 130.
42 Waldenfels, Erfahrung, 3.
43 Waldenfels, Spielraum, 16.
44 Cf. Waldenfels, Normalisierung, 30.
45 DBWE 6, 59. DBW 6, 44.

ture, humanity, tolerance and autonomy, taking their own self-images seriously.[46] In this way they can preserve their liberating character.

If one follows the step of the eidetic reduction, one can identify some distinctions which illustrate the direction of Bonhoeffer's understanding of "Wirklichkeit". At first, he refuses an empiristic, utility-driven concept of reality based on the pretended normativity of facts.[47] This attempt is exemplified by the picture of Sancho Panza. For Bonhoeffer, the servant of "the knight of the doleful countenance" is "the type of complacent and artful accommodation to things as they are".[48] Picking up Nietzsche's statement, Bonhoeffer notes twice that Sancho's personality is marked by a "servile attitude toward the facts".[49] Yet Bonhoeffer disapproves of Sancho's master's constructions of reality as "theoretical and phantastical".[50] Theoretically expressed, this access may be displayed in a twofold way: as abstractive or as idealistic.[51] Bonhoeffer sees the first (abstractive access) when reality will be conceptualised, since "God is not known in faith to be the ultimate reality".[52] He sees the second (idealistic access) when someone renders that God is the ultimate possible reality, yet, at the same time understands God only as a "religious concept". In this case "there is no reason why there should not be, behind this apparent 'ultimate' reality, a still more ultimate reality: the twilight or the death of the gods".[53]

Complementing these insights from the eidetic reductions, one may wish to pay attention to Bonhoeffer's distinctions in relation to the transcendental reduction. In my view, they produce a more interesting outcome for current systematic application due to their methodological impact. These distinctions – and here I can recall Moltmann's demand to interpret the *Ethics* from the perspective of Bonhoeffer's early systematic writings – can be traced back to the access to reality as examined and disapproved of in *Act and Being*. According to Bonhoeffer's "Habilitation", neither idealism and transcendentalism on the one hand nor essentialism and intentional phenomenology on the other can adequately acquire reality. Speaking with Hans-Richard Reuter, the first cluster cannot escape from the "Scylla of the circle of reflection", whereas the second falls into the "Charybdis of delusional reification ('Verdinglichungswahn')".[54] In theological terms: both

---

46　Cf. DBWE 6, 340f. DBW 6, 343f.
47　DBWE 6, 53f. DBW 6, 38f.
48　LPP, 217. DBW 8, 333.
49　DBWE 6, 222. 261. DBW 6, 221. 260.
50　Cf. Ott, Wirklichkeit und Glaube, 220.
51　Cf. DBWE 48f. DBW 6, 32f.
52　DBWE 6, 48.
53　DBWE 6, 48.
54　Cf. DBW 2, 176.

ways of constructing "Wirklichkeit" depend upon the reason of the "*homo incurvatus in seipsum*".[55] In opposition to such a "word perspective" unmasked by theological anthropology, Bonhoeffer insists that "man cannot place himself into truth".[56]

Having used the eidetic and transcendental reduction to reject these options for (re)constructing "Wirklichkeit", a deeper point of access to "Wirklichkeit" now opens up beyond them. Looking back on the central passage, it draws attention to the text's many idioms which are connected by the semantic field of communication. The challenge to discover the reality of the world by the significative difference of God's reality in Christ is understood as an "invitation" ("Angebot"). Although this invitation occurs overwhelmingly[57] to those who are affected by it, it is free of any violence. Additionally, Bonhoeffer sees this challenge as a disclosure – novel, donated access. This disclosure (preparing its own way) is *revelation*[58] – it does not only refer to the semantic field of light but also (through identification with the word of God) to the field of communication. It is from this perspective of communication that Bonhoeffer understands revelation, as we can see from his chapter "Ultimate and Penultimate Things". Here, the Ultimate is understood as the "ultimate word".[59] In other words, God's communicative self-disclosure (which Christians believe occurred in the life, words, acts, crucifixion and resurrection of Jesus Christ) offers those who are affected by God an extraordinarily novel disclosure of their own reality, thus leading them to new being. The true reality, as the reality of the truth, can only be *revealed*, i.e. it strikes us from outside[60] and powerfully opens our distorted reason. In other words, God's believed self-disclosure is communicative and *personal*, it has a "name"[61] and a told story. All of this serves to emphasise the most phenomenologically relevant reconstruction, viz., as theology interprets reality from "Christuswirklichkeit", all essentialist ontology will be founded in the ontology of communication. This is the dynamic mystery and mysterious dynamic offered by the "Wirklichkeit" *Gottes* in Jesus Christ to the reality of the world. The word creates being; the new word re-creates old being. In order better to visualise this dynamic conveyed by the expression "God's reality in Jesus Christ" or, in short, "Christuswirklichkeit" (the reality of Christ) I will not translate the term.

---

55 Cf. Tietz-Steiding, Kritik; Boomgaarden, Wirklichkeit.
56 Bonhoeffer, Witness, 73 (DBW 2, 75).
57 Cf. DBW 6, 34: "Die Frage nach der letzten Wirklichkeit versetzt uns also bereits in eine solche Umklammerung durch ihre Antwort, daß wir uns garnicht mehr entwinden können".
58 Cf. DBW 6, 43.
59 Cf. e.g. DBWE 6, 151. DBW 6, 142.
60 Cf. DBW 2, 132–134.
61 DBWE 6, 54f. DBW 6, 39f.

Due to the eminent importance of the "Christuswirklichkeit" as the grounding perspective of communicative ontology beyond empiristic, idealistic or essentialist descriptions of reality, we must dwell on this subject and unpack it more precisely: The methodological specification of this communicative ontology will be absolutely vital for the inner- and extra-theological justification of Bonhoeffer's comprehension of "Wirklichkeit". For this purpose, I will again take up the phenomenology of Waldenfels and introduce its decisive difference from the old phenomenology; this should help us to better reformulate the status of "Wirklichkeit" in Bonhoeffer's theology for our time. According to Waldenfels, the statement: "against the background of other societal and historic interpretations, a first person interprets something *as* something" is an incomplete formula or, more precisely, the formula lays its (groundless) foundation on: "facing the (strange) Other's 'Anspruch'".[62] Of course, this idea must be explained: Both for Bonhoeffer and Waldenfels, "Wirklichkeit" cannot be explained sufficiently by going back to the eidetic or transcendental reduction. "Wirklichkeit" (and here we must remember the dynamics of this concept!) originates from and occurs by a confrontation with the incident of strangeness. In a phenomenological perspective such strangeness can be reconstructed retrospectively as the occurrence of an inescapable, incomparable, inassimilable, refractory, asymmetric event. Characterising a strange event with these epithets does not imply that one is unable to deal with the event at all. Rather it emphasises that such "dealing" always means engaging with it in a second order manner; that it is continuously stamped by this event. It implies that the so-called first person is not the first (acting) person. In events experienced this way, the person is passive rather than active. Therefore the person's duty or, better, vocation consists in recognising the irrefutable, appealing, demanding and self-sufficiency-promoting expression: "*You* are the one being addressed!" All of us have had some experience in such vocations – in both love affairs and religious affairs.

The constitution of "Wirklichkeit" is most-deeply founded in those events in which we recognise the Other as a strange Other. While we may forget this deepest constitution of "Wirklichkeit" in our everyday lives, in situations of danger, misery or emergency we are brutally reminded of this real constitution and constitutional reality. Just remember the horrific pictures and stories of the people in New Orleans. Whenever we try to reconstruct the reality and we search for theoretical and/or practical orientation by empiricism, essentialism, idealism etc., such orientation finds its limit, its (often empirical, always transcendental) co-constitutional partner in the

---

62 Normally "Anspruch" is translated as "claim" or "demand". Here, I leave the term untranslated. I will provide an explanation for my reasoning below.

Other. Therefore, the expression "Anspruch" of the Other, which in this specific sense transcends or, better, precedes all traditional interpreted constitutions of reality, means the "beginning of communication", "appeal", "plea", "claim", "demand", and sometimes "pretension". Having acknowledged this group of connotations "Anspruch" conveys, I will not translate the term. In my opinion, that these different semantic elements are drawn together does not only seem to be an oddity of one language. It can be displayed in many phenomena from the world in which we live. Just imagining the situation of unrequited love immediately opens up the different connotations of "Anspruch".[63] Bearing this constitutional validity of the Other's "Anspruch" in mind, Waldenfels calls the ultimate dimension of the significant differences the *responsive difference*. Ultimately, "Wirklichkeit" will be construed by *responding* to the preceding "Anspruch" of the strange Other. Although we are practically familiar with these insights, we still lack the theoretical familiarity. Hence, Waldenfels points out that the understanding of response in this manner does not nullify traditional concepts of answering or replying. Rather, the response is more than these forms of communication:

Responding implies more than moments of knowledge, capacity, will or ought. It is more than only a combination of such factors, which could be uncovered in a factorial analysis. It is also more than pure performance that – considered in itself – resembles an execution.[64]

Conversely: In the end, understanding the response in this way expresses it as a gift that receives by giving.[65]

When Bonhoeffer raises this topic he not only speaks personally but reflects on the testimony of many other Christians when he argues that the experienced ultimate "Anspruch" can be summarised in terms of content as God's *assurance* and claim in Jesus Christ ("Zuspruch" and "Anspruch").[66]

---

63 While this concept has been warranted by many studies in communication theory, body theory, theory of order, cultural theories and so on, I cannot enter into all of them here.

64 Waldenfels, Antwortregister, 333, cf. 191.

65 Cf. Waldenfels, op. cit., 614.

66 Cf. Thesis II of the Theological Declaration of Barmen: "As Jesus Christ is God's assurance of the forgiveness of all our sins, so, in the same way and with the same seriousness he is also God's mighty claim upon our whole life". In order to avoid any misunderstandings: The phenomenological meaning of "Anspruch" has a wider extension than the dogmatic meaning according to Barmen II. In the Theological Declaration of Barmen, Anspruch is defined only by claim, which is a circumscription for the theological term "law". This is only one way in which God's word can strike us. Otherwise, as Barth points out, theology cannot consider the "Anspruch" of God's word other than as a "Zuspruch" (assurance): "That God speaks with us, this is at all events inherently a grace" (Barth, Evangelium, 4). Bearing this in mind, it must be admitted that we cannot avoid some linguistic intricacy due to combining different language systems. Nevertheless the issue behind this linguistic complexity should be coherent.

Responding to Jesus Christ's "Anspruch", understood in a comprehensive way, is what Bonhoeffer calls "Verantwortung":

> This life, lived in response[67] to the life of Jesus Christ (as the Yes and No to our life), we call *'responsibility'* [*'Verantwortung'*]. This concept of responsibility denotes the complete wholeness and unity of the response[68] to the reality that is given to us in Jesus Christ, as opposed to the partial answers that we might be able to give, for example, from considerations of usefulness, or with reference to certain principles.[69]

Upon reading this passage, one will now understand that instead of merely repeating how "Wirklichkeit" cannot be constituted according to Bonhoeffer, one can move on to an actual reformulation of his understanding. Bonhoeffer's communicative ontology – "world's reality *as* reality of Christ" – can then be described precisely in the following way: as "responding to the vital 'Anspruch' of Jesus Christ in our own constructions of reality in the world in which we live", while the "Anspruch" is believed and experienced to be irrefutable (and consequently, if one will, a *mystery*). This "Anspruch" is experienced as the *excess* of all of our attempts to give a response to the "word of the person of Christ"[70] as Bonhoeffer emphasises when he claims:

> Isn't it occasionally, perhaps, a more genuine reference to the ultimate – which God will speak in God's own time (to be sure, likewise only through a human mouth) – to remain consciously in the penultimate?[71]

Indeed, this sentence is found in a context where Bonhoeffer meditates upon the usage of language. Nevertheless it gives us an important hint: we often discover (and suffer from) the Ultimate in, with and under our own words and actions. Bonhoeffer sees the key task of Christian ethics as bearing witness to this responsive difference of "Wirklichkeit".[72]

There is not a great deal to be said against a thesis interpreting the "Christuswirklichkeit" as the "Anspruch" of the reality of the word; even if

---

67 The editors translate "Antwort" with "answer". In my opinion, this lacks the communicative dimension which "response" implies.
68 Cf. the previous footnote.
69 DBWE 6, 254. Cf. DBW 6, 254: "Dieses Leben als Antwort auf das Leben Jesu Christi (als Ja und Nein über unser Leben) nennen wir 'Verantwortung'. In diesem Begriff der Verantwortung ist die zusammengefasste Ganzheit und Einheit der Antwort auf die uns in Jesus Christus gegebenen Wirklichkeit gemeint im Unterschied zu den Teilantworten, die wir zum Beispiel aus der Erwägung der Nützlichkeit oder aus bestimmten Prinzipien heraus geben könnten".
70 Cf. DBW 2, 132: "Er [sc.: der Mensch in der Kirche] sieht seine Existenz einzig begründet durch das Wort der Christusperson".
71 DBWE 6, 152f. DBW 6, 144: "[I]st das bewusste Bleiben im Vorletzten nicht hier und da vielleicht der echtere Hinweis auf das Letzte, das Gott zu seiner Zeit selbst (freilich auch nur durch Menschenmund) sagt?".
72 Against this background the editors of the *Ethics* emphasise that "Bonhoeffer here develops an understanding of human beings not only as relational but also as responding" (DBWE 6, 254, note 27. DBW 6, 254, note 25).

one alludes to some remarks where Bonhoeffer describes reality in terms of the *recapitulatio*-Christology put forward by the Deuteropaulines.[73] Furthermore, nothing argues against the general idea of a communicative and responsive ontology – which means that Bonhoeffer formulates some of their content and consequences in the Platonic language of participation.[74] *Recapitulatio*-Christology and participation must be listed as second order events in order to articulate the preceding "Anspruch" under certain respects *ex post*.[75]

But is the *ex post* reconstruction of such an "Anspruch" adequate for the responsive constitution of "Wirklichkeit"? Since the "Christuswirklichkeit" has been experienced as an irrefutable "Anspruch", one must acknowledge that the question concerning legitimacy bears a meaning which follows the former "Anspruch". Elucidating this point once more with Waldenfels:

> The query, whether 'Ansprüche' are legitimate or not, does not mark the beginning. This question presupposes the existence of a legal or moral order in which the rights and duties are distributed with respect to a certain norm.[76]

Since the *quaestio iuris* simply arises after the preceding "whereupon" of the "Anspruch",[77] this "Christuswirklichkeit" can be understood as a "Zumutung".[78] The editors of the English version of the *Ethics* translate "Zumutung" as "demand". While this is ostensibly correct, "Zumutung" also refers to "Mut", or "courage". Consequently, the "Zumutung" of the "Christuswirklichkeit" not only implies a demand but also an assurance. In short, when such a "Zumutung" comes from the outside into our own view of the world, it causes a "rip in our webbing"[79] of reality: *"iustitia passiva!"*[80]

According to Bonhoeffer the responsive construction of "Wirklichkeit" under the "Anspruch" of "Christuswirklichkeit" never begins and ends in itself and therefore lacks the saturated quality of self-consciousness. This "fact" can be undermined if one regards the time, mode and content that the

---

73 Cf. DBW 2, 39. 54.
74 Cf. DBW 6, 38: "Teilbekommen an dem unteilbar Ganzen der Gotteswirklichkeit ist der Sinn der christlichen Frage nach dem Guten". Cf. DBW 6, 40. 61.
75 It is decisive that these dicta pay attention to the responsive difference in with and underlying their thoughts.
76 Waldenfels, Antwortregister, 575 (cf. ibid., 565). Cf. Bonhoeffer's analogous consideration, admittedly put forward in a peculiar epistemological context: "Nie gelangt man zur Wirklichkeit des anderen auf erkenntnistheoretischem und metaphysischem Wege. Wirklichkeit ist schlechthin unableitbar, nur gegeben, anzuerkennen, abzulehnen, nie zu begründen, gegeben aber auch nur der ganzen ethischen Person" (DBW 1, 218).
77 Cf. Waldenfels, Antwortregister, 355f. 557–563.
78 DBW 6, 33.
79 Waldenfels, Gedankengänge, 379.
80 DBW 2, 132.

ultimate word involves. In his chapter "The ultimate and penultimate things", Bonhoeffer understands the ultimate word as ultimate in regard to its quality[81] and its temporality.[82] This is correct if we reconstruct this "Anspruch" of God's ultimate word as the "gospel of the justification for the godless sinner by Jesus Christ".[83] The world is reconciled through this ultimate word.[84] A dynamic moment or advent occurs, which Bonhoeffer describes as "God's reality revealed in Christ becoming real among God's creatures".[85] This "becoming real"[86] of reality constitutes the mysterious difference of the "Christuswirklichkeit" which, as we will see, is far from an obscuration.

From the outside, the ultimate word of "Christuswirklichkeit" as assured reconciliation and justification breaks (as "Anspruch") into the interferences of our world's realities. Their fragmented nature does not have the ultimate word. Theologically speaking, this *fides ex auditu* or, in phenomenological terms, "*responsio ex auditu*"[87] averts the claim of system rationalities or, in Bonhoeffer's words, the claim of "autonomous spheres of life" ("Eigengesetzlichkeiten"[88]) acting as the ultimate reality. They receive their justification by being "gerichtet" – simultaneously convicted, then adjusted and brought forward: *iustitia aliena* in all attempts to find an ultimate method for forming life.[89]

Against this background Bonhoeffer distinguishes between "preparing the way"[90] and "method".[91] Bonhoeffer uses this term in order to group together all those vain attempts to comprehend reality without a responsive difference between "de-securing"[92] "Anspruch" and responding faith. This may occur in secular ways – such as in political totalitarianisms (which Bonhoeffer had in mind), or be promulgated by current ideologies like "healthism" or economism. Beyond these secular modes, Bonhoeffer also considers religious "methods". He mentions disapprovingly the "Lutheran or Pauline method for attaining the ultimate word".[93] Contrary to this method, "preparing the way" respects the foundational, responsive differ-

---

81   Cf. DBW 6, 140.
82   Cf. DBW 6, 141.
83   Jüngel, Rechtfertigung. Cf. in Bonhoeffer's writings e.g. DBW 6, 142.
84   Cf. DBW 6, 40. 49f.
85   DBWE 6, 49. DBWE 6, 34. Cf. DBWE 6, 40. 44. 61.
86   Cf. DBW 2, 79. Witness, 76: "God is always the 'coming', not the 'existing' deity".
87   Waldenfels, Antwortregister, 250.
88   DBWE 6, 264. DBW 6, 263.
89   Cf. DBW 6, 149–151.
90   Cf. DBWE 6, 163f.
91   Cf. DBWE 6, 149f.
92   Cf. Jüngel, Geheimnis, 227f.
93   Cf. DBWE 6, 149. DBW 6, 140.

ence between the ultimate and the penultimate. The difference in the vector of validity ("Geltungsvektordifferenz") is vital for this view: "Method is the path from the penultimate to the ultimate. Preparing the way is the path from the ultimate to the penultimate".[94] Both ways involve the performance of a *relation*: "The ultimate and the penultimate are closely bound to one another".[95] The difference occurs in the recognition and contemplation of this relation. Thus "preparing the way" is not an activity or capacity, but above all a passion. It is more passive than the passivity correlated to activity:[96] "To love God means simply to allow God to elect and conceive us in Jesus Christ. [...] As such, human love thus remains purely passive".[97]

Wherever the responsive difference is beneficently upheld in faith against the false "ultimate claims" of the penultimate, there the area of the penultimate can be valued in the following way: "Part of preparing the way is to respect the penultimate and to enforce it, because of the ultimate that is approaching".[98] Such a responsive "analogy of advent"[99] encourages us to deal with reality in a prosaic manner.[100]

Action in accordance with Christ is in accord with reality because it allows the world to be the world and reckons with the world as world, while at the same time never forgetting that the world is loved, judged, and reconciled in Jesus Christ by God.[101]

The crucial change of perspective (needed to regard the reality of the world in such a sober manner) is joined to the responsive difference which reconstructs the response as a mode of receiving: "Thus, in order that the word may come to me, my last act of preparing the way, the last deed in the penultimate, is that I go where it has pleased God to give that word".[102]

In this section we have approached Bonhoeffer's conception of "Wirklichkeit" by new phenomenological methods which are nevertheless still

---

94 DBWE 6, 178. DBW 6, 159.
95 DBWE 6, 168. DBW 6, 161.
96 Cf. Lévinas, Jenseits, 49; Waldenfels, Antwortregister, 345f.
97 DBWE 6, 336f. DBW 6, 340.
98 DBWE 6, 166. Cf. DBW 6, 158: "Es gehört zur Wegbereitung, das Vorletzte zu achten und inkraftzusetzen um des nahenden Letzten willen". Cf. his analogous remarks: "Aber vom kommenden Herrn her fällt schon ein Licht auf das Menschsein und das Gutsein" (DBW 6, 157). "Das Vorletzte muß um des Letzten willen gewahrt bleiben. Eine willkürliche Zerstörung des Vorletzten tut dem Letzten ernstlich Eintrag" (DBW 6, 152).
99 Jüngel, Geheimnis, 389f.
100 Cf. DBW 6, 237. 266. 326.
101 DBWE 6, 264. Cf. DBW 6, 263: "Wirklichkeitsgemäß ist das christusgemäße Handeln, weil es die Welt Welt sein läßt, weil es mit der Welt als Welt rechnet und doch niemals aus den Augen läßt, daß die Welt in Jesus Christus von Gott geliebt, gerichtet und versöhnt ist".
102 DBWE 6, 166. Cf. DBW 6, 158: "Soll also das Wort zu mir kommen können, so ist der letzte Akt der Wegbereitung, die letzte Tat des Vorletzten, daß ich dorthin gehe, wo es Gott gefallen hat, sein Wort zu geben".

connected to his own conclusion. At this point, we can conclude: Phenomenologically speaking, "Wirklichkeit" is understood and described adequately by significative differences. Therefore, "Christuswirklichkeit" and the reality of the world are not distinguished realms in our existing reality but primarily significative differences challenging each other. So, the "Christuswirklichkeit" (i.e. *Gottes* "Wirklichkeit" in Jesus Christ) proves to be an irrefutable, personally experienced "Anspruch" to believers to regard the reality of the world in the *light* of reconciliation (in other words: under the ultimate *word* of the justification). To believers, the "Christuswirklichkeit" occurs as the responsive difference to all attempts to exaggerate and claim penultimate things as ultimate things. This disclosure is exactly that which constitutes the mystery, in contrast to other understandings of "Wirklichkeit". This mystery is far from obscuration. On the contrary, due to its critical impact on many unwarranted claims it functions as a promoter of clarification. Its "Anspruch" is closer to me than I am to myself[103] (i.e.: my Self). Responding to this opening "Anspruch" is called "preparing the way". This primal passion offers us a chance to regard the world in a sober manner, thus empowering us to adequate action.

If we take this responsive refiguration of Bonhoeffer's conception of "Wirklichkeit" into account, we are then able to re-examine controversial issues in Bonhoeffer research: Christomonism and the difference between the ultimate and the penultimate are not a contrast. This may only be the case if one adheres to essentialist or idealistic interpretative schemes. With the perspective on a responsive ontology with regard to the ultimate "Anspruch", we can now speak of a monism, precisely a Christomonism. Yet, concerning other significative differences, our view of the world is also interfered with by many other orders and schemes. Additionally, the question whether Bonhoeffer tends more to the idea of a "royal reign of Christ" ("Königsherrschaft Christi") or to the "two kingdoms doctrine" finds a novel solution. If one starts with the decisive validity of the ultimate "Anspruch", only one (eschatologically qualified) reality exists; nevertheless existing system rationalities (interpreting something *as* something), as well as schemes and orders are harshly criticised if they take effect as "autonomous spheres of life" ("Eigengesetzlichkeiten"[104]).

If one applies established terminology, one finds that Bonhoeffer stands for a two kingdoms doctrine being hermeneutically subjected to a royal reign of Christ, understood responsively. The responsive difference of the "Christuswirklichkeit" provokes a disturbance in system rationalities concerning their own legitimacy. Consequently, there is nothing to be said

---

103 Cf. Jüngel, Geheimnis, 536.
104 DBWE 6, 264. DBW 6, 263.

against Hans-Richard Reuter's phrase that Bonhoeffer uses the method of deconstruction.[105]

According to Bonhoeffer's understanding of "Wirklichkeit", theological ethics in particular (together with other ethics) can play its part in an intrinsic and extrinsic authenticity because it is able to call upon a diverse semantic and pragmatic potential in order to sensibly draw distinctions.[106] In other words, by keeping in mind the responsive difference (of the "Christuswirklichkeit") in contrast to other significative differences, theological ethics observes (and re-constructs) "Wirklichkeit" – since observing means to draw distinctions. These distinctions mainly address the occurrence of "border violations" in certain system rationalities.[107]

The style of the proposed critical approach is nothing for theological ethics to be ashamed of, at any rate compared with other moral conceptions or interpretative schemes of reality. On the contrary, other ethical systems quite often practise their reflections completely disconnected from the world in which we live and, consequently, act in a forensic manner. In contrast, theological ethics is embedded in the religious environment. By belonging to such a cultural-linguistic approach of faith which does not characterise itself as irrational or antirational – to which the Christian faith practising the formula *fides quaerens intellectum* certainly belongs – Christian ethics is able to motivate and reproduce faith. Taking all this into account should not only hinder ethics as method, but also enable the unfolding of "ethics as formation". In the next section, I will examine this question in more detail.

2.3 "Preparing the way" as "formation" of the world

If the significance of faith consists in "preparing" the world as opposed to engaging with "method", and if all understanding of reality and all actions should be imprinted with the responsive difference of the "Christuswirklichkeit", then one can agree with Bonhoeffer that "Ethics as formation" has little to do with "planning and programs".[108]

Far from assuming that "preparing the way" lacks space for such activities, Bonhoeffer draws upon Luther to assert a primal passivity. He uses

---

105 Reuter, Nachwort, 181.

106 Cf. DBW 3, 80: "Die Grenze des Menschen ist in der Mitte seines Daseins, nicht am Rand; die Grenze, die am Rand des Menschen gesucht wird, ist Grenze seiner Beschaffenheit, Grenze seiner Technik, Grenze seiner Möglichkeit. Die Grenze, die in der Mitte ist, ist die Grenze seiner Wirklichkeit, seines Daseins schlechthin".

107 Since one has to make a further move, unfolding and justifying one's own interpretations of the world on the level of the penultimate.

108 DBWE 6, 93. DBW 6, 80.

one of Luther's well known anthropological statements to argue that passion precedes the correlation of activity and passivity: *"Prius est enim esse quam operari, prius autem pati quam esse. Ergo fieri, esse, operari se sequuntur"*.[109] In light of this statement, Bonhoeffer equates "ethics as formation" with "being drawn into the form of Jesus Christ, by *being conformed to the unique form of the one who became human, was crucified, and is risen*".[110]

To say that "[i]n Bonhoeffer's theology there is a close correlation between Christology and theological anthropology"[111] – and to view this correlation from the perspective of Chalcedonian Christology – is not really surprising. Yet, beyond this, it is also undeniably true that Christologically associated topoi such as "vicarious representative action" ("Stellvertretung"[112]) should not be read in terms of *imitatio Christi*. Responding to the "Anspruch" of God's Word in Jesus Christ arouses a formation that (being conformed to "the one who has become human") renounces all "superhumanity ['Übermenschentum'], [...] all struggle to be heroic or a demigod".[113] Instead, (being conformed to the Crucified) formation finds its closed identity judged and (conformed to the risen) renewed.[114] In no way does ethics as formation eliminate "purest activity".[115] Yet, it is understood as "passivity". In the end, an intrinsic part of responsive identity is its social constitution (in the church). This specific place has no primary entitlement in itself. Instead, "[t]he church is nothing but that piece of humanity where Christ really has taken form".[116]

How does this work practically? It will be helpful to outline some examples that can unpack "formation of the world" as a response to the "Christuswirklichkeit": The most inspiring considerations "After ten years" (written on New Year 1943) produced a set of moral attitudes and types under the title "Who stands fast?". These moral feelings and attitudes had all collapsed because of the "great masquerade of evil [that] has played havoc with all our ethical concepts".[117] Bonhoeffer has notable opinions on the collapse of the reasonable, on all moral fanaticism, on the conscience, and on duty, freedom, and private virtuousness. Many of his notions are quite remarkable, such as those on civil courage, on success,

---

109 WA 56, 177, quoted in DBW 2, 113.
110 Cf. DBW 6, 69–80.
111 Green, Ethical, 257.
112 Cf. DBW 6, 256–260.
113 DBWE 6, 94. DBW 6, 81.
114 Cf. DBWE 6, 84–96.
115 DBWE 6, 226. DBW 6, 224.
116 DBWE 6, 97. DBW 6, 84. Cf. DBW 6, 409.
117 LPP, 4. DBW 8, 20.

on folly, contempt for humanity, immanent righteousness, faith in the sovereignty of God in history, confidence, the sense of quality, sympathy, suffering, on perceptions of time, optimism, and on insecurity and death.[118] While each one deserves attention, from my systematic perspective I will focus on one particular feature: the framework for his thoughts. His remarks begin with a distinct reference to foundational, responsive difference:

> Who stands fast? Only the man whose final standard is not his reason, his principles, his conscience, his freedom, or his virtue, but who is ready to sacrifice all this when he is *called* to *obedient* and *responsible* action in *faith* and in exclusive allegiance to God – the *responsible* man, who tries to make his whole life a [*response*][119] to the *question* and *call* of God.[120]

While this opening passage is full of phrases provoking connotations from the semantic field of responsivity, the final remarks focus on formation in terms of "being conformed to Jesus Christ". The text concludes with notes on "the view from below".[121] It is this view that marks the preferential option for the disadvantaged – a main characteristic of the whole biblical and Judeo-Christian tradition. It was also the view of the real human being, Jesus Christ, as is seen in his preaching, actions, death and his irreversible, revealed and everlasting acceptance through God. Since this view is not to be mistaken for that of "those who are eternally dissatisfied",[122] it can open the way for a new sensibility:

> we must do justice to life in all its dimensions from a higher satisfaction, whose foundation is beyond any talk of 'from below' or 'from above'. This is the way in which we may affirm it.[123]

In any case, the view from below reminds us that forming the world as a response to the "Anspruch" of Jesus Christ fulfils itself in serving the Other. The "outcast, the suspects, the maltreated, the powerless, the oppressed, the reviled – [...] in short, [...] those who suffer"[124] are the people to whom "preparing the way" should be directed.

---

118 LPP, 4f. DBW 8, 20–38. Cf. DBW 6, 64ff.
119 Translation slightly altered: the editors translate "Antwort" with "answer", though "response" is more appropriate.
120 LPP, 5 (emphasis added). DBW 8, 23: "Wer hält stand? Allein der, dem nicht seine Vernunft, sein Prinzip, sein Gewissen, seine Freiheit, seine Tugend der letzte Maßstab ist, sondern der dies alles zu opfern bereit ist, wenn er im Glauben und in alleiniger Bindung an Gott zu gehorsamer und verantwortlicher Tat gerufen ist, der Verantwortliche, dessen Leben nichts sein will als eine Antwort auf Gottes Frage und Ruf".
121 LPP, 17. DBW 8, 38f.
122 LPP, 39.
123 LPP, 17. DBW 8, 38f.
124 LPP, 17.

In addition to this responsive phenomenology of virtues and vices, other distinctions are also conducive to "preparing the way". In general, a basis is provided for listening to the "polyphony of life".[125] On the one hand, the diversity of life would not be approved by a compromise: "Here the ultimate word is divorced in principle from all that is penultimate".[126] On the other hand, when penultimate things are ignored[127] by focusing on the ultimate, "serious tension"[128] will be released. It is worth mentioning here that Bonhoeffer appreciates both sides of the responsive difference, the "Anspruch" *and* the response. Analogous arguments can be found from the perspective of the theory of religions (on monasticism and the "cultural Protestant"[129]), cultural studies (on secularism in Europe and America), anthropology (on the differences between vitalism and mechanisation,[130] between rationalisation and biologisation,[131] between individual and social perspectives, as well as between the person and work[132]). By overemphasising one side of the relation, all these types have failed to account for the deconstructive difference of the "Anspruch" over against the penultimate. One may well criticise some empirical or systematic points in Bonhoeffer's distinguishing observations, or suggest that other issues (more relevant today) are passed over by Bonhoeffer. Yet the lesson to be learned from Bonhoeffer is that one must understand life's "serious tensions" as both an assurance and demand.

A further technique for dealing with the responsive difference on behalf of the "polyphony of life" is found in Bonhoeffer's heavily discussed doctrine of mandates. It is worth noting at the outset that several approaches do *not* meet the doctrine's challenge: for example, simply comparing Bonhoeffer's idea with its source (Luther's doctrine of *tres ordines*); asking whether Bonhoeffer adequately transformed this idea for today; or asking whether the range and amount of the mandates are sufficient. While these may all be legitimate issues,[133] if one truly wishes to rise to the challenge of the mandates today, then it must be noted that Bonhoeffer characterises the mandates neither as orders of preservation nor orders of creation. In this basic decision, Bonhoeffer delivers the theologically provocative message that a promise rests (at the least) on work, marriage, government and church. This

---

125 LPP, 303. DBW 8, 440.
126 DBWE 6, 154.
127 DBWE 6, 153. DBW 6, 144f.
128 DBWE 6, 129. DBW 6, 120.
129 DBWE 6, 57. DBW 6, 42. 291.
130 DBWE 6, 123. DBW 6, 114.
131 DBWE 6, 196. DBW 6, 191.
132 DBWE 6, 51. DBW 6, 36.
133 Cf. e.g. Honecker, Christologie.

is the surplus of a Christological perspective in contrast to the perspective of a theology of creation. Although there have been other theologies of creation that put forward some soteriological implications, e.g. Barth's topos of "creation as justification",[134] Bonhoeffer is wary of the notion of autonomous natural orders found in other influential creation theologies of his day:

> We speak of divine mandates rather than divine orders, because thereby their character as divinely *imposed* tasks ['Auftrag'], as opposed to determinate forms of being, becomes clearer.[135]

In opposition to such approaches, Bonhoeffer integrates two observations in order to cope with the systematically problematic status of the mandates:

First, he states that the topoi of the mandates are not divine in themselves. That means: work, marriage, government and church do not share a divine essence. They are divine only "as God's mandates".[136] Only by this assurance, claim and demand have they become what they are – they receive their being through responding to the "Anspruch" from the outside:

> Not because there *is* work, marriage, government, or church is it *commanded* by God, but because it is *commanded* by God, therefore it *is*. Only insofar as its being is subjected – consciously or unconsciously – to the divine task is it a divine mandate.[137]

Once again, significant differences can at first be understood via eidetic reductions but according to Bonhoeffer they finally have to point at the responsive difference. His language (full of communicative phrases) leads to this conclusion and invites us to oppose essentialist interpretative schemes or the schemes of autonomous structures. Again, the vector or argumentation (whether from the ultimate to the penultimate or vice versa) is decisive.

Second, besides these well-known main features, Bonhoeffer introduces an important methodological consideration. In *intentione operis* (which is not always identical with the author's intentions) this short remark prevents us from interpreting the doctrine of mandates as glorifying authorities. While the unfortunate link to "above/below" terminology[138] might promote

---

134 Barth, Dogmatik III/1, § 42.
135 DBWE 6, 68f. DBW 6, 55 (emphasis added).
136 DBWE 6, 69. DBW 6, 56.
137 DBWE 6, 69f. Cf. DBW 6, 56: "Nur als Mandate Gottes sind sie göttlich, nicht aber schon durch ihr faktisches Gegebensein in dieser oder jener konkreten Gestalt. Nicht weil Arbeit, Ehe, Obrigkeit, Kirche, *ist*, ist sie göttlich *geboten*, sondern weil sie von Gott *geboten* ist, darum *ist* sie, und nur sofern ihr Sein – bewußt oder unbewußt – dem göttlichen Auftrag unterworfen ist, ist es göttliches Mandat".
138 DBWE 6, 372ff. DBW 6, 375ff.

such an impression,[139] this problematic train of thought actually contradicts what Bonhoeffer himself says on the interrelation of the mandates:

Only in their being with-one-another ['Miteinander'], for-one-another ['Füreinander'], and over-against-one-another ['Gegeneinander'] do the divine mandates [...] communicate the commandment of God as it is revealed in Jesus Christ.[140]

As is stated in the Editor's Afterword to the German Edition: As Bonhoeffer "discloses their co-operative, subsidiary and polemic character",[141] the "responsive character" of his teaching[142] is displayed once more. Beyond any conceivable criticism concerning semantic and biographical backgrounds, this methodological keynote remains fruitful today. Why not transcend Bonhoeffer's semantic proposals? Why not discover other mandates, or rediscover some of Bonhoeffer's mandates in another way? All of this is conceivable if one respects the decisive precondition: to be aware of responsive difference. Such regard sets the course not only for dealing with moral questions but also for reflecting on ethical theory. Let us now look at this aspect of Bonhoeffer's theology.

2.4 The conducive limitation of a responsive ethics

Bearing in mind the responsive difference between the "Anspruch" of the "Christuswirklichkeit" and "preparing the way" as the response to that "Anspruch", we are now able to address plausibly the disclaimer presented by other ethical theories. It is a well-known fact that Bonhoeffer abandons nearly all classical ethical approaches: deontology, teleology, "ethics of goods", utilitarianism, virtue ethics and casuistry. Yet he deals with the key concepts of ethics such as duty, freedom, conscience, virtue, happiness, good (and evil), and norms. Bonhoeffer alleged that all ethical principles finally fail to offer sufficient orientation. Thus it is hardly surprising that in Bonhoeffer's *Ethics*, ethics seems to be a profoundly dubious enterprise. This may remind us of Luhmann's sceptical phrase: that the first task of ethics should be to caution against morals.[143] Bonhoeffer takes such scepti-

---

139 Cf. Dramm, Einführung, 156: "Die konservativen und patriarchalischen Elemente in Bonhoeffers politisch-gesellschaftlichem Denkradius sind vor dem Hintergrund seiner Zeit und seines familiären und sozialen Umfeldes [...] ganz und gar nicht ungewöhnlich. Ungewöhnlich hingegen ist, daß Bonhoeffer mit und trotz dieser konservativen Grundhaltung zu Konsequenzen in politischen Fragen gelangte, die diesen Konservativismus buchstäblich rücksichtslos transzendierten und – ebenso buchstäblich radikal außer Kraft setzten".
140 DBWE 6, 393. DBW 6, 397.
141 DBWE 6, 428. DBW 6, 433.
142 DBWE 6, 428. DBW 6, 433.
143 Cf. Luhmann, Paradigm, 41.

cism seriously and begins three passages with fundamental questions on the legitimacy of ethics. Presumably, these sections were considered for introducing the envisioned book.[144] Such a prominent position underlines once again the relevance of these qualms.

The intensive rejection of common ethical conceptions and methods suggests that Bonhoeffer's conclusion can be described as "situational ethics" (an expression admittedly introduced by Joseph Fletcher in the 1960s).[145] Indeed, some sections seem to support this view:

Responsible action is neither determined from the outset nor defined once and for all; instead, it is born in the given situation. The point is not to apply a principle that eventually will be shattered by reality anyway, but to discern what is necessary or 'commanded'.[146]

According to this excerpt, it seems possible to conclude that the key concept of responsibility should be subordinated to the approach of situational ethics. However, a precise examination of the text reveals slight differences which might call such an interpretation into question. Bonhoeffer only disputes the view that principles and norms might determine the ethical situation at all. This does not mean that they have no importance and that the situation bears the ethical orientation. A few lines before this passage, Bonhoeffer stresses these counter-questions, showing that, on the contrary, it is the responsive identity that bears the ethical situation: "The moment a person accepts responsibility for other people – and only in so doing does the person live in reality – the genuine ethical situation arises".[147] Furthermore, Bonhoeffer does not deny at all that one should normally heed moral orders and principles.[148] The extraordinary situation is simply the exception that proves the rule.

Responsibility is the key ethical concept for both normal and extraordinary situations. Bonhoeffer develops his ethics of responsibility by responding to the "Anspruch" of Jesus Christ. The bipolarity in the concept of responsibility (in that it binds through vicarious representative action as well as through accordance with reality, while also freeing through accountability and venture[149]) is Bonhoeffer's reading of conforming to the "Anspruch"

---

144 Cf. DBWE 6, 429.
145 Cf. Ott, Wirklichkeit, 231; Honecker, Einführung, 12.
146 DBWE 6, 221. Cf. DBW 6, 220: "Verantwortliches Handeln liegt nicht von vornherein und ein für allemal fest, sondern es wird in der gegebenen Situation geboren. Es geht nicht um die Durchführung eines Prinzips, das zuletzt doch an der Wirklichkeit zerbricht, sondern um das Erfassen des in der gegebenen Situation Notwendigen, 'Gebotenen'".
147 DBWE 6, 221. Cf. DBW 6, 220: "In dem Augenblick, in dem ein Mensch Verantwortung für andere Menschen auf sich nimmt – und nur indem er das tut, steht er in der Wirklichkeit – entsteht die echte ethische Situation".
148 DBWE 6, 272f. DBW 6, 272.
149 DBWE 6, 257ff. DBW 6, 256.

of Jesus Christ. While this understanding starts with a particular belief, it is by no means irrational. On the contrary, both its foundation and its justification are rationally comprehensible: This concept is justified in that it is capable of reconstructing the foundational, responsive trait of responsibility. Beyond the fundamental responsive difference it finds another constitutional "authority" that hinders the closeness of an ethical theory. This troublesome "opener" of distorted ethical theories is the concrete, not only the general, Other.[150] Like Arthur Rich many years later,[151] Bonhoeffer arranged the concept of responsibility by integrating humanity and appropriateness. Nevertheless, in cases of conflict, humanity has right of way (cf. Mk 2,27). The lack of ambiguity here can be traced back to the "Anspruch" of Jesus Christ:

> It is through Christ that the world of things and values is given back its orientation toward human beings, as was originally *intended* in their creation. The frequent talk about responsibility toward a cause is legitimate only within these limits.[152]

In other words: caring for the Other and an ethics of appropriateness are not inconsistent with one another. But such an ethic of responsibility (as it is conceived by Bonhoeffer) demands that one recognise the concrete Other as the essential corrective for action and institutional decisions. In the language of social ethics, Bonhoeffer's concept of responsibility (which starts by responding to the "Christuswirklichkeit") demands a straightforward application of equity. And again: equity finds its norm in the trouble of the Other.

We would be providing an inappropriate conceptualisation of Bonhoeffer's approach of responsibility[153] if we were to perceive it as the contradiction of an "ethic of disposition or intention",[154] or if we were to understand it as an ethic of sustainability. More radically, Bonhoeffer derives the foundation of responsibility from the idea of responsivity.[155] Such a foundation does not oppose these ethical conceptions, but for its assuring and demanding "Anspruch" it insists on the mysterious excess of "Wirklichkeit". In

---

150 Cf. Benhabib, Selbst, 148–177.
151 Cf. Rich, Wirtschaftsethik, 72ff.
152 DBWE 6, 260. DBW 6, 259: "Durch Christus erhält die Welt der Dinge und Werte ihre schöpfungsgemäße Ausrichtung auf den Menschen zurück. Die oft gehörte Rede von der Verantwortung für eine Sache hat ihr Recht nur innerhalb dieser Grenze".
153 Cf. DBWE 6, 254: "We thus define the term 'responsibility' with a fuller meaning than is the case in everyday usage and even in cases where it has become a highly defined ethical concept". Cf. DBW 6, 254: "Wir geben [...] dem Begriff der Verantwortung eine Fülle, die ihm im alltäglichen Sprachgebrauch nicht zukommt, selbst dort nicht, wo er eine ethisch höchst qualifizierte Größe geworden ist".
154 DBWE 6, 52. DBW 6, 36: "Gesinnungsethik".
155 Cf. DBWE 6, 254: "We live by responding to the word of God addressed to us in Jesus Christ".

non-theological language, the structure of responsibility (according to Bonhoeffer) can be reformulated as follows:

Responsibility isn't the capacity for beginning with oneself, but rather the inescapability that we start with the Other. Ecstasies – the term indicates a centrifugal drive – is overturned in exposition: I am outside, *au dehors*.[156]

As formally described in a phenomenological way, the responsive difference between the "Anspruch" of the "Christuswirklichkeit" and the claim of the Other reminds theological ethics of the starting point of all ethics, and thus a theological ethics of responsibility in Bonhoeffer's sense does not need to render homage to a situational ethics (which pretends to be norm-free) nor to deductive models of ethics. Rather, from Bonhoeffer's point of view, an ethics of responsibility grounded in a responsive identity should be grasped as a "concrete ethic".[157] It exceeds Krämer's approach of integrative ethics[158] since it does not only integrate deontology and teleology (as Krämer does), but also reflects on the communicative, immemorial ground. This strange topic[159] was the starting point of "is" and "ought". Concrete ethics, as Bonhoeffer understands it, is integrative ethics on a higher level since it takes its own, responsive limitation into account. It acknowledges its origin in this incomprehensible, yet self-imposing, ground. By conforming to this "Anspruch", it displays self-criticism as well as criticism of others, where the concrete Other seems to be subordinated to anonymous structures. Thus a responsive ethics is an ethics "*in accordance with reality*".[160]

With these vital differences in mind, an ethics of responsibility can provide ethical advice in an unpretentious and pragmatic way:

The goal is not to realize an 'absolute good'. Instead, the self-denial of those who act responsibly includes choosing something relatively better over something relatively worse, and recognizing that the 'absolute good' may be exactly the worst.[161]

Beyond the truism that times of crisis challenge ethics in different ways than in peaceful times, a Christian ethics of responsibility must always be conformed to the "Anspruch" of Jesus Christ. In all times it must serve the

---

156 Cf. Waldenfels, Gedankengänge, 335.
157 DBWE 6, 99. DBW 6, 86.
158 Cf. Krämer, Ethik.
159 In so doing, Bonhoeffer accomplishes Fischer's expectations: that theological ethics must talk about moral and other grounds (cf. Fischer, Gründe).
160 DBWE 6, 261.
161 DBWE 6, 261. Cf. DBW 6, 260: "Nicht ein 'absolut Gutes' soll verwirklicht werden, vielmehr gehört es zu der Selbstbescheidung des verantwortlich Handelnden, ein relativ Besseres dem relativ Schlechteren vorzuziehen und zu erkennen, daß das 'absolut Gute' gerade das Schlechteste sein kann".

"polyphony of life". Put very simply, and very truly: it should "help people *learn to live with others*".[162] This is true *con-crescere*.

3. Responding to the mystery

Bonhoeffer's *Ethics* is based upon a remarkable concept of "Wirklichkeit". At first glance, it seems to be construed much like all other schemes of "Wirklichkeit", namely in the formula: "something as something". Upon closer inspection, the significative difference, "Christuswirklichkeit", turns out to be an "Anspruch". This "Anspruch" is experienced as a call, an assurance and a demand. Those who are struck by it cannot avoid responding. The experience of this irresistibility is the phenomenological expression for the real constitution of "Wirklichkeit". In general terms, Bonhoeffer evolves a communicative and responsive ontology. His ontology also has a personal foundation beyond "act or being": namely, Jesus Christ. This is the function of the mystery of "Christuswirklichkeit". As a responsive difference, it provokes a dynamic in all world views. The "Anspruch" of "Christuswirklichkeit" is an invitation: "Let yourselves be conformed to *the unique form of the one who became human, was crucified, and is risen*". On the basis of such a constitutional passivity, an enormous amount of activity can arise. Through the calling "Anspruch" or mystery of God's reality in Christ there occurs a constant yet fruitful disquiet over against all attempts at exact orientation. From the assurance of the Word, which is believed to be ultimate, we should distance ourselves from all assumed claims of explaining the world in definite terms.

In summation, Bonhoeffer's ethics can be viewed as an important challenge both for Christian and non-Christian ethics. The responsive difference between the ultimate and the penultimate may be re-identified (and believed differently) in other religious or philosophical contexts. It leads to substantial societal consequences in a way that is, in addition, motivationally backed: displaying a sensitivity for the concrete Other, a sensitivity for the frontiers of system rationalities, and a sensitivity for equity.

Returning full circle, it should now be eminently clear that this approach is far from irrational. Furthermore, it does not simply convey redundancies over against secular ethics. One might take this opinion, but doing so ignores the semantic and motivational potential which religion has – and which secular ethics does not share.[163] This is no cause for *Schadenfreude*,

---

162 DBWE 6, 370. DBW 6, 372.
163 Cf. Habermas, Religion.

but it is a mandate to participate in the building of an open concept of overlapping consensus. In light of the assuring and demanding ultimate word, responding to the Other serves the polyphony of life. That is our part in the mystery, in a world come of age.

Bibliography

Primary Sources

BARTH, K., *Evangelium* und Gesetz, TEH 32, München 1935.
–, Die Kirchliche *Dogmatik*, Vol. III/1, Zollikon/Zürich ³1957.
BONHOEFFER, D., Sanctorum Communio. Eine dogmatische Untersuchung zur Soziologie der Kirche, Dietrich Bonhoeffer Werke, Vol. 1, ed. by J. von Soosten, München 1988 (= DBW 1).
–, Akt und Sein. Transzendentalphilosophie und Ontologie in der systematischen Theologie, Dietrich Bonhoeffer Werke, Vol. 2, ed. by H.-R. Reuter, München 1988 (= DBW 2).
–, Schöpfung und Fall, Dietrich Bonhoeffer Werke, Vol. 3, ed. by M. Rüter/I. Tödt, München 1989 (= DBW 3).
–, Ethik, Dietrich Bonhoeffer Werke, Vol. 6, ed. by I. Tödt/H.E. Tödt/E. Feil/C. Green, München 1992 (= DBW 6).
–, Ethics, Dietrich Bonhoeffer Works, Vol. 6, ed. by C. Green, transl. by R. Krauss/Ch.C. West/ D.W. Stott, Minneapolis 2005 (= DBWE 6).
–, Widerstand und Ergebung. Briefe und Aufzeichnungen aus der Haft, Dietrich Bonhoeffer Werke, Vol. 8, ed. by Ch. Gremmels/E. Bethge/R. Bethge/I. Tödt, Gütersloh 1998 (= DBW 8).
–, Letters and Papers from Prison. The Enlarged Edition, ed. by E. Bethge, transl. by R. Fuller/ F. Clark et al., New York et al. 1997 (= LPP).
–, *Witness* to Jesus Christ (Making of Modern Theology), ed. by J. de Gruchy, Minneapolis 1991.
HABERMAS, J., Zwischen Naturalismus und *Religion*. Philosophische Aufsätze, Frankfurt/M. 2005.
HUME, D., Traktat über die menschliche *Natur*, 3. Über Moral, Vol. 2, Hamburg 1978.
LÉVINAS, E., *Jenseits* des Seins oder anders als Sein geschieht, Freiburg 1992.
LUHMANN, N., *Paradigm* lost. Über die ethische Reflexion der Moral. Rede anläßlich der Verleihung des Hegel-Preises 1989, Frankfurt/M. 1990.
LUTHER, M., Werke. Kritische Gesamtausgabe ("Weimarer Ausgabe"), Weimar 1883ff.
WALDENFELS, B., Der *Spielraum* des Verhaltens, Frankfurt/M. 1980.
–, Einführung in die *Phänomenologie*, München 1992.
–, *Antwortregister*, Frankfurt/M. 1994.
–, Deutsch-französische *Gedankengänge*, Frankfurt/M. 1995.
–, *Topographie* des Fremden. Studien zur Phänomenologie des Fremden 1, Frankfurt/M. 1997.
–, Grenzen der *Normalisierung*. Studien zur Phänomenologie des Fremden 2, Frankfurt/M. 1998.
–, Bruchlinien der *Erfahrung*. Phänomenologie – Psychoanalyse – Phänomenotechnik, Frankfurt/ M. 2002.

Secondary Sources

ABROMEIT, H.-J., Das *Geheimnis* Christi. Dietrich Bonhoeffers erfahrungsbezogene Christologie, NBST 8, Neukirchen-Vluyn 1991.
BAYER, O., "Christus als *Mitte*". Bonhoeffers Ethik im Banne der Religionsphilosophie Hegels, BThZ 2, 1985, 259–276.

BENHABIB, S., *Selbst* im Kontext. Kommunikative Ethik im Spannungsfeld von Feminismus, Kommunitarismus und Postmoderne, Frankfurt/M. 1992.
BETHGE, E., Dietrich *Bonhoeffer*. Eine Biographie, München [6]1989.
BOOMGAARDEN, J., Das Verständnis der *Wirklichkeit*. Dietrich Bonhoeffers systematische Theologie und ihr philosophischer Hintergrund in "Akt und Sein", Gütersloh 1999.
CAPUTO, J.D., A *Sketch* of an Ethics without Ethics, in: E. Wyschogrod/G. P. McKenny (Ed.), The Ethical, Blackwell Readings in Continental Philosophy 5, Malden/Oxford 2003, 169–180.
DABROCK, P., Antwortender *Glaube* und Vernunft. Zum Ansatz evangelischer Fundamentaltheologie, Forum Systematik 5, Stuttgart/Berlin/Köln 2000.
DABROCK, P./KLINNERT, L./SCHARDIEN, S., *Menschenwürde* und Lebensschutz. Herausforderungen theologischer Bioethik, Gütersloh 2004.
DRAMM, S., Dietrich Bonhoeffer. Eine *Einführung* in sein Denken, Gütersloh 2001.
FISCHER, J., Über moralische und andere *Gründe*, ZThK 95, 1998, 118–157.
GREEN, C.J., Ethical theology and contextual *ethics*. New perspectives on Bonhoeffer's ethics, in: Ch. Gremmels/W. Huber (Ed.), Religion im Erbe. Dietrich Bonhoeffer und die Zukunftsfähigkeit des Christentums, Gütersloh 2002, 255–269.
–, Editor's *Introduction* to the English Edition, in: D. Bonhoeffer, Ethics (= DBWE 6), Minneapolis 2005, 1–44.
HONECKER, M., *Christologie* und Ethik. Zu Dietrich Bonhoeffers Ethik, in: M. Oeming/A. Graupner (Ed.), Altes Testament und christliche Verkündigung (FS A.H.J. Gunneweg), Stuttgart/Berlin/Köln/Mainz 1987, 148–164.
–, *Einführung* in die theologische Ethik, Berlin/New York 1990.
JÜNGEL, E., *Entsprechungen*. Gott – Wahrheit – Mensch, München [2]1986.
–, *Tod*, Gütersloh [5]1993.
–, Wertlose *Würde* – Gegenwärtige Gewissenlosigkeit. Erinnerung an den christlichen Ursprung lebensorientierender Begriffe, Frankfurter Rundschau vom 18. Februar 1997, 10.
–, Das *Evangelium* von der Rechtfertigung des Gottlosen als Zentrum des christlichen Glaubens, Tübingen 1998.
–, Gott als *Geheimnis* der Welt. Zur Begründung der Theologie des Gekreuzigten im Streit zwischen Theismus und Atheismus, Tübingen [7]2001.
KRÄMER, H., Integrative *Ethik*, Frankfurt/M. 1995.
KRAUSE, G., Art. Bonhoeffer, TRE 7, 1981, 55–66.
MAURER, E., Die *Gerechtigkeit* Gottes und die menschliche Gerechtigkeit. Die kritische Funktion der Rechtfertigungslehre in der evangelischen Ethik, in: P. Dabrock/T. Jähnichen/L. Klinnert/W. Maaser (Ed.), Kriterien der Gerechtigkeit. Begründungen – Anwendungen – Vermittlungen (FS Ch. Frey), Gütersloh 2003, 106–120.
MAYER, R., *Christuswirklichkeit*. Grundlagen, Entwicklung und Konsequenzen der Theologie Dietrich Bonhoeffers, AzTh 15, Stuttgart 1969.
MOKROSCH, R./JOHANNSEN, F./GREMMELS, CH., Dietrich Bonhoeffers *Ethik*. Ein Arbeitsbuch für Schule, Gemeinde und Studium, Gütersloh 2003.
MOLTMANN, J., *Herrschaft* Christi und soziale Wirklichkeit nach Dietrich Bonhoeffer, TEH N.F. 71, München 1959.
OTT, H., *Wirklichkeit* und Glaube, Vol. 1: Zum theologischen Erbe Dietrich Bonhoeffers, Göttingen 1966.
REUTER, H.-R., *Nachwort* des Herausgebers, in: D. Bonhoeffer, Akt und Sein. Transzendentalphilosophie und Ontologie in der systematischen Theologie (= DBW 2), München 1988, 163–185.
RICH, A., *Wirtschaftsethik*, Vol. 1, Gütersloh [4]1991.
RUSS, H.G., Empirisches *Wissen* und Moralkonstruktion. Eine Untersuchung zur Möglichkeit und Reichweite von Brückenprinzipien in der Natur- und Bioethik, Frankfurt/M. u.a. 2002.
SECKLER, M., *Fundamentaltheologie*. Aufgaben und Aufbau, Begriff und Namen, in: Handbuch der Fundamentaltheologie, Vol. 4, 1988, 450–514.
SLENCZKA, N., Die unvermeidbare *Schuld*. Der Normenkonflikt in der christlichen Ethik. Deutung einer Passage aus Bonhoeffers Ethik-Fragmenten, BThZ 16, 1999, 97–119.

SOOSTEN, J. von, *Nachwort* des Herausgebers, in: D. Bonhoeffer, Sanctorum Communio. Eine dogmatische Untersuchung zur Soziologie der Kirche (= DBW 1), München 1986, 306–324.

TIETZ-STEIDING, CH., Bonhoeffers *Kritik* der verkrümmten Vernunft. Eine erkenntnistheoretische Untersuchung, BHTh 112, Tübingen 1999.

–, Verkrümmte Vernunft und intellektuelle *Redlichkeit*. Dietrich Bonhoeffers Erkenntnistheorie, in: Ch. Gremmels/W. Huber (Ed.), Religion im Erbe. Dietrich Bonhoeffer und die Zukunftsfähigkeit des Christentums, Gütersloh 2002, 293–307.

TÖDT, H. E., Theologische *Perspektiven* nach Dietrich Bonhoeffer, Gütersloh 1993.

TÖDT, I./TÖDT, H.E./FEIL, E./GREEN, C., *Nachwort* der Herausgeber, in: D. Bonhoeffer, Ethik (= DBW 6), 413–456 (= Editors' Afterword to the German Edition, DBWE 6, 409–449).

WANNENWETSCH, B., *Gestaltwerdung* und Wegbereitung. Zur Aktualität von Bonhoeffers Ethik, VF 46, 2001, 56–64.

Barry Harvey

Accounting for Difference

Dietrich Bonhoeffer's Contribution to a Theological Critique of Culture

If Thomas Aquinas and Max Weber are to be believed, there are no villains in the epic tale of capitalism, only accountants.[1] According to Aquinas, the division of material goods in a commonwealth

> is not according to the natural law, but arose rather from human agreement which belongs to positive law [...] Hence the ownership of possessions is not contrary to the natural law, but an addition thereto devised by human reason.[2]

Weber expands on Thomas's point with respect to contemporary political economy when he locates the wellspring of the forces that drive capitalist markets, not in some mysterious natural or historical necessity – class conflict, for example – but in bookkeeping, a contingent operation of human intellect. According to Weber, capitalism only became a reality when procedures of accounting defined capital as something distinct from income, thus making possible its distinctive regime of accumulation.[3] Capital is therefore not something that was always dormant in "nature of things", but a concept which, in coordination with other factors, regulates to a significant extent the relationships of our modern and now postmodern world around the activities of production, consumption, and exchange.

Talking about accountants and the origins of capital may seem an odd way to begin an article on the idea of culture in the context of a volume on the theology of Dietrich Bonhoeffer, but I hope to show its relevance. "Culture", I shall argue, is a polysemic and ambiguous concept, the scope and significance of which are often taken for granted. It was devised and refined principally in Europe, and has genealogical links to the modern notion of "religion",[4] about which, as we all know, Bonhoeffer has much

---

[1] I am indebted to Nicholas Boyle for this way of putting the matter. Boyle, Who Are We Now?, 66.
[2] Thomas Aquinas, Summa Theologica, IIa. IIae. 66, A. 2.
[3] Weber, Vorbemerkung, cited by Boyle, Who Are We Now?, 66.
[4] More needs to be said in this regard, but we can begin by noting Paul Tillich's claim that "religion is the substance of culture, [and] culture is the form of religion." Tillich, Theology of Culture, 42.

to say.[5] The idea of culture represents a significant change in "bookkeeping procedures" with respect to the way the modern world accounts for human difference, defining it as something distinct from politics, which is the exclusive provenance of the nation-state and capitalist markets. In at least this strictly formal sense it is not necessarily contrary to what Bonhoeffer calls the natural, i.e., to that which in the created order is open to Christ. But if theologians are to use this concept we must do so carefully, lest we fail to note that as a product of liberal capitalism it accounts for difference in a manner that tends, sometimes subtly, sometimes abruptly, toward the unnatural, toward that which has closed itself off against the coming of Christ.[6]

If nothing else, I hope in this essay to remind us that there is no innocent use of any concept, that all theoretical endeavors serve an agenda, advancing a social project that may or may not be open to Christ. But beyond that I shall argue that when making an inquiry into the concept of culture we must concern ourselves both with the general question of human difference *and* the particular way liberal capitalist society deals with the other. What is needed on both counts is not a theology of culture (which would inevitably grant the concept an architectonic role it does not deserve), but a theological critique of the concept not unlike Karl Barth's and Bonhoeffer's critiques of "religion".[7] In what follows, then, I shall argue that "culture" is one of a series of concepts that emerge in conjunction with the rise of the secular sphere, which is probably the single most important working hypothesis of our post-whatever-it-is world. One of the principal functions of the concept of culture is to differentiate, classify and position strategically the wondrous diversity of human existence within this secular domain, so that it might conform to the practices and institutions with dominant power. Bonhoeffer's contribution to a critique of this process resides not in any theory of culture (he has none to offer), but in a theological framework around which to construct such a critique.

How a society accounts for difference is vital, for as the poet Wallace Stevens once observed, human beings live in their description of a place, not the place itself.[8] In our time the concept of culture has emerged as a central life-world category by which dominant power works constructively[9]

---

5   LPP, 279–282. 285–287. 311f. 325–329. 336f. 341f. 344–346. 359–362. 380–384.
6   DBWE 6, 173–175.
7   See Barth, Church Dogmatics I/2, 280–361.
8   Stevens, April 4, 1945 letter to Henry Church, Letters, 494.
9   Muslim anthropologist Talal Asad disputes the claim that hegemonic power necessarily suppresses difference in favor of unity, or that power always abhors ambiguity: "To secure its unity – to make its own history – dominant power has worked best through differentiating and classifying practices." Asad, Genealogies of Religion, 17. See also de Certeau, The Practice of Everyday Life.

to differentiate and classify otherness. We simply cannot treat this concept as a given, but must see it as a distinctive way of describing difference that strategically positions it vis-à-vis the two most important powers organizing spaces today – the modern nation-state and the global market. That something should perform this work should not be particularly controversial, since dominant regimes typically take upon themselves the task of constructing a "world" big enough to encompass all human beings. The poet Virgil, for example, claimed that it was Rome's destiny "to rule Earth's peoples [...] to pacify, to impose the rule of law, to spare the conquered [and] battle down the proud."[10] Nor should Christians expect the rulers and authorities of this world to act otherwise. After all, Jesus told his followers on the night before his crucifixion that Gentiles kings lord it over their subjects, and then claim that they do so for their benefit (Luke 22,25).

This gospel passage reminds us as well that throughout history all peoples have of necessity formulated ways to account for the other, each with their own rules of inclusion and exclusion. Jews, including Jesus, referred to non-Jews as Gentiles, a term with pejorative connotations, at least in some circles. In like manner the Greeks and Romans referred to non-Greek speakers as barbarians, literally, as those who say nothing but "bar-bar-bar" (and who therefore were obviously uncivilized). Liberal capitalism is no exception. What is significant in this otherwise mundane fact is the particular way that accounting for difference is done. To quote an old proverb, the devil is in the details, and he has been exceptionally busy.

In his book *Beyond Anthropology*, Bernard McGrane contends that Europeans and more generally self-identified "Westerners" have used four broad paradigms to describe and interpret non-European peoples. Up to the sixteenth century, the frame of reference was Christianity, and the other was a pagan who inhabited a space that lent itself to demonization, since the only space of salvation was in the body of Christ. During the Enlightenment, the Christian paradigm was supplanted by one that positioned otherness in terms of epistemology, using categories such as ignorance, error, superstition to account for the difference between the European (who was rational, cultured, civilized) and the non-European. The Enlightenment paradigm too eventually gave way, replaced in the nineteenth century by one that privileged a certain narration of time as the "scientific" arbiter of difference, arranging it in terms of past and present, stages of development, the primitive and the advanced.[11]

---

10   Virgil, The Aeneid, VI.850–3, 190. Augustine's contention that the earthly city is governed by the *libido dominandi*, the lust to mastery thus applies with equal force to liberal capitalism. Augustine, City of God, I.Pref., 3.

11   McGrane, Beyond Anthropology, ix–x. As Kenneth Surin points out, McGrane's archaeology of the concept of culture is not without its problems, but it does effectively chart a potent

In the twentieth century, says McGrane, difference was no longer demonized as pagan, or described derisively as primitive and superstitious, or relegated to an earlier step in the process of social evolution, surviving, as Zygmunt Bauman puts it, into the present on false pretenses and ultimately doomed to extinction.[12] The dominant paradigm instead became "culture". According to McGrane,

[w]e think under the hegemony of the ethnological response to the alienness of the Other; we are, today, contained within an anthropological concept of the Other. Anthropology has become our modern way of seeing the Other as, fundamentally and merely, culturally different.[13]

As a result of this development, says Kenneth Surin, difference has been "democratized", such that the non-European other is no longer a relic of another time. The radical democratization of difference authorizes us to insert the other into "our" present, to transform her or him into "our" contemporary, always of course on "our" terms: "The non-European 'other' is still 'different' of course, but now (s)he is *merely* 'different'."[14]

This is not say that previous modes of dealing with the other have disappeared altogether. Residual elements of previous eras have been folded into the cultural paradigm. The events of 11 September 2001 have resuscitated the practice of demonizing the other, now in the form of "fundamentalist" or "radical" religion, which is then linked immediately with that most dreaded of concepts: terrorism. This way of describing the current state of affairs is part of a larger narrative, according to which there is a dichotomy between the religious and the secular, and that the former is irrational and dangerous, and must be constantly reigned in by "rational", that is, secular political power. Delimiting the human condition in this manner establishes an other who is essentially irrational, fanatical and violent, which in turn authorizes coercive measures against this Other. In our time and place

the Muslim world especially plays the role of religious Other. *They* have not yet learned to remove the dangerous influence of religion from political life. *Their* violence is therefore irrational and fanatical. *Our* violence, by contrast, is rational and peacemaking, and sometimes regrettably necessary to contain *their* violence.[15]

---

historical trajectory in the authorizing discourse of modern secular society. I am indebted to Surin, both for bringing McGrane's work to my attention and for his lucid summation of it. Surin, A Certain "Politics of Speech", 73f.

12 Bauman, Postmodern Ethics, 39.
13 McGrane, Beyond Anthropology, x.
14 Surin, A Certain "Politics of Speech", 74, author's emphasis.
15 Cavanaugh, Sins of Omission, 35, author's emphasis.

The not-so-subtle message is that the only good religion is one in which everyone acts like good cultural Protestants, that is, as those who do not take their religion seriously.

The claim that the other becomes "merely different" under the aegis of the idea of culture may seem an unduly harsh indictment of what most people take to be a straightforward concept, but it accurately describes what has happened to difference in a society that has organized itself around the working hypothesis of the secular, that is, a space free from all traces of transcendence, a domain in which what is truly and fully human can be understood *etsi deus non daretur*, even if God does not exist.[16] This is a strong claim, and it requires some historical context. During the Middle Ages, which, though never a Christ-centered world, was certainly Christ-haunted,[17] the notion that there is an autonomous space of the purely "human", distinct from that of the sacred, the essential features of which are knowable in full, at least in principle, would have been incomprehensible. Human beings could not live except by the vision of God – and that vision depended totally on God's good pleasure.[18] Women and men were created with a natural desire to see and participate in God, but that desire could only be realized by God's gracious initiative. And apart from participation in the divine life made flesh in Jesus Christ, the human being – created in God's image and in possession of reason that reflects the very Word himself – effectively disappears, undoing the work of God.[19]

Participation in the reality of the triune God, moreover, was not confined to a marginal realm of "religion" sequestered from the reality of the world, that is, from the workings of politics, economics and the like. Medieval society formed a complex space comprised of intersecting associations – church, civil authorities, monasteries, guilds, clans and towns. The duties and rights that men and women owed to each other were not conferred by a omnicompetent, centralized state – an institution that effectively disconnects persons from local encumbrances in order to establish a direct rela-

---

16 Traditionally the Latin *saeculum* did not originally designate a space or realm separate from the religious or sacred, but a time. Theologians used the term to refer to the temporal period between fall and eschaton, and after the coming of Christ to the overlap of the two ages in the here and now. The secular thus denotes that period in the story of creation when temporal authorities were mandated to pursue certain legitimate yet limited goods to preserve fallen creation, e.g., restraining evil through the use of coercive justice, facilitating the production and exchange of material goods through the institutions of private property, and in general maintaining social cohesion.

17 An expression I borrow from the American Catholic novelist Flannery O'Connor, which she uses to describe the American South in the mid-twentieth century. See O'Connor, Some Aspects of the Grotesque in Southern Fiction, in: Collected Works, 815, and: The Grotesque in Southern Fiction, in: Mystery and Manners, 44.

18 De Lubac, The Mystery of the Supernatural, 179.

19 See, for example, Athanasius, On the Incarnation, 31f.

tionship to the sovereign center of power – but were embedded in these overlapping associations of which they were members. Each person and association were regarded as wholes that also constituted parts of a larger whole, generating a complex conception of space that was conceived on the Pauline theology of the body of Christ.[20]

Beginning around the thirteenth century, however, what was once a complex, integrated space of lived existence was gradually sub-divided into quasi-autonomous spheres of influence: state, market, family, religion, and of course "culture". Due to contingent operations of intellect analogous to the changes in bookkeeping that distinguished capital from income, an existence unrelated to the transcendent became imaginable. The secular as the space of the purely human, with its spheres of differentiation, was instituted and imagined "both in theory and in practice", that is, as both social construct, preeminently by the practices of statecraft and capitalist accumulation, and as intellectual concept, articulated principally by the modern social sciences – political science, political economy, sociology and anthropology.[21] The world as social scientists typically describe and explain it is therefore not how things with human beings in their complex relationships have always worked in reality, but a historically constituted set of social roles, disciplinary techniques, material forces, and institutional structures which, in their efficient anonymity, are both the instrument *and* effect of human intelligence and artifice.

Two working hypotheses that were essential to this newly constituted space of the secular had to do with the realms of "religion" and "culture". Both concepts need to be examined in relation to each other and to the social and historical circumstances that accompanied their invention and development. With respect to the idea of religion, prior to the fifteenth century no one used this idea in the distinctively modern sense, having to do with the private beliefs and sentiments of individuals that have little or no direct bearing on public life, and which therefore become in a very real sense optional in a way that, say, science is not.[22] When the Latin *religio* does occur in medieval writings (which is rare) it either refers to the rule or discipline of monastic life,[23] or to an acquired virtue similar to that of

---

20   Milbank, The Word Made Strange, 268–292; Gierke, Associations and Law, 143–160; Cavanaugh, Theopolitical Imagination, 99f. Elements of this tradition are reflected in Bonhoeffer's understanding of the difference between Anglo-Saxon and German conceptions of human rights, contending that the language of rights must be set in a social framework that recognizes the fact that one's existence as an individual and one's membership in various social groupings are constitutively bound to each other. DBWE 16, 528–533.

21   Milbank, Theology and Social Theory, 9.

22   Asad, Genealogies of Religion, 51. Here I dispute Bonhoeffer's contention that the whole history of Christian preaching and theology rests on the religious *a priori*. See LPP, 280.

23   Southern, Western Society, 214; Asad, Genealogies of Religion, 39 n. 22.

sanctity, a disposition which – in concert with other virtues – directs the faithful to know and love God: "the activity by which man gives the proper reverence to God through actions which specifically pertain to divine worship, such as sacrifice, oblations, and the like."[24] In either sense the term presupposed a context of practices embodied in the communal life of the church.

Beginning in the fifteenth century, however, the doctrinal and moral convictions that had been fostered by church teaching were gradually separated from the life and language of Christ's ecclesial body, and reconceived as abstract systems of beliefs which could be embraced voluntarily by individuals about what is ultimately true and important in their lives, but without the need to participate in the worship and witness of the church. Nicholas of Cusa laid much of the groundwork for this transition in the first half of the fifteenth century by reconceiving different traditions as the result of epistemic limitations of finite human beings, with a single, infinite reality standing behind the heterogeneous expressions. He thus speaks of "one religion in the multiplicity of rites". According to Peter Harrison, it is clear that

> Cusanus does not mean one 'religion' in the modern sense, for that would imply an end to the 'diversity of rites'. Yet neither is he using the term in the limited sense of 'monastic rule'. Instead, he seeks to promote the view that diverse religious customs (the accidents of 'religion', if you will) conceal a true or ideal 'religion'. This *'una religio'* is the unattainable truth about God – the Platonic ideal of which all existing belief systems are but shadowy expressions. The faithful of all nations and creeds should persevere in their particular expressions of piety in the firm belief that the one true 'religion' is the basis of them all.[25]

Marsilio Ficino builds on Cusanus's Platonic speculations in his 1474 book *De Christiana Religione*, positing *religio* as a human impulse or propensity common to all women and men, "the fundamental distinguishing human characteristic, innate, natural, and primary." For Ficino, *religio* names the Platonic ideal of genuine perception and worship of God, which Wilfred Cantwell Smith translates as "religiousness". The various historical manifestations of this instinct, the varieties of pieties and rites that we now call religions, are all just more or less true approximations of the one true *religio* divinely implanted in the human heart.[26] That which directs us to know and love God is thus interiorized and naturalized, made a matter of an inward awareness or affection orienting individuals toward the transcendent, an innate, pre-linguistic disposition only indirectly related to any particular

---

24 Thomas Aquinas, Summa Theologica, IIa. IIae. 81, A. 2.
25 Harrison, "Religion" and the Religions, 12.
26 Harrison, op. cit., 12f; Smith, The Meaning and End of Religion, 32ff.

ecclesial context.[27] It is only a few short steps from here to the fully developed theological conception of religion that we find, for example, in the work of Friedrich Schleiermacher.

The concept of culture emerged in Europe at approximately the same time. Through the fifteenth century its etymological Latin forerunner, *cultura*, was typically reserved for talking about what farmers and gardeners did, the tending of natural growth. Human beings cultivated crops and animals, but not people. It was only in the sixteenth and early seventeenth centuries that this abstract term designating a method of husbandry was metaphorically extended to describe the process of human development, especially the improvement of mind, of moral sensibility and aesthetic taste.[28] Francis Bacon and Samuel Pufendorf resuscitated the idea of *cultura animi* from Cicero's *Tusculan Disputations*: "just as a field, however good, cannot be productive without cultivation, so the soul cannot be productive without teaching. So true it is that the one without the other is ineffective. Now the cultivation of the soul is philosophy [*cultura autem animi philosophia est*]; this pulls out vices by the roots and makes souls fit for the reception of seed, and commits to the soul and, as we may say, sows in it seed of a kind to bear the richest fruit when fully grown."[29]

From this metaphorical extension arose the first modern use of the abstract noun "culture" in both French and English to demarcate a process of intellectual, spiritual and aesthetic development and refinement. As one might expect, an aristocratic sense of what counts as proper cultivation attached itself quite early to this use of the concept, with unmistakable class and colonialist connotations. To be counted among the "cultured" or "civilized", particularly in Britain and France (and extending eventually to America in the West and Russia in the East), came to be associated with conceptions of enlightened rationality, a sign that one had been formed in the manner of Europe's new social elites who would manage society from a universal, cosmopolitan perspective. The cultured person possessed through habituation a refined, educated soul with a claim to distinctive social status by virtue of his intellectual training and aesthetic sensibilities.[30]

In Germany the relationship between the ideas of culture and civilization was configured somewhat differently due to the influence of at least two different impulses. There tended to be a more nationalistic character to the related notions of *Bildung* and *Kultur*, as German intellectuals resisted French claims to the universality of its notion of a movable Enlightenment. Intellectual, artistic, and spiritual achievements were often singled out as

---

27 Cavanaugh, Theopolitical Imagination, 33.
28 Williams, Keywords, 87.
29 Cicero, Tusculan Disputations I.v.13, 150–160. See Tanner, Theories of Culture, 4.
30 Tanner, op. cit., 4; Williams, Keywords, 87f.

Germany's bulwark against French-dominated internationalism, in part because it was thought that they constituted a higher form of achievement than any civilization imposed from those outside Germany, but especially because they manifested a spirit that was distinctively German. Johann Gottfried von Herder objected in particular to the suggestion that there was a universal and unilinear process of human development to be identified with dominant European civilization, and in a decisive linguistic innovation insisted that it was necessary to speak of "cultures" in the plural.[31] Kathryn Tanner thus states that "[t]he distinctively German character of its *Kultur* interrupted the uniformity of Enlightenment civilization as an ideal for all peoples."[32]

Also embedded in the emerging concept of *Kultur* was a Romantic critique of the notion of a single, enlightened rational order. The notion of "civilization" that was held in such esteem in Britain and France was frequently regarded in Germany as artificial in comparison with "nature". Natural human needs and impulses were seen as more basic to life and therefore to be elevated above the artificial manners of politeness and elegance. There developed an interest in "folk cultures", which were held to be closer to nature and thus offered an alternative to "civilization", which was regarded as "mechanical", the product of an abstract rationalism and the inhumanity of the industrial revolution. The emphasis of the culture-concept thus shifts from the rational cultivation of an enlightened intellect to the activities and achievements of literary and artistic endeavor: literature, music, dance, food, clothing and the like. The concept of "civilization" was accordingly associated with political and economic practices and institutions, which were seen as human artifacts, whereas *Kultur* was reserved for referring to the highest intellectual and artistic achievements in German society.[33]

The range of the culture-concept was extended once again, this time to name that which stood between human beings and the machines and technologies that had been invented to tame Nature, but which increasingly had imprisoned men and women within the iron cage of modern instrumental rationality.[34] As the nineteenth century progressed the concept's meaning increasingly became intransitive and self-contained, much like Aristotle's concept of *praxis*, which had the effect of privatizing everything that was classified under the concept as a matter of personal taste instead of public

---

31 Williams, op. cit., 89f.
32 Tanner, Theories of Culture, 9f.
33 The fluidity of the concept allowed some authors to reverse this relationship, "culture" being used to talk about material development and "civilization" spiritual. Williams, Keywords, 89f.
34 See Weber, The Protestant Ethic, 181.

fact. The aim of culture was no longer to accomplish some end, but simply to do something well, namely, to cultivate certain standards of thought and feeling, or as Matthew Arnold put it, "inward spiritual activity",[35] emphasizing "levels of excellence in fine art, literature, music and individual personal perfection."[36] With Arnold the link to the concept of religion that Barth and Bonhoeffer sought to criticize becomes more apparent.

The plural form "cultures" leads to a third and more recognizably anthropological sense of the concept, specifying a particular way of life, occasionally of humanity in general,[37] but more often of a particular people. It is here that the concept plays a central role in the ethnological discourses of the modern secular world, the emergence of which initiated a time of unparalleled social change brought about by colonialism, the rise of modern science and technology, the emergence and expansion of the political institution of the modern nation-state, and the development of capitalist modes of accumulation and consumption, all of which led to the widespread encounters between, and then the massive displacements of whole populations. In the face of such rapid and radical diversification, says Raymond Williams, the idea of culture was a general reaction to a general and major change in the conditions of common life in liberal industrial society. The basic element of this concept was its effort at total qualitative assessment. Changes in the whole form of a common life necessarily focused attention on it. Unlike particular changes, which only modify specific habitual actions, general change drove a people back to look at general designs as a whole. In short, says Williams, "[t]he working-out of the idea of culture is a slow reach again for control."[38]

Anthropologist Talal Asad extends Williams's insights in a study on the development of the concept of culture in Britain in the late nineteenth and twentieth centuries, particularly as it related to the nonwhite populations of the British empire. Asad contends that the culture-concept was "part of a language of controlled reconstruction [...] according to the dictates of liberal reason." Its aim was to identify, study and normalize the traditions and *mores* of subject peoples for the purpose of integrating them into modern (i.e., Western) civilization by way of "amalgamation" and "persuasion". Talk of "amalgam" implies the notion of original, "pure" cultures coming into contact with each other to create a new, emergent, and more progressive historical identity. The dynamics of the culture-concept extends to recent discussions about multiculturalism, which has essentially to do with

---

35   Arnold, Culture and Anarchy, 44.
36   Jenks, Culture, 9.
37   This is the sense of the term that one finds in Niebuhr's influential but problematic Christ and Culture, 29–39.
38   Williams, Culture and Society, 295.

the proper theoretical and practical coordination of dominant (i.e., European) and subordinate (native) cultures. There is to be equal respect and tolerance for all, but the realities of political and economic power require the subordinate, which is less "progressive", to adjust to the dominant and more progressive culture.[39] (Recent suggestions both in academia and the popular press that Islam needs its own "Renaissance" – European history once again serving as the norm for what constitutes genuinely civilized development – are only the latest examples of how a secular society accounts for difference.)

In the post-industrialized countries of Europe and North America, writes Slavoj Zizek, the concept of culture names the field of beliefs and practices that have been disowned, i.e., "all those things we practice without really believing in them, without 'taking them seriously'" (or at least, which we should not take seriously). In matters of religion, for example, most people no longer "really believe", though they may still follow (some) traditional rituals and mores, to show respect for the "lifestyle" of the community to which they belong: "'I don't really believe in it, it's just part of my culture' effectively seems to be the predominant mode of the disavowed or displaced belief characteristic of our times." What *is* a "cultural lifestyle", writes Zizek, "if not the fact that, although we don't believe in Santa Claus, there is a Christmas tree in every house, and even in public places, every December?" If such claims seem overstated, why then do most people not include science within the ambit of culture? Is it not because it is all too real, something we cannot hold it at arm's length, and thus it is not "cultural"? Is this not why those of us who pride ourselves on being "cultured" derisively dismiss fundamentalist believers as barbarians, as anticultural, as a threat to culture, because "they dare to *take their beliefs seriously*?" All those who lack some kind of cognitive or interpretive distance to their beliefs, who live it immediately, we perceive as a threat to culture:

Recall the outrage when [...] the Taliban forces in Afghanistan destroyed the ancient Buddhist statutes at Bamiyan: although none of us enlightened Westerners believe in the divinity of the Buddha, we were outraged because the Taliban Muslims did not show the appropriate respect for the 'cultural heritage' of their own country and the entire world. Instead of believing through the other, like all people of culture, they really believed in their own religion, and thus had no great sensitivity toward the cultural value of the monuments of other religions – to them, the Buddha statues were just fake idols, not 'cultural treasures'.[40]

The danger that Zizek risks in making this point, of course, is that some might hear him trying to excuse, or worse, justify the actions of the Taliban,

---

39 Asad, Genealogies of Religion, 248–253.
40 Zizek, The Puppet and the Dwarf, 7f.

which I do not take to be his aim. What he is attempting to show are the theoretical and practice dilemmas that attend the attempt to account for difference by means of the concept of culture. What we get is two versions of multiculturalism, the difference between which is only a matter of degree. I too risk being misunderstood at this point, for there are few concepts more widely celebrated or politically axiomatic in our time than those of pluralism and multiculturalism, particularly among intellectuals and in such culture industries as the mass media and entertainment providers. For one even to raise a question about them is to be regarded by some as *prima facie* evidence that he or she is prejudiced, biased, blind, and hateful, the enemy of difference and tolerance, of humanity itself. And yet it is a risk that I must make, precisely for the sake of difference.

One version is what one social critic calls boutique multiculturalism, which is the pluralism of ethnic restaurants, weekend festivals, and high profile flirtations with the other that the novelist Tom Wolfe once satirized as "radical chic". Boutique multiculturalists can never really take seriously the particularity of other traditions, because they stipulate that the core convictions and practices of the other be regarded "as icing on a basically homogeneous cake." Wed as they are to an essentialist anthropology, boutique multiculturalists see differences not as basic to who and what women and men are, but as commodities to be consumed, tourist stops to be visited, exotic cuisines to be sampled, in short, as accessories to a standard model of universal humanity as defined by the regime of liberal capitalism.[41] Such pluralism rejects the force of actual diversity at precisely the point where it makes the strongest claim on its most committed members, and prescribes instead a rational essence for the other which enforces a superficial respect that so many in our shrinking world rightly find insulting.

There is another type of multiculturalism that is more serious, because it seeks to value difference in and for itself. This postmodern version recognizes that the politics of equal dignity advocated by boutique multiculturalism is just too easy, too facile. Ascribing to everyone the identical basket of immunities and entitlements on the premise that "deep down" all of us are essentially the same (autonomous maximizers of self-interest), utterly fails to account for the particular and substantial ways in which persons, groups, and traditions differ. For these strong multiculturalists, nurturing particularity and diversity through tolerance, not adherence to some purported universal quality such as our status as autonomous rational agents, is a first principle of both personal morality and public policy.[42]

---

41 Fish, Boutique Multiculturalism, 382.
42 Fish, op. cit., 383.

Nevertheless, the time will always come for a serious pluralist when the stranger will act in a way that resists her or his "proper" place, i.e., incorporation into the larger whole ordered by the nation-state and the global market. "Confronted with a demand that it surrender its view point or enlarge it to include the practices of its natural enemies – other religions, other races, other genders, other classes – a beleaguered culture will fight back with everything from discriminatory legislation to violence." One need only think of the way that the Taliban compelled women to wear the *burkha*, or the ethnic cleansing that took place in Kosovo. In such situations the dilemma for serious multiculturalists quickly becomes evident. Either they must stretch their tolerance so that it includes the intolerance of a group that they personally abhor, thus rejecting tolerance as their first principle, or they condemn the intolerance, in which case they no longer advocate difference at the point where it is most obviously at stake.[43] Whereas the boutique pluralism of the modernist is explicitly imperialist, the strong form of pluralism shows itself to be implicitly so, in spite of its best intentions to affirm difference and tolerance.

Far from providing a viable solution to reconciling profound differences and disagreements, pluralism and multiculturalism represent yet one more comprehensive doctrine added to the fragmented, contentious mix (and thus they do not even name our present predicament accurately). They create a façade of diversity masking an underlying uniformity that sets human life in a liberal capitalist society apart from previous forms of social life. In some ways multiculturalism is a sign of the impatience of our society in the face of seemingly intractable difference, hoping desperately that a formal principle can transform itself (and us) into meaningful substance through some sort of procedural alchemy.[44]

When defined by means of the culture-concept, otherness, because it is now "merely" different, no longer makes a difference. In this regard the three senses of the concept – a general process of intellectual, spiritual and aesthetic development, the particular way of life of a people, and artistic activity and production – though seemingly disparate, actually work hand in glove to render politically and economically inert the practices, customs, habits and rites of other peoples. That is to say, they are made to conform to the contours of production and consumption privileged by liberal capitalist society. Once traditional activities and dispositions are classified as cultural, and thus no longer part of the constitutive – which is to say, *political* – practice of a people, then artistic expression is virtually the only marker

---

43 Ibid.
44 The metaphor of alchemy to describe the modern belief that form can turn itself into substance I take from Mensch/Freeman, The Politics of Virtue, 5.

remaining to identify the way of life of the other.[45] Moreover, the significance of such expression is then privatized, either around the "cultivation" of individual sensibility (in the style of Arnold, i.e., "inward spiritual activity"), or sequestered within "cultural enclaves".[46] Either way, the other is "normalized", made into a happy, useful, productive, and safe subject, in the social and political sense of the term.[47]

Finally, the democratization of difference by way of the normalizing project of "culture" is a necessary condition for commodifying the customs, convictions, rites and habits of the world's peoples, turning them into raw materials for what Theodor Adorno and Max Horkheimer call the culture industries – means of mass communication such as movies, television, and popular music, distribution systems (cable and satellite systems, telecommunications firms and of course the Internet), data processing networks such as computer software and hardware interests, and marketing and advertising firms, and educational institutions.[48] These endeavors account for the majority of the world's output of shared images, stories, information, news, entertainment, and the like, which are the stock and trade of the formative practices that are intrinsic to every society. They exert an inordinate influence on how people relate not only to the processes and products of political and economic activity, but also to each other, both the neighbor with a face and the anonymous producer of goods that lives quite literally on the other side of the globe.[49]

---

45   Unfortunately, too many reflexively identify politics as a practice with statecraft, which is that form of political practice and theory which stipulates that the sphere where men and women come together to form a political association finds its highest expression in the nation-state. This definition invests the state with virtually unlimited political sovereignty over society, thus privileging it as the fulcrum of all social and political order and change. Underwriting the practice of liberal statecraft is the absence of any substantive conception of the common good, which effectively reduces politics to a set of procedures for protecting and promoting individual's pursuit of self-interest in the marketplace of desire and consumption. Bonhoeffer comes close to breaking the hold statecraft has on our political imagination when in *Discipleship* he says that, "[s]ince the church-community is the city on the hill, the 'polis' [...] established on this earth by God and marked with a seal as God's own, its 'political' character [*"politischer" Charakter*] is an inseparable aspect of its sanctification. The 'political ethics' [*"politische Ethik"*] of the church-community is grounded solely in its sanctification, the goal of which is that world be world and community be community, and that, nevertheless, God's word goes out from the church-community to all the world, as the proclamation that the earth and all it contains is the Lord's." DBWE 4, 261f.
46   Clifford Geertz, for example, identifies religion as a cultural system, which assigns to it an essentially cognitive function, having to with what he calls "reality maintenance". See his The Interpretation of Cultures, 87–125.
47   Lentricchia, Criticism and Social Change, 1f.
48   Horkheimer/Adorno, The Culture Industry: Enlightenment as Mass Deception, in: Horkheimer/Adorno, Dialectic of Enlightenment, 120–160, and Adorno, The Culture Industry. See also Budde, The (Magic) Kingdom of God.
49   Consider the way that, for example, television, with its titillating combination of sight and sound, its evocative appeals to the emotions rather than to the intellect, and its never-ending

With respect to the process of intellectual, spiritual and aesthetic development, these industries are quickly undermining every other kind of intellectual, moral and spiritual cultivation inherited from the past. Indeed, something that Bonhoeffer foresaw at the end of his life, the disappearance of the past, is quickly becoming a reality in the hands of the culture, bringing us to the brink of nothingness, *das Nichts*. Speaking in apocalyptic tones, Bonhoeffer declares that, "[e]verything that exists is threatened with annihilation. This is not one crisis among others, but a conflict of ultimate seriousness."[50] In face of *das Nichts*,

> the question about a historical heritage that we must make our own, use in the present, and pass on to the future is snuffed out. There is no future and no past. There remains only the present moment rescued from nothingness and the desire to grasp the next moment. Already yesterday's concerns are consigned to forgetfulness, and tomorrow's are too far away to obligate us today.[51]

Bonhoeffer concludes, perhaps with a touch of irony, that "[n]othingness binds itself to us and nothingness puts us in its debt."[52]

What, then, does Bonhoeffer offer to a theological critique of this concept of culture? It is certainly not a well-developed theory of the term; as I noted at the outset, there is nothing at stake theologically for him in it. Indeed, given the size of the corpus, it is intriguing to note how seldom culture and its cognates actually appear in his writings. He is familiar with its multiple connotations, including its more aristocratic implications, which at times he embraces, for example, when he laments the fact that cultural life (*geistige Existenz*) has become fragmented, a torso, that everyone is just a technician, even in music and the other arts.[53] Paul Lehmann observes in this regard that Bonhoeffer was thoroughly "German in his passion for perfection, whether of manners, or performance, or all that is connoted

---

stream of images and ideas, dominates the social ecology of capitalism. As the cornerstone of the expansion of global culture industries (together with the Internet), it intrudes into nearly every space of everyday life, crowding out other formative influences in the lives of young people, including the practices of the church. Television has an unparalleled ability to captivate our attention for extended periods of time in powerful images and deceptively subtle messages that take very little effort to understand. In a process known as fragmentation, images, ideas, and personalities are extricated from their conventional referents, and then recombined and reshuffled to confer novel meanings to products and consumption opportunities. Commercial television programming, taking features of a past or contemporary, "exotic" culture (music, dance, dress, language, stories, images) and recycling them with those extracted from other peoples to form disjointed images and impressions with no purpose other than to entice viewers and sell products, is so prevalent in our society that our perceptions and dispositions have been profoundly affected.

50   DBWE 6, 127.
51   DBWE 6, 128.
52   "Nichts haftet und nichts behaftet." DBW 6, 120, my translation. In the English edition it is rendered: "Nothing is fixed, and nothing holds us." DBWE 6, 129.
53   LPP, 219.

by the word *Kultur*. Here, in short, was an aristocracy of the spirit at its best".[54]

On other occasions Bonhoeffer can be highly critical of these connotations, stating that a culture (*Bildung*) that breaks down in the face of danger is no culture.[55] At yet other times he uses the term in a generic sense, as seen in his discussion of the mandates, where he employs it as a synonym for labor.

As we consider Bonhoeffer's work we need to remind ourselves that there are two distinct though related aspects to this discussion: the fact of difference for which the modern world seeks to account (and which every society must do), *and* its way of accounting for difference as "cultural". With respect to the latter, from Bonhoeffer's perspective we should classify the culture-concept as a product of what he calls natural reason, which he develops in connection with the notions of the ultimate and the penultimate. He invokes the idea of the natural as a mediating concept, treating it as distinct from the created, in order to take into account of the fallenness of humankind, and also from the sinful, to include in it the created. By entering into natural life, Christ transforms it into the realm of the penultimate, that is, that which is directed toward the ultimate – justification, salvation and the renewal of creation. The concept of the natural thus denotes a moment of independence and self-development for the created as such, with a relative freedom appropriate to natural life. Within this freedom, however, "there is a difference between its right use and its misuse, and this is the difference between the natural and the unnatural; there is therefore a relative openness and a relative closedness for Christ." The natural is therefore that within creation that is directed towards the coming of Christ, while the unnatural is that which has closed itself off against Christ's coming.[56]

The categories of natural and unnatural function typologically in Bonhoeffer's work, as anticipations and refusals, respectively, of redemption. The natural can therefore not be defined or understood apart from the event of grace. On its own, the natural cannot compel the coming of Christ (and hence it is truly unmerited grace), nor can that which is unnatural make it impossible: "in both cases the real coming is an act of grace."[57] The incarnation can never serve, then, as God's affirmation of the natural in abstraction from the cross and resurrection. The humanity of Jesus does not mean the ratification of the established world and of the human as it is. There can be no greater error than to separate the three elements of the event of grace:

---

54   Cited by Bethge, Dietrich Bonhoeffer, 155.
55   LPP, 193.
56   DBWE 6, 163.
57   DBWE 6, 173f.

"In the becoming human we recognize God's love toward God's creation; in the crucifixion God's judgment on all flesh; and in the resurrection God's purpose for a new world."[58] In Christ God judges our conceptions of what it takes to make and to keep human life human, and offers in their place the decisive definition in Jesus' life and passion.[59]

The emphasis here is on preserving the goodness and beauty of what God has created. "The natural", Bonhoeffer writes, "is that form of life preserved (*erhalten*) by God for the fallen world that is directed towards justification, salvation and renewal through Christ." Formally the natural is determined by God's intention to preserve the world and direct it towards Christ, and hence in this aspect can only be discerned in relation to Christ. Materially the natural is itself the form of preserved life, embracing the whole of humanity. Reason belongs to the material dimension of the natural as the source of knowledge of itself. It is not a divine principle of knowledge and order that can raise human beings above the natural,[60] but is itself a part of a fallen creation preserved by God, and thus wholly embedded in the natural. Its function is to take in (*vernehmen*) as a unity that which is whole and universal in reality. The natural and reason are thus correlated with each other, the former as the form of being of the preserved life, the latter as the form of its awareness. Reason is suited to this task because it too is fully implicated in the fall, hence it "perceives only what is given in the fallen world, and, indeed, exclusively according to its content."[61]

As a deliverance of natural reason, the concept of culture accomplishes two distinct but interrelated aims. First and positively, it registers the marvelous, wondrous diversity that is God's work of creation. This is the preserving function of which Bonhoeffer speaks, and it is a work that should not be overlooked or minimized. As Aquinas states, diversity is at the heart of the creative intention of God, who

brought things into being in order that His goodness might be communicated to creatures, and be represented by them; and because His goodness could not be adequately represented by one creature alone, He produced many and diverse creatures, that what was wanting to one in the representation of the divine goodness might be supplied by another. For goodness, which in God is simple and uniform, in creatures is manifold and divided; and hence the whole universe together participates the divine goodness more perfectly, and represents it better than any single creature whatever.[62]

---

58 DBWE 6, 157.
59 See Yoder, The Politics of Jesus, 99.
60 Or as Bonhoeffer puts it, "God's 'beyond' [*das "Jenseits" Gottes*] is not the beyond of our cognitive faculties. The transcendence of our epistemological theory [*die erkenntnistheoretische Transzendenz*] has nothing to do with the transcendence of God." LPP, 282.
61 DBW 6, 166f. DBWE 6, 174f.
62 Thomas Aquinas, Summa Theologica, Ia. 47, A. 2

This appreciation for diversity extends to the manifold customs, creations, convictions, rites and habits of humankind. According to Augustine, the achievements of human industry, agriculture, navigation, the arts, drama, hunting, weapons, medicines, culinary arts, communication, oratory and poetry, astronomy, even the ingenuity of philosophers and heretics in defending their errors and false doctrines, are wondrous and astonishing.[63]

At the same time, however, preservation exacts a high cost from diversity. A range of activities, institutions and virtues of the world's peoples that were once constitutive of an entire way of life – orchestrating the exchanges and relationships that took place within families and clans, villages and towns – are now consigned to the domain of culture, where they are to a significant extent precluded from intruding on the operations of either the state or the market. In our time these are the institutions that have seized almost unlimited proprietary authority in the organization of human life from the global down to the intimate (one thinks here, for example, of the recent efforts of the French government to ban the wearing of "conspicuous" religious paraphernalia in public schools). For something to be classified as "cultural" turns it into an "artifact" that is no longer part of a living whole, but something that belongs in a museum.[64]

Second and more problematically, then, the concept of culture serves to render the awe-inspiring diversity of human life politically inert, i.e., no longer facets of the constitutive practice of a people. This transformation is necessary if these differences are to be compatible with liberal capitalism's regime of accumulation and its modes of regulating virtually all aspects of day-to-day life. The question thus becomes, how does Bonhoeffer help us respond to the three-fold sense of the culture-concept in ways that avoid modernity's tendency toward the nothingness? A good point of departure may be found in his criticism of the concept of the "religious *a priori*" of humankind. He states in a series of letters to Eberhard Bethge in April and May 1944 that the whole history of Christian preaching and theology rests on this *a priori*. He then asks: "But what if one day it becomes clear that this *a priori* does not exist all, but was a historically conditioned and transient form of human self-expression [...]?" In response Bonhoeffer contends that in place of this contingent form of human self-expression we must attend to the church, not as a sequestered enclave unconcerned about the rest of the world around it, but as that body which mediates the mystery of God in Christ in the middle of the human village.[65]

This turn to the church may seem counter-intuitive, serving only to promote further division and suspicion among and between peoples, but I dis-

---

63 Augustine, City of God, XXII.24, 1162.
64 See Grant, Research in the Humanities, in: Grant, Technology and Justice, 97–102.
65 LPP, 280. 282. 286.

agree. Here we should heed what Bonhoeffer says at the conclusion of the preface to *Discipleship*:

> Today it seems so difficult to walk with certainty the narrow path of the church's decision and yet remain wide open to Christ's love for all people, and in God's patience, mercy and loving-kindness [...] for the weak and godless. Still, both must remain together, or else we will follow merely human paths.[66]

The editors to *Discipleship* rightly point out that the reference to "the church's decision" relates specifically to the Confessing Church and its decision to resist incorporation into the Reich Church, but I maintain that it also has a broader application, encompassing the question of how we deal with all that is entailed for a secularized world in the culture-concept.[67] These "human paths", he states in a lecture given to his students at Finkenwalde on the interpretation of the New Testament, will invariably lead Christians back to "Constantine's covenant with the church", which will in turn result in "a minimal ethic". When this occurs, the existence of the Christian becomes the existence of the citizen, and the nature of the church vanishes into the invisible realm: "But in this way the New Testament message was fundamentally misunderstood [and] inner-worldliness became a principle."[68]

What would it look like to implement in and through the church all that the secular world seeks to classify and control with the concept of culture? With respect to processes of "cultivation", i.e., of intellectual, spiritual and aesthetic development, it is significant that in several of his last letters Bon-

---

66   DBWE 4, 40. Bonhoeffer makes it clear throughout his career that the role of the church in a fallen world is crucial to the work of the gospel. In a lecture on interpreting the New Testament he states that "the church is the city on the hill. [...] It has to define its limits. It has to sever heresy from its body. It has to make itself distinct and to be a community which hears the Apocalypse." Bonhoeffer, No Rusty Swords, 324. Such comments confirm his oft-repeated insistence on the visibility of the church, such as the following from *Sanctorum Communio*: "The church is God's new will and purpose for humanity. God's will is always directed toward the concrete, historical human being. But this means that it begins to be implemented *in history*. God's will must become visible and comprehensible at some point in history." DBWE 1, 141.

67   Bonhoeffer eventually came to see that the narrow path of the church's decision was not a temporary measure in response to the church crisis of the 1930s, though that was the precipitating event. He writes in a 1940 letter to Eberhard Bethge that one of the most pressing issues raised by the Confessing Church's struggle with Nazism had to do with the institutional structures that support sound teaching. Can an authority for the church be established that is grounded in Scripture and confession alone now that the separation from papal and from secular authority in the church has taken place? If such authority cannot be constituted, Bonhoeffer concludes, then the last possibility of a Protestant Church has passed by. There are then only a few alternatives: a return to Rome or submission to the state church, or the path into isolation, i.e., the "protest" of true Protestantism against false authorities. DBWE 16, 78.

68   Bonhoeffer, No Rusty Swords, 324. This lecture was reconstructed in part from Bethge's notes.

hoeffer refers to the secret or arcane discipline in connection with the critique of religion. In his letter of 30 April 1944, for example, he asks what does it mean to be part of the *ek-klesia*, those who are called out, not to view things from a religious point of view, but as those who belong wholly to the world?[69] In such circumstances Christ is no longer an object of religion (nor, I would add, an object of culture), but the Lord of the world. It may well be in such circumstances that the secret discipline, which protects the mysteries of the faith from profanation, will take on a new importance.[70] The reference to the arcane discipline naturally leads us to think of the experiment in Christian community at Finkenwalde, the *Bruderhaus*. The practices that Bonhoeffer implemented there were a short-lived but important attempt to "cultivate" disciples in the way of Jesus, free from the profanation of the Nazi regime. I am reminded in particular of his love for African-American spirituals, which he acquired from his time in Harlem, and of the fact that he played recordings of these songs for the seminarians.[71] There is in fact a vital connection between these spirituals and the practice of the arcane discipline. Prior to the abolition of slavery in the American South, slaves needed to find a private place where their singing and shouting would not attract undue attention. An ex-slave preacher recalls what it was like to worship in these circumstances:

Meetings back then meant more than they do now. Then everybody's heart was in tune and when they called on God they made heaven ring. It was more than just Sunday meeting and then no more Godliness for a week. They would steal off to the fields and in the thickets and there, with heads together around a kettle to deaden the sound, they called on God out of heavy hearts.[72]

These secret meetings were necessary due to the legal restrictions against assemblies by slaves without white oversight, and also because of widespread dissatisfaction with the worship and preaching in white churches. "While the great majority of White Christians condoned slavery, saying it was permitted or even ordained by God," writes James Cone, "black slaves contended that God willed their freedom and not their servitude." They thus took every opportunity to steal off into the woods at night, risking serious injury and death, to sing, preach and pray for their liberation. And when the

---

69 I take Bonhoeffer's contention that Christians belong wholly to the world to be making the same claim that Augustine advances in *City of God* when he speaks of the mixing of the pilgrim city of God and the earthly city in the present time. Augustine makes clear what he means by this, namely, that Christians must endure the same hardships and make use of the same range of goods as the citizens of the earthly city, and moreover, that they do so according to a different faith, a different love, and a different hope. Augustine, City of God, XVIII. 54, 907f.

70 LPP, 281. 286.

71 See Bethge, Dietrich Bonhoeffer, 150.

72 Cited by Rawick, From Sundown to Sunup, 40.

slaves worshipped with their masters, they typically put on a "good front" so that their oppressors would think of them as pious and good. As Cone puts it,

> [t]he 'real meetin' and 'the real preachin' was held in the swamp, out of the reach of the patrols. An ex-slave, Litt Young, tells of a black preacher who preached 'obey your master' as long as her mistress was present. When the mistress was absent, she said, 'he came out with straight preachin' from the Bible'.[73]

In these secret meetings, described by Albert Raboteau as the "invisible institution",[74] the displaced children of Africa drew on the music, dance and modes of story telling of their native homelands to cry out to God in singing and shouting, preaching and dancing. As Bonhoeffer would put it, they encountered the mystery of God, not at the boundaries where human powers give out, but in the middle of the concerns and celebrations of their village, even as that village was compelled to come together in clandestine gatherings around the "prayin' ground" and the "hush harbor".[75] "Go down, Moses", they sang, "Way down in Egyptland/Tell old Pharaoh/To let my people go." And so they sang and danced around the "overturned pot", assuring each other that the God who had rescued the children of Israel from the hand of the oppressor would one day deliver them as well.

In this way they were shaped and sustained by a hope that was not rooted either in personal experience of freedom or in pragmatic calculations of how it might be achieved, and which therefore could not be falsified by seemingly endless delay or apparent defeat. They did not attempt to specify when God's triumph over the death, sin and evil that surrounded them would come, or by what mechanism it would be achieved. It was a way of reasoning that rejected any correlation between the ultimate victory of Jesus that would set right all things under heaven and on earth, and attempting by whatever means might be available to bring about that victory:[76] "Weep no more, Martha,/Weep no more, Mary,/Jesus rise from de dead,/Happy Morning."

In Bonhoeffer's love for spirituals we see the link between two of the uses made of the culture-concept, referring on the one hand to the process of intellectual, spiritual and aesthetic formation, and on the other to the works and practices of artistic activity, in this case, music and dance from Africa. But it is crucial to note that the *kind* of "cultivation" of persons through artistic expression determines to a great extent the use made of

---

73 Cone, Speaking the Truth, 88.
74 Raboteau, Slave Religion.
75 Cone, Speaking the Truth, 133.
76 See Yoder, The Power Equation, the Place of Jesus, and the Politics of King, in: Yoder, For the Nations, 136.

such expression, both positively and negatively. In this case the aim was not to achieve "levels of excellence in fine art, literature, music and individual personal perfection", as Arnold puts it, but to sustain faith, hope and charity among the exiled sons and daughters of Africa in a time of oppression and suffering. Unfortunately, what was created and passed along in these secret meetings has increasingly become in the hands of the culture industries "useful cultural capital" servicing the consumerist demands of the ever-expanding commercial regime of the global market.[77]

Bonhoeffer's interest in, and understanding of intellectual, moral and aesthetic formation is also manifested in his response to a comment by Bethge that links culture and death together with a reference to Socrates:

> I'm not sure how well I would come to grips with the situation if I saw what is really at stake. Education [*Bildung*] and death Socratic? The educated man as the one who has no illusions and does not deceive himself in activity or does not put up with it, but who knows how to overcome in Christian faith?

Bonhoeffer writes back:

> Your reference to Socrates in connection with the theme of culture and death may be very valuable; I must think about it. The only thing I am really clear about in the whole problem is that a 'culture' that breaks down in the face of danger is no culture.[78]

If I may be permitted to expand on this observation, the only culture that is finally worth having is one that is grounded in, and derives its nourishment from cross and resurrection. I seriously doubt that either the state or the market is interested in that kind of "cultivation" of persons.

Finally, how should Christians account for difference, for the other, for the broad spectrum of diversity among the tribes and languages, peoples and nations of the earth, if not with the concept of culture? For those called to participate in the mystery of the revelation of God in the human being Jesus Christ, in whom the reality of the world has already been borne, accepted and reconciled in the reality of God,[79] we first must resolve, at least initially, to let the other *be* genuinely other, to be strange and alien to us. This a response that may sound foreign to some, trained as most of us were in the modern university, which is predicated on the assumption that the only limits to understanding are the limits of being itself. In such a context naming someone as a stranger is regarded as an insult, rather than as an

---

77 Jennings, Harlem on My Mind. I have in mind a recent commercial on American television by a global company using the format of a typical African-American worship service to sell basketball shoes.
78 LPP, 183. 193f.
79 DBWE 6, 55.

opportunity both to show hospitality (or be gracious houseguests), and to be instructed further in the wondrous diversity of God's world.

In the fields of cultural and social anthropology the presumption that there are no real limits to our understanding of the other, and therefore no person or group is truly a stranger, often takes the form of an analogy between "culture" and "language", or more concretely, a "text". When we put matters this way, writes Edmund Leach in support of this proposition, we

> come to see that the essential problem is one of translation. The linguists have shown us that all translation is difficult, and that perfect translation is usually impossible. And yet we know that for practical purposes a tolerably satisfactory translation is always possible even when the original 'text' is highly abstruse.[80]

This analogy stipulates that a fundamental and relatively accessible commensurability exists between all "cultures", which again effectively functions to transform all difference into *mere* difference. Under the influence of the culture-concept, then, otherness becomes – in spite of our good intentions – a matter of indifference.[81]

I am not arguing for an *a priori* incommensurability, which would in effect say that the practices, habits, rites and convictions of different groups and peoples are so constituted that even communication is impossible with those who see the world differently. Those who would advance this point of view conclude that differences among diverse groups of human beings go "all the way down", and are therefore ineradicable. Conversion from one form of life to another could then only be

> the result of a non- or extrarational cause or process, and the shift would put the convert as completely outside his or her former view as he or she had been completely inside it before.[82]

From this standpoint it is virtually impossible to know what would count as a good reason either to subscribe to certain beliefs and practices, or to refrain from embracing others.

Rowan Williams, in a series of reflections on the biblical accounts of the trial of Jesus that are very reminiscent of Bonhoeffer's own work, notes that it is often our most-well meaning efforts to deal with the other, the outsider, the stranger, which serve only to exacerbate the problem. We take it for

---

80 Leach, Ourselves and Others, 772.
81 This is a problem faced by both modern and postmodern treatment of difference. Jacque Derrida's declaration, for example, that, *"Tout autre est tout autre"*, "every other is totally other", collapses otherness and difference altogether, and renders the term unintelligible. As Denys Turner observes, either difference is univocal, that is, absolutely indifferent, or equivocal, which makes all difference completely different, and again it becomes a matter of *mere* difference. Derrida, On the Name, 76; Turner, Faith, Reason, and the Existence of God, 165–169.
82 McClendon and Smith, Convictions, 8f.

granted that the way we manage such matters is right and normal, and that others should manage them in precisely the same way. It is particularly difficult, he writes, to resist the desire to bring the other into "our" world, "our" language, "our" time, "our" text. This is not to say that the outsider is necessarily right, nice or superior, only that by her or his very presence the stranger puts into question our way of accounting for the diversity of human existence, our way of making the world turn out right and manageable.[83]

Allowing the other to remain a stranger initially forces us to recognize that the limits of reason are not the limits of being. As Asad observes, knowledge *about* local peoples is not itself local knowledge, nor is it universal in the sense of being accessible to everyone.[84] Moreover, a world ordered in significant part by the *libido dominandi*, the lust to mastery,[85] and increasingly by aimless production and conspicuous consumption, requires frequent reminders that is woefully incomplete and needs to be enlarged in ways beyond all planning and control.[86] The church as the body of Christ – Christ-existing-as-community – has been gathered together by the Spirit in large part to serve as a laboratory for these kinds of encounters, not for the purpose of promoting "pluralism", but as both result and sign of having been "caught up in the way of Jesus Christ, into the messianic event."[87]

What are the theological warrants for this approach to the other? One obvious possibility is the concept of the *imago dei*. In *Creation and Fall* Bonhoeffer asserts that the divine image is not an innate potential or possibility or structure of human existence, but a constitutive relationship in which God sets us, given *through* the other. The likeness between God and humankind thus consists of the *analogia relationis*, the analogy of relationship. The possibility and actuality of this relationship, writes Bonhoeffer, is grounded in God's own triune life: "God is in humankind as the very image of God in which the free Creator looks upon the Creator's own self." The creature set in this image is free only as each exists in relation to the other, in being bound to the other:

The creatureliness of human beings is no more a quality or something at hand or an existing entity than human freedom is. It can be defined in simply no other way than

---

83 Rowan Williams, Christ on Trial, 57. 59. 65.
84 Asad, Genealogies of Religion, 9.
85 Augustine, City of God, I. Pref., 3.
86 Williams, Christ on Trial, 61f.
87 LPP, 361f. Bonhoeffer may have something along these lines when he ponders whether it is possible to recover a concept of the church as providing an understanding of the area of freedom, consisting of art, culture (*Bildung*), friendship and play, which would re-establish a form of aesthetic existence in the world. For this to happen would require a link to the Middle Ages. LPP, 193.

in terms of the existence of human beings over-against-one-another, with-one-another, and in-dependence-upon-one-another.[88]

But we need to proceed cautiously here when attempting to fashion an understanding of the other around the notion of the *imago dei*. The desire to ask about the beginning may be the innermost passion of our thinking as creaturely beings, imparting reality to every genuine question we ask, and yet no sooner is the question of the beginning put before us than our thinking, in its desire to reach back to the beginning, is thrown back on itself, spending its strength like huge breakers crashing upon a rocky shore.[89] Bonhoeffer's metaphor of waves shattering on the shore is particularly apt, for the early church fathers frequently spoke of the effect of sin as the shattering of the image which all human beings shared, for it was the same mysterious participation in God which caused the soul to exist that also constituted the primordial unity of humankind. Maximus the Confessor speaks of original sin as the breaking up of the natural unity of humankind into a thousand pieces. Humankind, which should constitute a harmonious whole, in which what is mine and what is thine should involve no contradiction, has been transformed into a multitude of individuals, as numerous as the grains of sand on the seashore, full of violence and enmity: "And now we rend each other like the wild beasts."[90]

Something of this understanding of the *imago dei* is present in Bonhoeffer's theology. He contends that the shame that fallen human beings feel is both an acknowledgement of, and a protest against disunion, estranged not only from God, but from other human beings, from all other created things, and even from themselves: "Shame is the irrepressible memory of disunion from their origin. It is the pain of this disunion, and the helpless desire to reverse it. Human beings are ashamed because they have lost something that is part of their original nature and their wholeness; they are ashamed of their nakedness. Just as in the fairy tale the man is ashamed because of his missing shadow, so human beings are ashamed because of the lost unity with God and one another." The unity of the human person as well as that of humankind as a whole thus consists, not in its own autonomy (which is the marker of its fragmentation), but in Jesus Christ. This coincides with his claim in *Creation and Fall* that, "[o]nly in the middle, as those who live from Christ, do we know about the beginning."[91]

The concept of the image of God is thus insufficient by itself to treat the shattered unity of humankind in a fallen world. In Bonhoeffer's terms, the

---

88 DBWE 3, 63–66.
89 DBWE 3, 25–28.
90 Maximus the Confessor, Questions to Thalassios, covering letter and q. 64, cited by de Lubac, Catholicism, 33f.
91 DBWE 6, 278. 303; DBWE 3, 62.

imago dei has become the *sicut deus*, the one like god, a condition which promises only death: "human beings who are *sicut deus* human beings can no longer live – they are in a state of death." In this state we encounter an irreducible juxtaposition. There is on the one hand the *imago dei*, humankind existing for God and the neighbor, bound to the word of the Creator and deriving life from the Creator. On the other there is the *sicut deus*, similar to God in its self-generated knowledge of good and evil, existing without limit, acting out of its own aseity, its solitude, living on the basis of the divide (*Zwiespalt*) between good and evil. This divide is resolved only by the *agnus dei*, the Lamb of God, "who is God incarnate, who was sacrificed for humankind *sicut deus*, in true divinity slaying its false divinity and restoring the *imago dei*."[92]

It is in Christ, then, that the mystery of the diversity of humankind is rightly cultivated, and it is in the church, Christ-existing-as-community, that the Spirit universalizes the particularity of Jesus among the shattered fragments of *imago-dei*-become-*sicut-deus*, gathering together a people from every tribe and language and people and nation (Revelation 5,9) to be the living members of the body of Christ, not for its own sake, but for the sake of a world that even in its violence and rebellion God has never stopped cherishing.[93] In this fellowship neither the whole nor the individual member is simply a function of the other. On the contrary, baptism and eucharist establish a new mode of social relations that, unlike the boutique egalitarianism prescribed by liberal capitalism, does not treat us as faceless integers of production and consumption. With their incorporation into the body of Christ through water, wine and word persons receive what the New Testament calls a spiritual gift – the distinctive singularity of personal existence in the body politic of Christ. Difference is therefore not embraced for its own sake, to be consumed as yet one more commodity, but so that all might share in one calling – to be for the sake of the world sign, foretaste and herald of the destiny of all things in God's new creation.

Put somewhat differently, it is the work of the Holy Spirit to repeat differently (and therefore precisely) what Bonhoeffer calls the polyphony of life[94] in the whole Christ, *totus Christus*, consisting of both head and body,[95] mediated through gathered Christian communities throughout the globe. The Spirit's labor is an ongoing, a never-ending endeavor, because times and circumstances change. New characters, social settings, and historical events are constantly being incorporated within the ebb and flow of time

---

92 DBWE 3, 113.
93 See Buckley, A Field of Living Fire, 91. 97.
94 See LPP, 303.
95 Augustine, First Homily on First John, in: Augustine, Later Works, 261.

around its center. The meaning of this process is therefore never fixed, but continues to unfold in the style of a historical drama that is never over and done with. The unity of this drama's story line resides not in the sameness of its performance, but in timely transpositions of the rhythms and progressions of human acting and relating which God had decisively set into motion in the life, passion and triumph of Jesus.

Bibliography

Primary Sources

ATHANASIUS, *On the Incarnation*, Crestwood, NY 2000.
AUGUSTINE, The *City of God* Against the Pagans, ed. by R.W. Dyson, New York 1998.
–, *Later Works*, ed. by J. Burnaby, Philadelphia 1955.
BARTH, K., *Church Dogmatics* I/2: The Doctrine of the Word of God, transl. by G.T. Thomson/ H. Knight, Edinburgh 1956.
BONHOEFFER, D., Sanctorum Communio: A Theological Study of the Sociology of the Church, Dietrich Bonhoeffer Works, Vol. 1, transl. by R. Krauss/N. Lukens, Minneapolis 1998 (= DBWE 1).
–, Creation and Fall: A Theological Exposition of Genesis 1–3, Dietrich Bonhoeffer Works, Vol. 3, transl. by M. Rüter/I. Tödt, Minneapolis 1997 (= DBWE 3).
–, Discipleship, Dietrich Bonhoeffer Works, Vol. 4, transl. by M. Kuske/I. Tödt, Minneapolis 2001 (= DBWE 4).
–, Ethik, Dietrich Bonhoeffer Werke, Vol. 6, ed. by I. Tödt/H.E. Tödt/E. Feil/C. Green, München 1992 (= DBW 6).
–, Ethics, transl. by R. Krauss/Ch.C. West et al., Dietrich Bonhoeffer Works, Vol. 6, Minneapolis 2005 (= DBWE 6).
–, Conspiracy and Imprisonment 1940–1945, Dietrich Bonhoeffer Works, Vol. 16, transl. by L.E. Dahill, Minneapolis 2006 (= DBWE 16).
–, Letters and Papers from Prison, transl. by R.H. Fuller/J. Bowden et al., New York 1971 (= LPP).
–, *No Rusty Swords*: Letters, Lectures and Notes, 1928–39, ed. by E.H. Robertson, New York 1965.
CICERO, M.T., *Tusculan Disputations*, transl. by J.E. King, Cambridge, MA 1971.
NIEBUHR, H.R., *Christ and Culture*, New York 1951.
ST. THOMAS AQUINAS, *Summa Theologica*, transl. by the Fathers of the English Dominican Province (rev. ed.), New York 1948.
VIRGIL, *The Aeneid*, transl. by R. Fitzgerald, New York 1990.

Secondary Sources

ADORNO, T. W., *The Culture Industry*, ed. by J.M. Bernstein, London 1991.
ARNOLD, M., *Culture and Anarchy*, ed. by S. Lipman, New Haven, CN 1994.
ASAD, T., *Genealogies of Religion*: Discipline and Reasons of Power in Christianity and Islam, Baltimore 1993.
BAUMAN, Z., *Postmodern Ethics*, Cambridge, MA 1993.

BETHGE, E., *Dietrich Bonhoeffer*: A Biography (rev. ed.), ed. by V.J. Barnett, Minneapolis 2000.
BOYLE, N., *Who Are We Now?* Christian Humanism and the Global Market from Hegel to Heaney, Notre Dame, IN 1998.
BUCKLEY, J.J., *A Field of Living Fire*: Karl Barth on the Spirit and the Church, Modern Theology 10, 1994, 81–102.
BUDDE, M., *The (Magic) Kingdom of God*: Christianity and Global Culture Industries, Boulder, CO 1997.
CAVANAUGH, W.T., *Sins of Omission*: What "Religion and Violence" Arguments Ignore, The Hedgehog Review 6, 2004, 34–50.
–, *Theopolitical Imagination*: Discovering the Liturgy as a Political Act in an Age of Global Consumerism, New York 2002.
CONE, J.H., *Speaking the Truth*: Ecumenism, Liberation, and Black Theology, Grand Rapids, MI 1986.
DE CERTEAU, M., *The Practice of Everyday Life*, transl. by S.F. Rendall, Berkeley 1984.
DE LUBAC, H., *Catholicism*: Christ and the Common Destiny of Man, transl. by L.C. Sheppard/ E. Englund, San Francisco 1988.
–, *The Mystery of the Supernatural*, transl. by R. Sheed, New York 1998.
DERRIDA, J., *On the Name*, ed. by Th. Dutoit, Stanford, CA 1995.
FISH, S., *Boutique Multiculturalism*, or Why Liberals Are Incapable of Thinking about Hate Speech, Critical Inquiry 23, 1997, 378–395.
GEERTZ, C., *The Interpretation of Cultures*: Selected Essays, New York 1973.
GIERKE, O., *Associations and Law*: The Classical and Early Christian Stages, transl. by G. Heiman, Toronto 1977.
GRANT, G., *Technology and Justice*, Notre Dame, IN 1986.
HARRISON, P., *"Religion" and the Religions* in the English Enlightenment, New York 1990.
HORKHEIMER, M./ADORNO, TH.W., *Dialectic of Enlightenment*, transl. by J. Cumming, New York 1972.
JENKS, CH., *Culture*, London 1993.
JENNINGS, W., *Harlem on My Mind*: Dietrich Bonhoeffer, Racial Reasoning, and Theological Reflection, unpublished paper.
LEACH, E., *Ourselves and Others*, TLS, 1973, 771–772.
LENTRICCHIA, F., *Criticism and Social Change*, Chicago 1983.
MCCLENDON, JR., J.WM./SMITH, J.M., *Convictions*: Defusing Religious Relativism (rev. ed.), Valley Forge, PA 1994.
MCGRANE, B., *Beyond Anthropology*: Society and the Other, New York 1989.
MENSCH, E./FREEMAN, A., *The Politics of Virtue*: Is Abortion Debatable? Durham 1993.
MILBANK, J., *Theology and Social Theory*: Beyond Secular Reason, Cambridge, MA 1990.
–, *The Word Made Strange*: Theology, Language, Culture, Cambridge, MA 1997.
O'CONNOR, F., *Collected Works*, New York 1988.
–, *Mystery and Manners*: Occasional Prose, ed. by S. Fitzgerald/R. Fitzgerald, New York 1969.
RABOTEAU, A. J., *Slave Religion*: The "Invisible Institution" in the Antebellum South, New York 1978.
RAWICK, G.P., *From Sundown to Sunup*, Westport, CN 1972.
SMITH, W.C., *The Meaning and End of Religion*: A New Approach to the Religious Traditions of Mankind, New York 1962.
SOUTHERN, R.W., *Western Society* and the Church in the Middle Ages, Harmondsworth 1985.
STEVENS, W., *Letters*, ed. by H. Stevens, New York 1966.
SURIN, K., *A Certain "Politics of Speech"*: "Religious Pluralism" in the Age of the McDonald's Hamburger, Modern Theology 7, 1990, 192–212.
TANNER, K., *Theories of Culture*: A New Agenda for Theology, Minneapolis 1997.
TILLICH, P., *Theology of Culture*, New York 1959.
TURNER, D., *Faith, Reason, and the Existence of God*, New York 2004.
WEBER, M., *The Protestant Ethic* and the Spirit of Capitalism, transl. by T. Parsons, Boston 1985.

–, *Vorbemerkung* zu den Gesammelten Aufsätzen zur Religions-Soziologie, in: Weber, Soziologie: Weltgeschichtliche Analysen. Politik, Stuttgart 1973, 340–356.
WILLIAMS, RAYMOND, *Culture and Society*: 1780–1950, New York 1959.
–, *Keywords*: A Vocabulary of Culture and Society (rev. ed.), New York 1983.
WILLIAMS, ROWAN, *Christ on Trial*: How the Gospel Unsettles Our Judgement, Grand Rapids, MI 2000.
YODER, J., *For the Nations*: Essays Public and Evangelical, Grand Rapids, MI 1997.
–, *The Politics of Jesus*: Vicit Agnus Noster (2nd ed.), Grand Rapids, MI 1994.
ZIZEK, S., *The Puppet and the Dwarf*: The Perverse Core of Christianity, Cambridge, MA 2003.

Peter Manley Scott

Postnatural Humanity?

Bonhoeffer, Creaturely Freedom and the Mystery of Reconciliation in Creation

> Nature has always been the ultimate bio-terrorist (Maria Zambon, Health Protection Agency, UK).[1]

> We further affirm that core values and principles, such as respect for human rights and human dignity, freedom, equality, solidarity, tolerance, [deleted: respect for nature] ... are essential for peaceful coexistence and cooperation among states (US version of the 2005 United Nations draft summit agreement).[2]

1. Introduction: Discerning the mystery

Can the Christian doctrine of creation be maintained in our ecologically distressed times without abridgement and in ways that are properly contextual? Some such requirement is posed by the later Bonhoeffer's searching after non-religious or secular interpretation in Christian life and theology. The desire for a secular theology is not a form of self-censorship in which Christianity seeks to offer "public" (that is, publicly acceptable) as opposed to preferred "religious" or Christian reasons. Instead, the search for a secular theology of nature involves a new form of theological discernment (with implications for both theological method and style): the overcoming of metaphysical, partial and individualistic interpretation of nature.[3] Not least, the mystery of reconciliation will need to be elaborated always in relation to practice: the real is *not* the rational but is rather re-founded in the saving reality of the crucified and resurrected Christ. Ecological realities – what-

---

[1] Cited in R. McKie, Nature, the most deadly bio-terrorist of all, New Statesman Vol. 133/4, No. 4719/20, January 2005, 59.
[2] As reported by J. Borger, Road map for US relations with the rest of the world, The Guardian, 27 August 2005, 19. In the final version, "respect for nature" is reinstated.
[3] Cf. Scott, Age.

ever these may be – are not matters for passive resignation but active engagement: the mystery of reconciliation invites the rethinking and re-relating of ecological relations in a Christological thought. (This, as we shall see, needs to be distinguished from forms of activism.) However, yet again, the theological task is not to apply some putative insights from the doctrine of creation but rather to rethink and relearn the doctrine of creation in this contested field. The theological task is therefore not to apply the mystery of reconciliation to the doctrine of creation but to attempt to rediscover and relearn the dynamics of reconciliation in creation.

I begin by indicating the ways in which I shall use the term, mystery. Through this essay, I shall be using the concept of mystery in three senses, two of which may be sourced directly to Bonhoeffer's writings. First, the primary sense refers to the mystery of reconciliation: God's saving action in Jesus Christ, the mystery of divine action; second, the mystery of living from centre and boundary, and the place of non-human nature in that: the mystery of participation in a common realm; third and last, the mystery of praxis: the mystery of postnatural reconciling work or activity in the shared realm of humanity and nature.

Throughout this essay, I shall be using the phrase, "postnatural humanity". This phrase identifies a default position for which I shall be arguing: of humanity in nature and nature in humanity. In my view, the doctrine of creation points to this default position. In this way, I seek to differentiate my position from "natural humanity" and "unnatural humanity". What do I mean by this? There is a tendency in ecological discourses – which I have analysed exhaustively elsewhere – to interpret ourselves in relation to the human – or in relation to nature. Indeed, Bonhoeffer does the first on occasion:

> Our immediate environment is not nature, as formerly, but organization. But with this protection from nature's menace there arises a new one – through organization itself. But the spiritual force is lacking. The question is: What protects us against the menace of organization? Man is again thrown back on himself.[4]

In this example, we begin from the human, refer to the non-human and then return to the unnatural human. A different strategy relocates humanity within nature and thereby proposes a natural humanity. Postnatural humanity – my preferred term – is an attempt to free anthropology from these strategies of personalism and naturalism and argue that humanity is in nature and that nature is both for and exceeds humanity.[5] Humanity is always post*natural*: following after non-human nature; and *post*natural: transcending non-human nature.

---

[4] LPP, 380.
[5] I define personalism as the attempt to understand "humanity as other than nature" and naturalism as stressing "the place of humanity in nature". For more detail, see Scott, Nature.

In the following, I argue that Bonhoeffer is a helpful guide in the development of an account of mystery that supports a theology of postnatural creatureliness. To establish this, I explore a number of instances of Bonhoeffer's presentation of creatureliness, primarily in *Creation and Fall* and *Ethics*. In other words, I track discussions of creatureliness in Bonhoeffer's literary legacy rather than discussions of mystery. As might be surmised, I detect an ecological deficit in Bonhoeffer's theology. In the final section I seek in a preliminary way to remedy this deficit by drawing together the mystery of reconciliation and the mystery of praxis. In such fashion, I begin the process of specifying some of the shape of "postnatural humanity". Now, however, it is time to stop the throat clearing and turn directly to Bonhoeffer's doctrine of creation.

2. Reading Bonhoeffer's doctrine of creation

Previously, I have sought to provide a systematic presentation of Bonhoeffer's theology of nature.[6] I am less convinced now that the interpretation of Bonhoeffer requires the effort to render his literary/theological legacy into a whole. Nor shall I speculate on other factors – formational, etc. – as to why Bonhoeffer might have been interested in the theme of nature. For my purposes it is enough to note that the theme of nature appears early in Bonhoeffer's theological writings – often associated with the theme of life – and persists into the prison writings. It is likely that the reference to nature is resourced by the Lutheran *Christus in nobis* structure of Bonhoeffer's theology that tempers Barth's actualism by reference to the temporal outworking and stability of community. Such community is always an ecological community, as Bonhoeffer sometimes avers. In what follows, I shall work from the premise that Bonhoeffer does discuss the theme of the mystery of reconciliation in creation, and in what follows I offer some textual evidence in support of this judgement.

There are important continuities in context between that of *Creation and Fall* – a theological exegesis of Genesis 1–3 first presented as a series of lectures in 1933 – and the present time. Bonhoeffer notes that technology "wars against" the given rhythm of the day and is furthermore writing in the context of the misuse of the concept of orders of creation[7] by the *Deutsche Christen* party. Similarly, the extensive employment of technology in our day carries the implicit charge that the non-human (and more recently, the

---

6   Cf. Scott, Ecological.
7   Cf. Scott, Creation, 341f.

human) is insufficiently productive. Furthermore, in some political discourses on ecology – deep ecology is a good example[8] – there persists the appeal to a static "nature" to which humanity must conform or with which it must identify, a harshly restrictive interpretation of the ecological rule that "Nature knows best" (Barry Commoner).

In addition, Bonhoeffer hints that the doctrine of creation provides a reflective path to consideration of the triune God. Writing of the ordered rhythm of God's creation, Bonhoeffer notes "the rhythm that is both rest and movement [...] and so points forever to God's giving and taking, to God's freedom beyond rest and movement – that is what the day is".[9] We encounter here a vital point: the character of the triune God as the source of a dynamic rhythm of createdness is one aspect of the doctrine of creation; theology is resourced by attention to the liveliness of God that in triune freedom is the source of "order" but always present in judgement on that order from the action in freedom of God. The resulting account of "order" is complex: through the affirmation of "the day" and the employment of the term, "rhythm", Bonhoeffer affirms an ordering. However, the freedom of God acts as a qualifier to this order: elsewhere, I have written that Bonhoeffer affirms the "disorganisation" – but not the disorderedness – of creatureliness.[10] Perhaps it would be more accurate to argue that what Bonhoeffer affirms is creaturely *disorderliness*. The nature of God and the nature of order, and their relationship, will be re-considered below.

The Fall remains an important point of discussion for the mystery of reconciliation in creation. Bonhoeffer does not claim that the Genesis text indicates that the "truly given" disorderliness can be "read off" creation. Instead, he argues that the irruption of evil points to the cross of Christ:

The theological question is not a question about the origin of evil but one about the actual overcoming of evil on the cross; it seeks the real forgiveness of guilt and the reconciliation of the fallen world.[11]

Given that the fallen world is in need of reconciling, Bonhoeffer argues that no natural features are unambiguous, as the following quotation indicates: "The protest that appeals to the natural character of sexuality is unaware of the highly ambivalent character of every so-called 'natural' aspect of our world".[12] We are thereby presented with an epistemological discontinuity between the fallen world and God's originary ordering and are offered a clue in the cross of Christ that directs us to the mystery of reconciliation.

---

8   Cf. Scott, Nature, 63–88.
9   DBWE 3, 49.
10 Scott, Ecological, 418.
11 DBWE 3, 120.
12 DBWE 3, 125.

That is, we are directed towards the mystery of practice rather than the unknowability of the world.

In Bonhoeffer's reading, furthermore, God's cursing of Adam confirms the disunity between the human and the non-human: "[T]he word directed to Adam proclaims the destruction and dividedness of the original relation between humankind and *nature* and the alienation that takes its place."[13] Once more, in the context of such alienation a Christological clue is offered:

> How should Adam know that, in this promise of death, already the end of death, the resurrection of the dead, was being spoken of? How could Adam hear announced already in the peace of death, and returning to mother earth, the peace that God wishes once more to conclude with the earth, the peace that God wishes to establish over a new and blessed earth in the world of the resurrection?[14]

If we now move backwards, as it were, to sections of Bonhoeffer's commentary exploring the pre-lapsarian state, I propose to discuss two matters: first, Bonhoeffer's account of human freedom and, second, the opaque and difficult contrast he draws between centre and boundary.

Freedom: Interpreting Genesis 1,26–27, Bonhoeffer argues in favour of the concept of freedom as the identifying mark of the *imago dei*. Claiming that "[w]e in no way wish to deny humankind's connection with the animal world – on the contrary",[15] Bonhoeffer argues for an *analogia relationis* in which the freedom of humanity is defined as "the existence of human beings over-against-one-another, with-one-another and in-dependence-upon-one-another".[16] Of course, this affirmation places Bonhoeffer in a difficulty: *analogia relationis* operates here as a comparative notion indicating the difference between humanity and world. Nonetheless, Bonhoeffer also wishes to affirm a connection between humanity and world.

To achieve this, he proposes a distinction between "freedom *for*" and "freedom *from*". The human being is for another human being in the duality of relationship and yet seeks freedom from the non-human. This "freedom from", so Bonhoeffer argues implicitly, maintains the difference between the human and animals and world but indicates the ways in which the human is bound to the non-human. Bonhoeffer writes:

> [I]n my whole being, in my creatureliness, I belong wholly to this world; it bears me, nurtures me, holds me. But my freedom from it consists in the fact that this world, to which I am bound like a master to his servant, like the peasant to his bit of ground,

---

13 DBWE 3, 134.
14 DBWE 3, 136.
15 DBWE 3, 62.
16 DBWE 3, 64.

has been made subject to me, that over the earth which is and remains my earth I am to *rule*, and the more I master it, the more it is *my* earth.[17]

In short, he proposes a practical and moral connection between the human and other creatures that is based on an ontological disjunction. Rule is secured by an ontology of "freedom *from*".

The strengths and weaknesses of this position are apparent. An important strength is an affirmation of human responsibility. However, it seems odd to address ecological dependencies only in terms of a structure of responsibility, that is, without attention to the natural reality that is being responded to. In fact, Bonhoeffer's position is based upon a prior, undeclared, decision about the nature of this natural reality. We can appreciate this if we consider an argument by Marxist philosopher Reiner Grundmann in support of the metaphor, the "mastery of nature". Formally, the argument is identical to Bonhoeffer's: Grundmann calls for the further mastery of nature on the grounds that in the perfection of such "mastery" lies deliverance from ecological terrors. Indeed, Grundmann appeals to the image of the violinist practising her craft: any deficiencies in the violinist's performance we attribute, so Grundmann argues, to her lack of mastery of the musical instrument. The same issue, he claims, is at stake in the consideration of the mastery of nature: any deficiencies in ecological performance must be addressed by attention to the further mastery of nature and not by calling into question the "true" human vocation to master nature.

The difficulty with this type of argument – and this difficulty applies to Bonhoeffer as well as to Grundmann – is that unhappily nature is not best understood in its entirety by reference to the metaphor of a violin. For buried in the appeal to the metaphor is a decision about the nature of nature: as already shaped in advanced ways for human purposes and ends. It transpires that the comparative strategy in turn rests upon an ontology based in the relation of artist to instrument or farmer to already cultivated land. In other words, the task of the human is to domesticate an already domesticated nature, to shape a nature pre-shaped (by whom?) for human purposes. What nature is in its relations to the human is already established but goes undeclared.

Analogy: Is it possible to argue for a more ecologically friendly reading of Bonhoeffer's position by suggesting that the concepts of "freedom for" and "freedom from" both refer to human relations to nature? That is, may it be argued that humanity is free *for* as well as free *from* nature? An answer to this question requires an exploration of the meaning of *analogia relationis*. In what sense is an analogy of relation being offered here?

---

17   DBWE 3, 66.

Analogy has commonly – going back to Aristotle – been understood in two ways: analogy of proportion, and analogy of attribution. Although both are concerned with the distribution of a specified property or matter, these characterisations function rather differently.

Analogy of proportion often takes the form a : b :: c : d. That is, "a" is to "b" as "c" is to "d": if the values of "a", "b" and "c" are known, then the different value of "d" can be established.

> Thus, if a = 2, b = 4, and c = 6, we may derive the value of d as being 12. But we can derive the value of d thus if and only if we know in what relation of proportion "a" stands to "b" [here multiplication by 2]. [...] Given, then, the values for three of the variables and a definition of the proportions in which they stand to one another, we can derive, by analogical argument, the value of the fourth.[18]

The value of "d" is not the same as that of the earlier values but can be established proportionately.

In that the concept of freedom is to be understood in relation to God and human creatures, I think that Bonhoeffer's *analogia relationis* works by way of proportionality for the central question is: how is the concept of freedom to be understood with reference to God and human creatures? Given that the analogy is governed by a concept of revelation, how does one infer from divinity to humanity? In that Bonhoeffer proposes an analogy of relation the answer lies in the act of freedom, so to speak. Thus, in a thoroughly *pro nobis* – incarnational – construal, Bonhoeffer argues that as God is free for human beings so human beings are free for other human beings. Certainly, in adopting Bonhoeffer's exegesis, Karl Barth understood the analogy in this manner, that is, of proportion:

> In this relationship [of freedom] which is absolutely given and posited there is revealed freedom and therefore the divine likeness. As God is free for man, so man is free for man; but only inasmuch as God is for him, so that the *analogia relationis* as the meaning of the divine likeness cannot be equated with an *analogia entis*.[19]

Clifford Green agrees with this judgement as part of a more elaborate interpretation:

> It is a *particular* relationship which constitutes the *imago*: just as the true Lordship of the Creator is God's being free for the creation, so the true humanity of God's creatures is co-humanity in being free for others on the basis of their freedom for God through Christ.[20]

---

18   Turner, Existence, 203.
19   Barth, Dogmatics III/1, 195.
20   Green, Sociality, 192.

Evidently an analogy of proportion is being employed here, in which being-free-for-others is related to relations between human beings. Furthermore, Green helpfully reinforces the reference to the human by noting that the incarnation of God in Christ is constitutive of correct interpretation of Bonhoeffer's *analogia relationis*.

To return to the original question, is it possible to interpret Bonhoeffer's position in more ecologically benign ways? That is, is it possible to understand human beings as being free-for the non-human as well as being free-from? This seems difficult to maintain on account of Bonhoeffer's argument that humans are free-for other humans who are also free-for. The structure of human responsibility is indeed responsive. Bonhoeffer appears to be offering an account of human-nature relations in which nature, we might say, is inert. Constitutive of humanity is freedom which nature lacks; struggling to be free from nature is in this perspective understandable in that nature suffers from a deficit; indeed, what nature lacks is the condition of sociality and participation and is thereby marked as always different from the human. The neo-Kantian echoes are clearly audible in this personalist strategy.

Would a more helpful strategy be to employ the second style of analogical thinking, the analogy of attribution? Aristotle famously employed this analogy to argue that all things insofar as they are enjoy the quiddity of substance. Would it be possible to employ the notion of freedom in such an analogy by arguing that all things, in that they exist, are free? As such, freedom would then be as a transcendental category in which all being participates.

Setting aside the matter as to whether such an understanding brings the use of analogy too close for actualist comfort to *analogia entis*, it is doubtful whether this understanding can easily be related to Bonhoeffer's position. Bonhoeffer employs the notion of freedom as part of a contrastive strategy that identifies the distinctiveness of the human in contrast with that of nature. It is difficult to see how an identifier of the human can also function as a transcendental category that identifies being *qua* being in which all entities, insofar as they exist, participate. This opinion is confirmed by the judgement that Bonhoeffer makes in *Christology* that nature does not sin but rather may expect to have its curse lifted from it.[21] In other words, being cursed suggests that nature does not have freedom to sin.

The nature of responsibility: For the ecological interpreter of Bonhoeffer, the problems are doubled in that Bonhoeffer next adopts a post-lapsarian perspective and proceeds to offer an Hegelian excursus. The reference to master/servant, quoted above, has a clear philosophical reference: the

---

21   Bonhoeffer, Christology, 64.

"lord/bondsman" section in Hegel's *Phenomenology of Spirit*. As in Hegel, Bonhoeffer argues that in the dialectic, the servant is also somewhat lord, thus:

Technology is the power with which the earth seizes hold of humankind and masters it. And because we no longer rule, we lose the ground so that the earth no longer remains our earth, and we become estranged from the earth.[22]

The estrangement is here doubled: there is, first, the estrangement from nature found in technological power; and, second, the estrangement from nature in the attempt at ruling. The recent development of GM crops may provide an instance of the dialectic. (1) Alteration of what is "natural" or stable in the genetic composition of a seed renders nature into an alien rather than a fellow creature. (2) The cultivation of GM crops raises the prospect of the permanent contamination of other plants, etc. which suggests a sort of "polluting" of the agricultural environment in ways that reinforce human estrangement from that environment. As we seek to make "nature" more productive through technological means, we realise that our efforts may lead to permanent changes in the natural environment in ways that are not beneficial to us. Despite our ability to engineer genes, nature is not under our control and somehow "resists" us. Thereby we are confounded by our efforts at the mastery of nature. We may savour the irony: nature cannot be fully controlled through technology and yet even our failures in control renders alien the non-human.[23]

Nonetheless, a difficulty resurfaces. I have already suggested that the account of creatureliness presented here may not be theologically robust: a nature already shaped for the human somehow escapes human control through technology. Nature is always a dominated nature and never a bestowing nature except that, under conditions of estrangement, nature "bestows" the domination of slavery through technology. We have already encountered the basic error in this argument: the relationship between the human and non-human nature is conceived in terms of the artist and her materials. In that it suggests and/or requires the pre-shaping of nature, the analogy does not hold because nature does not come already organised in the way that the analogy requires.

And what, for Bonhoeffer, is the remedy? This is more promising:

Without God, without their brothers ands sisters, human beings lose the earth. [...] For those who have once lost the earth, however, for us human beings in the middle, there is no way back to the earth except via God and our brothers and sisters.[24]

---

22 DBWE 3, 67.
23 See further, Scott, Anarchy.
24 DBWE 3, 67.

True to his earlier commitments, Bonhoeffer links reconciliation between the human and nature to God and yet as mediated by human beings. There is no way back to the earth except via God and the human. So we are offered a conventional model in which humanity mediates nature to God. Once more, this argument stresses human responsibility and – although Bonhoeffer does not say so – permits the identification of human injustices in human relationships with nature. Additionally, by this means Bonhoeffer refuses a turn to naturalism: by stressing that the way to nature is by God and human beings, Bonhoeffer makes difficult the transposing of natural categories into human affairs.

However, there need be no diminishment in responsibility or a weakening of the refusal of natural categories if nature is assigned an unmediated relationship to God. The quotation above could be expanded thereby with my addition presented in italics:

For those who have once lost the earth, however, for us human beings in the middle, there is no way back to the earth except via God and our brothers and sisters. *And for those who have once lost their brothers and sisters, for us human beings in the middle, there is no way back to our brothers and sisters except via God and our world.*

On this expanded view, human beings may mediate nature to God and nature may mediate human beings to God. What is crucial is that both ways are "via God", as Bonhoeffer puts it. It is the reference to God that secures the structure of responsibility and denies biocentrism and anthropocentrism by re-establishing these on a new, postnatural, basis.

On such a post-critical reading of Genesis, I see no persuasive reason why nature has to be understood as *pre-shaped* nor humanity considered as seeking only freedom *from* nature. In the biblical narrative, we are presented with a sequence of creaturely forms that ends in the human, indicating only a habitat of the human and the need for humanity to transform its habitat. And although the discussion of freedom is central to the narrative – and I shall return to it below – to make the decision that humanity exercises an intra-human "freedom for" and a "freedom from" *ad extra* strikes me as being an interpretation more conclusive than can be established from a reading of the text *simpliciter*. Later, I shall be proposing an ecologised freedom that builds upon and incorporates Bonhoeffer's insights.

Centre/boundary: In an exegesis of the second, Yahwist, creation narrative, Bonhoeffer stresses the relationship between human creatureliness and freedom. Arguing that human beings have "life from God and *before* God", Bonhoeffer maintains that life is given to the human not as a kind of addition but as a gift related to the totality of human existence. As the totality of human life is enacted in freedom, the human being receives life in its freedom. "The life that human beings have happens in an obedience that issues from freedom."[25] The source of that life is the centre, who is God. Human freedom and boundedness are thereby complementary: human freedom is directed towards the centre, so to speak, and yet lives from that centre. The human creature does not have its freedom as a sort of facility nor does it occupy the centre and grasp at its life. As Bonhoeffer summarises God's address, "You are a free creature, so now be that. You are free, so be free; you are a creature, so be a creature."[26] In such fashion, Bonhoeffer argues for the "interrelatedness of freedom and creatureliness" in which life and freedom, gift and obedience, living from God and for God are to be understood as complementary. Thus centre and boundary cohere in the duality of life and freedom.

Such Scriptural wisdom may go unheard in our contemporary context. Against a tendency to construe the limitation or boundedness of the human in relation to the margins – which are then understood as a challenge to human artifice and technology – Bonhoeffer proffers a "picture" of humanity limited by the centre, of the enactment of "centredness" through the freedom of obedience. Consider this excerpt:

> The human being's limit is at the center of human existence, not on the margin; the limit or constraint that people look for on the margin of humankind is the limit of the human condition, the limit of human technology, the limit of what is possible for humanity. The boundary that is at the centre is the limit of human reality, of human existence as such. Knowledge of the limit or constraint on the margin is always accompanied by the possibility of failing to know any internal limit.[27]

Indeed, at one point, Bonhoeffer discusses this matter of the infrastructural relationship of life and freedom in terms of freedom from and freedom for.

Of course, Bonhoeffer is discussing a pre-lapsarian section of the narrative. It is not to the purpose to develop a series of recommendations from this interpretation. Indeed, it would be difficult to do so because the problem adumbrated above returns: what is the relationship between human life and other life? And why should the exercise of freedom in relation to other life always be in terms of freedom *from*? Bonhoeffer insists on the creatureliness, the earthiness of human life but always under the rubric of "freedom from". Yet this disjunction between human freedom and non-human activity fits poorly with his affirmation of bodiliness and turns the centre into a "magical" place where God lives. However, even in this pre-lapsarian saga, is not God at the centre of a *garden*, present in a specific *environment*? If we construe the matter differently at this point, God as the source and giver of creaturely life then appears to work without reference to the situatedness

---

25   DBWE 3, 84.
26   DBWE 3, 85.
27   DBWE 3, 86 (italics removed).

of freedom as if freedom of action may stand as an adequate description of freedom.

In a way this essay's key theological problem emerges clearly: how can one live freely *from* God (as the giver of life), *for* God (in obedience) and *before* God (in our post-lapsarian world) without taking shortcuts? These shortcuts include over-emphasising "from God" and so falling into over confidence in moral matters; over-emphasising "for God" and so stressing law before grace; and over-emphasising "before God" and so falling into an "orders of creation" mistake.

In order to stress a different position – that is, to insist that to begin from the human is always already to begin from the natural – Bonhoeffer's language of centre/boundary is helpful. What is useful in Bonhoeffer is the relation between the goodness of God and human freedom although it is under specified in relation to social and ecological tendencies. It is to the further specification that Bonhoeffer offers in *Ethics* that I now turn.

3. Mandates: trajectories of creaturely freedom

In a previously published account of Bonhoeffer's presentation of creatureliness in *Ethics*, I overlooked the mandates and instead concentrated on the discussion of "natural life".[28] In that there is a type of "naturalisation" operative in discussions both of natural life and the mandates, overlooking the mandates no longer seems to me to be defensible. In other words, in both discussions Bonhoeffer is exploring ethical aspects given in and by the stability of human creatureliness.

Natural life: What, for Bonhoeffer, is "the natural"? In the discussion in *Ethics*, Bonhoeffer wishes to speak of "relative differences within a fallen creation" as a way of resisting "arbitrariness and disorder" in natural life.[29] Put differently, Bonhoeffer is concerned with the matter of natural *order*: is there a givenness to human life – a givenness that is natural to human life – which Protestant theological ethics needs to rediscover? In that human beings participate in natural life "by nature" such participation must be understood as universal; natural life is thereby an interpretation of post-lapsarian creatureliness.

Three concepts of nature are operative here. Such natural life is already formed, thus participating in the sense of $nature_1$, that the natural precedes human artifice: the natural "has already been set and decided and in such a

---

28 Cf. Scott, Ecological.
29 DBWE 6, 172.

way that the individual, the communities, and the institutions receive their respective share in it".[30] Such natural life is a construal of a universal human creatureliness, thus drawing on the sense of nature$_2$, that humanity participates in such creatureliness by its nature; that such natural life inheres in the human: "[T]he natural is determined by the form of preserved life itself as it embraces the whole human race".[31] Such natural life might also be understood in the sense of nature$_3$, that such creatureliness participates in the wider creatureliness of the albeit fallen creation: various interpretations of natural law maintain such a view by arguing that certain interests in life, etc. are shared by human and non-human creatures.[32] What is truly natural to the human can thereby be identified by reference to that nature which creatures share.

In fact, Bonhoeffer partly refuses this third sense of nature by connecting the natural with the incarnation of God in Jesus Christ:

> Natural life [...] receives its confirmation only through Christ. Christ has entered into natural life. Only by Christ's becoming human does natural life become the penultimate that is directed toward the ultimate. Only through Christ's becoming human do we have the right to call people to natural life and to live it ourselves.[33]

Although it is the task of fallen reason to identify the content of the natural,[34] the formal recognition is by Christ, thus:

> Formally, the natural is determined by the preserving will of God and by its orientation toward Christ. Its formal side, then, can only be recognized by looking at Jesus Christ.[35]

It would take us too far from the substance of this essay to enquire whether in the discussion of natural life Bonhoeffer adheres to his own method.

Throughout the discussion of natural life, Bonhoeffer is concerned with what we may call the rights of human life. As such, the discussion is not directly concerned with the theme of this essay, the mystery of reconciliation in creation. However, there are similarities between this discussion and the mandates that are worth noting; the similarities are concerned not with content but with approach. We can begin our discussion of the mandates by noting that Bonhoeffer is here concerned with the same problem that he addresses in the discussion of "natural life": is there any direction or givenness in the commandment of God? Again, we are concerned with the prob-

---

30   DBWE 6, 175.
31   DBWE 6, 174.
32   See Scott, Creation, 339–341.
33   DBWE 6, 174.
34   The continuities between Bonhoeffer's position and natural moral law ethics are evident, as he himself notes: DBWE 6, 175, note 1.
35   DBWE 6, 174.

lem of order in Christianity which, as Karl Rahner observes, is always concerned with an "ordination to the good".[36]

Mandates: In the writing of *Ethics*, the manuscript "The Concrete Commandment and the Divine Mandates" seems to have been composed rather late. Although Bonhoeffer appears to have moved away from his opening concern with "ethics as formation" towards an ethics based on God's commandment, his early concern to delineate the direction, order and stability of Christian ethical enquiry remains evident. It seems that in developing his account of the divine command, Bonhoeffer was heavily influenced by the section "The Commandment of God" in Karl Barth's *Church Dogmatics* II/2. Of Barth's discussion, Nigel Biggar has written:

> [I]t would appear that a divine command comes like a thunderbolt out of heaven, brooking no questioning, displacing all thinking. It alone *decides* what is right. It is utterly concrete, requiring no further human reflection to give it specific form, but only human consent to realize it.[37]

In this regard, divine command theory has frequently been criticised for its irrationalism.

Of course, such an orientation (let us leave aside the question as whether this is true to Barth or not – Biggar regards it as untrue, certainly in the light of *Church Dogmatics* III/4) coheres poorly with Bonhoeffer's approach. As we have already seen, the presentation of the natural life is an attempt to present differences in human creaturely life rather than obscure all such differentiation by reference to revelation and, in addition, Bonhoeffer argues that reason, although fallen, determines the content of natural life. Nor is it likely that Bonhoeffer's experience in the conspiracy, and the moral dilemmas posed by that, were easily attended to by ethical reference to a thunderbolt from heaven. As Barth will put it later, under the rubric of "special ethics", the issue is "whether anything can be known about the horizontal, the permanence, continuity and constancy of the divine command and human action".[38] In the discussion of the divine mandates this is indeed Bonhoeffer's concern.

I have already claimed that some procedure of "naturalisation" is evident in the presentation of the mandates. One way of putting this is to say that in the discussion of natural life Bonhoeffer is working with two meanings of nature and one reference to Christ. However, in moving from "natural life" to the discussion of mandates the balance is altered: now there are two references to Christ and one to nature. The alteration is with the first sense of nature: the mandates are given but not in the sense that these mandates

---

36 Rahner, Art. Order, 1111.
37 Biggar, Barth's, 215.
38 Barth, Dogmatics III/4, 18.

are natural and as such precede human artifice. Indeed, it is such a position that Bonhoeffer wishes to avoid. We can readily appreciate why because if the status of being "beyond artifice" is granted to the mandates, then it would be hard to discriminate between the mandates and the "orders of creation" that Bonhoeffer had rejected in the mid 1930s. For, as he noted, once such orders are naturalised, almost anything can be justified:

One need only hold out something to be God-willed and God-created for it to be vindicated for ever, the division of man into nations, national struggles, war, class struggle, the exploitation of the weak by the strong, the cut-throat competition of economics.[39]

To accept such naturalisation would thus be a concession to a "romantic conservatism" that Bonhoeffer consistently refuses.

In order to resist such naturalisation, Bonhoeffer argues that the mandates are commanded by Christ:

The divine mandates depend solely on God's one commandment as it is revealed in Jesus Christ. They are implanted in the world from above as organizing structures [...].[40]

Of course, for Bonhoeffer the mandates offer a universal claim, thus drawing on the sense of nature$_2$, that humanity participates in such creatureliness by its nature: all of human life is engaged thereby in that the commandment's claim "on human beings and the world through the reconciling love of God is all-encompassing".[41]

Strictly, there is no reference in the discussion of the mandates to the sense of nature$_3$, that such creatureliness participates in the wider creatureliness of the-albeit fallen-creation. As with natural life, Bonhoeffer offers instead a theological rather than an anthropological referent: occupiers of a mandate are vicarious representatives holding a commission from God. The final criterion here is Jesus Christ. Having said that, Bonhoeffer also holds to the view that the mandates are given by the unity of God; they are sourced to and resourced by God's one commandment. The mandates therefore have to be taken together: each implies the other, presumably because each depends on the one command.

Only in their being with-one-another, for-one-another, and over-against-one-another do the divine mandates of church, marriage and family, culture, and government communicate the commandment of God as it is revealed in Jesus Christ.[42]

---

39 Bonhoeffer, No Rusty Swords, 161.
40 DBWE 6, 390.
41 DBWE 6, 388.
42 DBWE 6, 393.

In effect Bonhoeffer reprises a point from *Creation and Fall*: The freedom of humanity is defined as "the existence of human beings over-against-one-another, with-one-another and in-dependence-upon-one-another".[43] It is therefore as if the mandates share a common nature or a common horizon, bringing to mind the sense of nature$_3$. Of course, the reference *ad extra* is to God but the question of the commonality (if any) of the mandates is raised: is any commonality to be sourced to the unity of God's command and/or is there some commonality of human action to which we should also pay attention? Furthermore, we encounter once more the hint that Bonhoeffer's account of creatureliness may offer a reflective path to the one God – more on this in the next and final section.

An ecological framing? The effect of this Christological framing of the mandates is to subject them to a procedure of "naturalisation". That is, although Bonhoeffer only draws on one sense of nature, this, plus the fact there is no discussion as to whether these mandates are adequate to the task of interpreting contemporary complex-simple modern societies, secures a certain givenness to the mandates. Such givenness is a problem in a way that differs from the givenness of natural life. That is, while humans are always embodied they are capable of offering very different ways of organising socially and politically. We must ask whether these mandates are the best way of understanding the stability of human life in a period rather different from Bonhoeffer's. In essence, I am posing the question: what are "mandates" under the conditions of an emerging globality? Of course, God's will is not to be confused with any particular order, but God does resource orderings. How is that to be thought?

First, a reference to the ecological is an essential *precondition* for interpreting the mandates – human living must be understood by comprehensive and consistent reference to the biosphere. In other words, reference to the ecological conditions of human life raises the matter of human nature and in what ways such human nature "opens out" onto non-human nature. "The End of God's Ways is Bodily Existence"[44] is theologically true if the theme of the bodily is understood in terms of ecological relations between the many "bodies" of animals, plants and the inorganic.

Second, the mandates need to be understood as activities rather than as structures. (Does such an emphasis on activity rather than structure bring us close to one of Karl Barth's questions to Bonhoeffer's presentation of the mandates:

Would it not be advisable, then, to begin with the more cautious question what we have to learn from God's Word concerning this constancy rather than rushing on to

---

43   DBWE 3, 64.
44   DBWE 3, 121, paraphrasing F.C. Oetinger.

the rigid assertion of human relationships arranged in a definite order, and the hasty assertion of their imperative character?[45])

If, for example, as a counterpart to the catholicity of the Church, globalisation was deemed to be a mandate, this cannot be understood abstractly or by focussing on structure. What would require theological scrutiny are global *activities* that are always carried through in specific places, that is, with both economic and ecological components. Global trade would here be a key theme: a way of exploring just economic relationships between people as well as the global imperative towards greater conversations between peoples that might be understood positively as constitutive of global trading.

Third, under global conditions, the mandates need to be extended by reference to the global. (The previous point supports this judgement also.) That is, although the mandates are not "natural", they enjoy a universal horizon, which in contemporary circumstance would need to be interpreted in relation to the global. For the mandate of government, for example, the matter of global governance and international law is raised. The discussion of the legal basis for the 2003 US-UK invasion of Iraq nicely presents one of the many difficulties in this area: in the context of the (in)security of the supply of non-renewable energy (a global issue), the British attorney general – the UK government's most senior law officer – discussed whether breaches in a Security Council resolution could be determined by an individual state as "a matter of objective fact" or whether only the Council could make a determination regarding breaches.[46] The US has maintained the first position, the UK the second. Establishing which position is correct takes us to the heart of discussions regarding the legality of the operation of global governance.

Fourth, a counterpart accompanies each of the mandates: for work, it is non-work and non-paid work, including care of children, the elderly and the infirm; for marriage, it is alternative parenting and sexual arrangements (this mandate is very important as it opens onto human nature and nature); for government, it is self-government, as suggested by anarchism; for church, it is other religions.[47] These counterparts are, if you like, secured by the mandates themselves: each dispensation calls into being a companion. With regard to the mundane mandates, reference to what is by nature hu-

---

45   Barth, Dogmatics III/4, 22.
46   Advice, dated 7 March 2003, from Attorney General Peter (Lord) Goldsmith to British Prime Minister Tony Blair under the title *Iraq: Resolution 1441*. Available at www.number-10.gov.uk/output/page7445.asp.
47   Of course, beyond the mandates and their counterparts are distortions of the mandate: exploitative work, pornography, etc.

man and its relationship to non-human nature discloses a penumbra without which the mandates lack comprehensiveness. This penumbra also participates in the mandate commandment although not in the same way as the mandate itself. Thus, for example, because homosexual sex and homosexual relationships are not under the mandate does not mean that they are excluded from the mandate. The mandate normalises and thereby does not exclude this "broken middle"; instead, through such normalising the mandates stabilise activities of the "broken middle", granting dignity to them. Through such a conferral what is excluded are injustices in the counterparts and what is permitted is ordination to the good. The brazenness and uncertainty of activities within the "broken middle" are partially overcome and reoriented in their own truth to the truth of God's commandment. In return, the activities of the penumbra offer a broader context for mandated activities and may raise questions to a mandate about the justice of activities directly under the mandate itself.[48] For example, dignified homosexual relationships may call into question those heterosexual relationships that, although formally heterosexual and therefore under the mandate, betray freedom and justice.

Fifth, reference to the biosphere and the ecological conditions of human life checks a tendency towards hierarchy in the presentation of the mandates. One way of approaching this issue would be to note one of Karl Barth's criticisms of Bonhoeffer's account of the mandates. In *Church Dogmatics* III/4, Barth queries whether Bonhoeffer's fondness for affirming relationships of superiority and inferiority in the mandates may be considered as biblical. Barth writes: "Is the notion of authority of some over others really more characteristic of the ethical event than that of the freedom of even the very lowest before the very highest?"[49] Transferred to an ecological context, what sense does it make to affirm in a settled and permanent way the superiority of the human over the non-human? We are returned to the questions raised earlier concerning Bonhoeffer's understanding of the freedom of the human.

Although it would be possible to explore the cogency and relevance of each of the mandates, including – given the emergence of postliberal theology – the Church, this is too large an agenda for one essay. So, in the next and final section of this essay, I want here to note that the problem identified in the discussion of freedom in *Creation and Fall* here resurfaces: the mandates of work, marriage and family, and government have little ecological reference. How might reference to the ecological situatedness of the

---

48 Marriage is the trickiest mandate as sexuality is the most "given" form; work, government and church have more varied and variable forms.

49 Barth, Dogmatics III/4, 22.

human be construed theologically as a first move in seeking to render the mundane mandates more convincing?[50]

4. The mystery of reconciliation in creation: the praxis of citizens, representatives and agitators

So far I have argued that to enquire after the mystery of reconciliation in creation will require the development of Bonhoeffer's account of creatureliness. What remains important and convincing about Bonhoeffer's account is the emphasis on the earthly character of human answerability and the orientation towards moral concretion evident in the discussion of the mandates.

What remains less satisfactory is what I shall call the Christological overdetermination of Bonhoeffer's anthropology. By such overdetermination, Bonhoeffer begins by identifying the Christological aspect, freedom, in which non-human nature does not share: "Created freedom then means [...] that God's self enters into God's creation."[51] The Christological-incarnational shape of this theological position is evident: this "then" is not a temporal reference but rather indicates that the *Christus pro nobis* structure of Bonhoeffer's account of creatureliness is foundational for his understanding of the human person. Freedom in kenosis begets human freedom, so to speak. The concentration on the human is plain: the soteriological dynamic, explored analogically, identifies the human. In that the ecological referent is understated, how might Bonhoeffer's anthropology be developed in order to overcome such understatement? The freedom of humanity is defined as "the existence of human beings over-against-one-another, with-one-another and in-dependence-upon-one-another".[52] How can this be reframed to include over-against, with and in-dependence-upon nature?

I suggest that a way forward may be found if a theological anthropology is developed in rather fuller conversation with the concept of God: a three-fold/trinitarian anthropology of *citizen*, *representative* and *agitator*. In making this move, as I hope to show, I wish to honour Bonhoeffer's insight into *analogia relationis* and incorporate his account of vicarious, representative action. In developing this position, it is important to begin – as Bonhoeffer

---

50 It is important to note that the manuscript "The Concrete Commandment and the Divine Mandates" breaks off abruptly before any detailed consideration of the three mandates of work, marriage and family, and government.
51 DBWE 3, 63.
52 DBWE 3, 64.

argued – with the reconciling work of God in Christ as providing the theologically most secure epistemic access: it is to the theme of vicarious, representative action that I turn first.

In one of his working notes for *Ethics*, Bonhoeffer writes: "[C]ivil servant, soldier, minister, scholar. *Principle of vicarious representative action*: one for the other – fights, works, administers, studies".[53] This, so to speak, is the creaturely aspect of the reconciling dynamic of Christ's work; representatives are exemplars of Christ's objective sacrifice. If Christ's sacrifice rescues the actuality of creatures from pride-ful forgetfulness of the ecological conditions of the human habitat towards "living out of the roots of creaturely being" (Colin Gunton), representative actions enable others to overcome such forgetfulness. (Such forgetfulness may take many forms including, paradoxically, the attempted "mastery of nature", in which human creatures struggle to forget or set aside their creatureliness. In that such forgetfulness is often called stewardship, efforts to repristinate the notion of stewardship must also be rejected.) To be a representative requires acting for the other or representing them. A representative is not a substitute and should not obscure the one for which she acts. Instead, a representative seeks vicariously to relate or present the interests of another. We are familiar enough with this role when a doctor represents the interest in life of a patient who for a medical reason cannot speak for herself or when elected officials in an indirect democracy represent their electors in democratic deliberations. The task of the representative in this discussion is to remind postnatural humanity of its situatedness in nature, of its "interweaving" (Daniel Hardy) in its natural conditions.

However, it is not from being a representative alone that knowledge of creaturehood is solely to be gleaned. To appreciate more fully of what we are being reminded we should turn to the doctrine of creation to explore the ecological aspects of creaturehood by reference to *analogia relationis*. Relocated to the doctrine of creation from the doctrine of reconciliation, this analogy does not now direct our attention to incarnation but rather the situatedness of the human as a representative of other nature. In what senses does the human creature share a nature with other creatures so as to be able to assume the role of the representative? (Clearly, the issue here is not expert knowledge or vocation, as my examples of a doctor and an elected official might suggest, for neither of these examples refers to a shared nature between the human and other kind.)

Rather, being a representative has an originary and ontological foundation, to which the creation narratives in Genesis point, in the interdependence of the human and the non-human. *Imago dei* is here understood as eco-

---

53 DBWE 6, note 2, 388f.

citizenship, that is, humanity is in God's image and likeness[54] through its participation in the citizenry of a commonwealth. In this rather hurried proto-exegesis of Genesis, I think that the entirety of the narrative needs to be attended to: creation is seen as the emergence of a sequence of forms that culminates in the human. I find little merit in, for example, Karl Barth's literalistic and over-specified reading whereby he argues that the only division in humanity that we may assert from Genesis 1–3 is that between male and female. Although I appreciate the political consequences that Barth draws, this sort of "hard" reading forgets that such a "saga-esque" reading is a "mythic" interpretation from which such definite conclusions cannot be drawn. Interestingly, Rosemary Radford Ruether makes a similar case although to a different purpose: for Ruether, social organisation can be read directly off the Genesis narratives as it can from other creation narratives extant in the Ancient Near East.[55] In my view, such creation texts are not transparent in this fashion and require a rather more sophisticated style of ideology critique. Against such hard readings, I recommend an interpretation that acknowledges the mutual interrelatedness of human life presented as a logical sequence through a series of "days". A key theme here is that creaturely life is participatory life.

I find no objection to understanding this participation by Bonhoeffer's preferred term of *sociality*. Language does not therefore mark the difference between the human and the non-human but rather the intensive concentration of the dynamic of sociality is where we should look to discern the difference. Here it is important to maintain that the dialectic between the human and the non-human is both quantitative and qualitative: if the human linguistic capacity is qualitatively different from most of the higher animals this must be understood as a capacity based on a quantitative relation: in the flex of the dialectic, the distinctiveness of the human is then founded on the quantitative social relations between the human and the non-human. To follow Murray Bookchin at this point, the non-human is not a point of departure for the development of the human but remains the *co-condition* of the development of the human.[56] It is on this basis – and only on this basis – that the human represents the non-human. The human acts as a representative of the non-human to present the common relations between the human and non-human based in participation in social life. This, we might say, is the default position in the doctrine of creation: postnatural humanity is always after nature in the senses of both exceeding yet also following na-

---

54 It remains unclear as to whether different aspects of the matter are referred to in the dual description of "image" and "likeness".
55 Radford Ruether, Healing, chapter 1.
56 Bookchin, Ecology, 33.

ture. The human represents such common creatureliness in any circumstance where such commonality is questioned or denied. Humanity and nature may thereby be understood as *citizens* in a common realm.

This brings me, finally, to the theme of redemption and the identification of the human as agitator. For the human agitates against attempts to separate humanity from non-human nature in ways that deny the profundity of human participation of the human in the non-human. Instead, the agitator recommends the dialectic of friendship and the entanglements of mutual aid. As such, the theological position being developed is anti-modern. What does "anti-modern" mean in this context? Here I am following Bruno Latour's analysis in *We Have Never Been Modern*: whereas modern discourse has operated strategies of ontological hygiene that function to keep separate and purify Nature and Society, a different sort of discourse – which Latour terms "amodern" – is now required to indicate that the objectification of nature and the subjectification of society are not two separate processes but are rather intertwined, intermixed.[57] The role of the agitator is to protest against the practices of ontological hygiene.

The mystery of reconciliation is therefore coincident with the mystery of praxis. The mystery of reconciliation identifies us as nature's representatives and therefore as ecological citizens and thereby as agitators (to agitate whenever citizenship is denied). The hiddenness of the mystery of the reconciling God in creation *etsi Deus non daretur* is not the evacuation of Christian meanings but the attempt to re-relate these afresh in the inhospitable circumstances of modernity – that is, to develop a moral/practical position – towards a threefold anthropology. Reconciliation does not here mean a "realistic" acceptance of what is: being reconciled is not the acceptance of contemporary circumstance, a position that Raymond Williams once mocked as "long term adjustments to short term changes". Reconciliation is not resignation to our present social order therefore. Instead, being reconciled means the attempt to act as nature's representative in order to defend a common citizenry and to agitate where such citizenry is obscured or denied.

This threefold anthropology is grounded in the revelation of Christ: through the defence and development through agitation of a common citizenry there is participation in the reconciling work of Christ for others.

> In Christ we are invited to participate in the reality of God and the reality of the world at the same time. [...] But I find the reality of the world always already borne, accepted, and reconciled in the reality of God. That is the mystery of the revelation of God in the human being Jesus Christ. [...] What matters is *participating in the reality of God and the world in Jesus Christ*.[58]

---

57 Latour, Modern.
58 DBWE 6, 55.

By such reconciling work the citizen seeks to participate anew in the blessing of a common citizenship and to agitate for the redoubling of that blessing as a form of eschatological anticipation. Moreover, this postnatural humanity grounded in the revelation of Christ refers also to the Creator and the Spirit. To be a representative is to represent a common citizenry and to agitate for the re-establishment of that citizenry towards the future of the Kin-dom of God. If the above is right, we are also offered a reflective path to God. God is the source of the social nature of the citizenry, renews community and resources the agitation towards the fellowship of citizens in community. In sum, this God is triune.

Whether such a threefold anthropology of postnatural humanity can be amplified to support a renewal of the divine mandates, and thereby achieve the degree of concretion that Bonhoeffer searched for, remains an open question. Is it possible to develop a theological ethics that is both ecologically concrete yet also rather more provisional than the scheme of mandates proposed by Bonhoeffer? Perhaps some encouragement may be had from Bonhoeffer's commitment to understanding the commandment of God as always concrete (or otherwise not a command or not of God). Thereby, the importance of the reconsideration of the interpretation of God as triune against the horizon of ecological and economic distress emerges as a key theological task. Living intelligently and wisely in the mystery of reconciliation in creation requires the development of theology as a "science" of postnatural humanity.

Bibliography

Primary Sources

BARTH, K., *Church Dogmatics* III/1, transl. by J.W. Edwards/O. Bussey/H. Knight, Edinburgh 1958.
–, *Church Dogmatics* III/4, transl. by A.T. Mackay/T.H.L. Parker et al., London/New York, 2004.
BONHOEFFER, D., Creation and Fall. A Theological Exposition of Genesis 1–3, Dietrich Bonhoeffer Works, Vol. 3, ed. by J.W. de Gruchy, transl. by D.S. Bax, Minneapolis 1997 (= DBWE 3).
–, *Christology*, transl. by J. Bowden, London 1978.
–, Ethics, Dietrich Bonhoeffer Works, Vol. 6, ed. by C. Green, transl. by R. Krauss/Ch.C. West/D.W. Stott, Minneapolis 2005 (= DBWE 6).
–, Letters and Papers from Prison, ed. by E. Bethge, transl. by R. Fuller/F. Clark et al., London 1971 (= LPP).
–, *No Rusty Swords*, transl. by J. Bowden, London 1970.

Secondary Sources

BIGGAR, N., *Barth's* trinitarian ethic, in: J. Webster (Ed.), The Cambridge Companion to Karl Barth, Cambridge 2000, 212−227.
BOOKCHIN, M., The Philosophy of Social *Ecology*. Revised Edition, Montreal/New York 1991.
GREEN, C.J., Bonhoeffer. A Theology of *Sociality*. Revised Edition, Grand Rapids/Cambridge 1999.
LATOUR, B., We have never been *Modern*, London 1993.
RAHNER, K., *Art. Order*, Encyclopedia of Theology: Concise "Sacramentum Mundi", London 1999.
RADFORD RUETHER, R., Gaia and God: An Ecofeminist Theology of Earth *Healing*, London 1993.
SCOTT, P., Nature in a World come of *Age*, NBl 79, 1997, 356–368.
−, A Political Theology of *Nature*, Cambridge 2003.
−, Christ, Nature, Sociality: Dietrich Bonhoeffer for an *Ecological* Age, SJTh 53, 2000, 413–430.
−, *Creation*, in: P. Scott/W.T. Cavanaugh (Ed.), The Blackwell Companion to Political Theology, Oxford 2004, 341–342.
−, *Anarchy* in the UK? GM crops, political authority and the rioting of God, Ecotheology 11, 2006, 32–56.
TURNER, D., Faith, Reason and the *Existence* of God, Cambridge 2004.

Niels Henrik Gregersen

The Mysteries of Christ and Creation

"Center" and "Limit" in Bonhoeffer's *Creation and Fall*
and *Christology* Lectures

1. Introduction

Even though Bonhoeffer's writings often have an immediate appeal and freshness, they nonetheless continue to pose difficulties for their interpreters. It is sometimes difficult to establish a clear picture of the inner relation between his writings, so different in style and content, and in addition many passages are formulated in such a condensed form that the interpreter has to divine their exact meaning.

One reason for this state is that Bonhoeffer developed his theology on the basis of different theological resources that he combined in the process of writing without always sorting out the provenance of central ideas such as "religion", "revelation", "mystery", or even the "Word of God". Bonhoeffer's work must therefore be read intertextually, that is, as part of an ongoing conversation with other theologians from whom he absorbed ideas but then used for his own purposes. Not least the figures of Martin Luther and Karl Barth were important for the formation of Bonhoeffer's thought, and for good reasons Bonhoeffer's relation to Luther and Barth has been at the center of Bonhoeffer scholarship. Can the this-worldly orientation of Bonhoeffer's theology, especially in the later phase of his *Ethics* and *Prison Letters*, be explained from his use of the Lutheran principle of *finitum capax infiniti?* So Regin Prenter.[1] Or may Bonhoeffer's critical attitude towards religion and metaphysics be explained, at least in part, from a continuous influence of Karl Barth's early dialectical theology on Bonhoeffer's theology, while Bonhoeffer continued to struggle, mostly silently, with Karl Barth's later theology? So Andreas Pangritz.[2]

---

[1] Prenter, Bonhoeffer.
[2] Pangritz, Barth. – A concrete example of the Barth-Bonhoeffer entanglement can be found in the *Christology* lectures (1933), where Bonhoeffer refers to the three forms of the presence of Jesus Christ today (as Word, Sacrament and Church) without mentioning Karl Barth's distinction between the three forms of the Word (preached, written and revealed) in *Church Dogmatics* I/1 § 4 (1932). See below, section 5.

The evaluation of the exact influence of such tacit cross-references accompanies any interpretation of Bonhoeffer's work. This article, however, has a more limited scope. My concern will first and foremost be intra-textual in that I will concern myself primarily with Bonhoeffer's *Creation and Fall* from 1932/33 and his *Christology* lectures from 1933. It is thus the middle period of Bonhoeffer's work, from about 1932 to 1940, on which I concentrate my attention. However, this middle period of Bonhoeffer's work cannot be understood without reference to his earlier academic work. Already in his early dissertation, *Sanctorum Communio* (1927), Bonhoeffer coined the famous term "Christ existing as community". Christ is where his body and members are. Later on, in his *Lectures on Christology* (1933), he developed a corresponding interpretation of the Chalcedonian dogma. He thus wanted to answer two questions in tandem: *Who* is Christ, and *Where* is He? In line with the dogma, Bonhoeffer affirmed Jesus as the hypostatic union of God and humanity, while adding that the very essence of Christ is to be there "for us", so that he is never to be thought of without his body, the community of Christ. His "being there for us" is not an accidental effect of the nature of Jesus Christ, but belongs to his very *esse*. Moreover, the place of Christ is not only for his church, but for the world of creation at large. In effect, the dwelling-place of Jesus Christ is not only humanity, but the whole space-time continuum. In this way, Bonhoeffer combined an existential approach ("Christ for me") and a community-oriented approach ("Christ for us"), which towards the end of his career was extended into a more universalist approach ("Christ for the world").

Correspondingly, in *Creation and Fall* (1932/33) Bonhoeffer presents the concepts of "center" and "limit" as anthropological concepts. As I am going to argue, this interpretation of Genesis 2 should be seen in the context of the Christological position, which he then explicated in his *Christology* lectures. Even though we have them only through the transcripts of his students, these lectures have rightly been accorded a central role in the interpretation of Bonhoeffer's work.[3] For while they reaffirm Bonhoeffer's earlier insistence on "Christ as existing as community", they mark an important step towards a more embracing vision of Jesus Christ as the one who stands in for human beings, whether or not they belong to the Christian community.

In the same vein, I will argue that some of the tensions in Bonhoeffer's *Creation and Fall* are in fact addressed, and to some extent solved, in his *Ethics* from the 1940's. Here the presence of Christ in the worldly realm is asserted in a way that one cannot find as clearly expressed in the middle period of his work.

---

3   Bethge, Bonhoeffer, 265, and Feil, Theologie, 171f.

The tensions between Bonhoeffer's texts thus raise the more general question of the scope of his Christology and of the exact nature of his Word-of-God theology. The existence of intratextual tensions between Bonhoeffer's works, however, requires a critical evaluation of the theological positions taken in his works each individually. After all, no theology is a one-person affair, and no theologian is without limits. Taking Bonhoeffer seriously means discussing his theology as a contribution to the self-reflection of Christian faith in a present-day setting. Like any other theology, Bonhoeffer's work must be judged by what he *actually says*, by what he does *not* say, and what he *could* and perhaps *should* have said.

2. Intra-textuality and inter-textuality in Bonhoeffer research

It is well-known that the great historian of doctrine and professor in systematic theology in Berlin, Reinhold Seeberg (1859–1935), introduced Bonhoeffer to the thought of Hegel during the formative years 1925–27. Seeberg was also the supervisor of Bonhoeffer's dissertation, *Sanctorum Communio. Eine dogmatische Untersuchung zur Soziologie der Kirche*, which he defended in 1927, when he was only 21 years old, and proceeded to publish in revised form in 1930. Throughout this volume we find the aforementioned phrase, *Christus als Gemeinde existierend*, "Christ existing as community".[4]

This term clearly echoes Hegel's concept of God existing as community: "Thus the community itself is the existing Spirit, the Spirit in its existence, God existing as community".[5] Yet the positive influence of Hegel's *Lectures on the Philosophy of Religion* on Bonhoeffer's own ecclesiology is only ambiguously attested in *Sanctorum Communio*. In the published text (1930) Bonhoeffer certainly recognizes that the notion of "Christ existing as community" is a "modification" of the Hegelian concept; this was not admitted in the original dissertation of 1927.[6] Bonhoeffer also recognizes that the idealist movement from Schleiermacher to Hegel rightly put emphasis on the idea of the community, but he criticized idealist philosophy for erasing the concrete ethical persons of the community, and for neglecting the ontological difference between the Spirit of God and the human community:

---

4   DBWE 1, 141. DBW 1, 87.
5   Hegel, Philosophy of Religion, Vol. III, 331. Bonhoeffer taught a seminar on these lectures in 1933, see Rumscheidt, Formation, 58.
6   DBWE 1, 189. DBW 1, 126. Cf. editor's note 184 in DBWE 1, 189, note 171. DBW 1, 268.

we [sc. Bonhoeffer] understand the term 'corporate life' [*Gesamtleben*] and 'real' in a significantly different sense. We understand both as ethical categories, whereas in idealist philosophy they are partly biological, and partly metaphysical categories.[7]

Whether it is a correct conclusion that Schleiermacher's concept of corporate life erases the concrete personhood in favor of biological categories, or that Hegel's metaphysics is without concern for the ethical person, is questionable but need not concern us here. My point here is only that Bonhoeffer tends to express his own positions by placing them in a stark contrast to views that have inspired his own thought in the first place. By inserting "Christ" for "God", and the church for the community, the young Bonhoeffer wanted to point out that only the Christian church is the dwelling-place of Christ.

God established the reality of the Church, of humanity pardoned in Jesus Christ – not religion, but revelation, *not religious community, but church.* This is what the reality of Jesus Christ means.[8]

Bonhoeffer not only changed the common denominator "God" for "Christ", he also argued that the body of Christ is not to be equated with any phenomenon of culture or religious organization. Thus the *Sanctorum Communio* is constantly accompanied by a double-edged sword, on the one hand directed against the Roman Catholic concept of the church as an "organism" (whereby not only Christ, but also the Church exists prior to its members), and on the other hand against idealistic conceptions of spirit, where Spirit is assumed to be self-identical and transpersonal, while the concrete characteristics of the believer and the believer's community are erased.[9] The reality of Jesus, as Bonhoeffer said in an address on "Jesus Christ and the Essence of Christianity" on December 11, 1928, is a matter of life, not of the "churchiness" of groups: "we understand Christ only if we commit ourselves to him in a stark 'Either-Or'. He did not go to the cross to ornament and embellish our life. If we wish to have him, then he demands the right to say something decisive about our entire life".[10]

Bonhoeffer's earliest and most characteristic theological vision is thus both positively and negatively informed by his reception of Hegel. Accordingly, an important task for the Bonhoeffer-interpreter is to clarify, as far as

---

7   DBWE 1, 198. DBW 1, 132.
8   DBWE 1, 153. DBW 1, 97.
9   DBWE 1, 141: "[…] the body of Christ exists only through Christ 'above' and 'before' all individuals. The theory of organism in Roman Catholicism, biology, or the philosophy of the state ranks the collective above the individual. For Paul, only Christ exists 'before' and 'above' the individuals. He looks at the church from the perspective of the collective person [Gesamtperson], that of 'Christ existing as church-community [Gemeinde]'". DBW 1, 87.
10 Bonhoeffer, Jesus Christus und das Wesen des Christentums, translated after: Bonhoeffer, Jesus Christ, 53.

possible, the specificity of Bonhoeffer's texts through the intertextual cross-references that he is either alluding to or hiding. Having made such clarifications, however, a new difficulty emerges for the interpreter of Bonhoeffer. For Bonhoeffer does speak in different styles, depending on the situation and the theological problems that he is committed to solve.[11] Thus an intra-textual reading of Bonhoeffer's work may serve as a remedy for solving tensions across the different contexts in which he spoke.

I am commenting on this difference between inter-textual and intra-textual interpretations of Bonhoeffer here, because I believe that a similar strategy of intra-textual correlation can be used in elucidating the tensions between *Creation and Fall* from 1932/33 and the *Christology* lectures from 1933. But it also seems clear that no Bonhoeffer reader should take for granted that he always took the appropriate theological decisions. If so, the task for a future Bonhoeffer scholarship should not only be to show the inner coherence of his work, but also identifying the incoherencies and blind spots of his writings. In what follows I want in particular to argue that some of Bonhoeffer's theological shortcomings may derive from a too general criticism of philosophical metaphysics, and, within his theology, from an over-use of Christological concepts and a corresponding under-use of Trinitarian resources.

3. Bonhoeffer's Christocentric doctrine of creation in *Creation and Fall*

In his "Introduction" to *Creation and Fall*, Bonhoeffer states rather uncompromisingly: "Only the church, which knows of the end, knows also of the beginning".[12] The doctrine of creation, in other words, cannot be dealt with adequately from the perspective of Jewish or any other religious faith tradition, for the Christian church alone knows about the fall, and only the church knows that the new creation will emerge on the basis of the dying of the old creation. In an oblique reference to the cross and resurrection of Christ, Bonhoeffer says,

---

11 What, for example, is the relation between our commitment to Christ, and the fact that we, *if* we are in the body of Christ, are ruled by Christ, and not ruling ourselves, as suggested by *Sanctorum Communio*? This is the question that Bonhoeffer is struggling with in *Discipleship*, where he indeed came up with a solution. Our commitment is here seen as "the first step" of obedience under the call of Christ, and only after our first step of willingness is the true discipleship under the rule of Christ possible, DBW 4, 50: "Mit dem ersten Schritt ist der Nachfolgende in die Situation gebracht, glauben zu können". DBWE 4, 62.

12 DBW 3, 21; English translation after DBWE 3, 22.

[t]he church therefore sees the beginning only in dying, from the viewpoint of the end. It views the creation from Christ; or better, in the fallen, old world it believes in the world of the new creation, the new world of the beginning and the end, because it believes in Christ and in nothing else.[13]

Bonhoeffer is here clarifying the epistemic perspective from which he is going to pursue his interpretation of Genesis 1–3. However, he is also raising a more general dogmatic claim, saying that a christocentric doctrine of creation is the only adequate theology of creation. Bonhoeffer's epistemological stance thus involves a stark ontological claim. For the church speaks of the end of the world, "as if it had already happened", since the world "has already been judged".[14] As a matter of fact, Bonhoeffer speaks in a language of extermination about the created but fallen world. The world is destined to die, and is already dead from the perspective of the church. The *creatio nova* apparently happens through an annihilation of the old world, in order that the new world may shine forth. There is no discussion of the possibility of a *creatio nova ex vetere*, that is, on a new creation emerging out of old creation.

This becomes evident in Bonhoeffer's correlation of the doctrine of the creation *ex nihilo* with the resurrection of Jesus Christ. That the God of creation is the same as the God of resurrection is already expressed by Paul in Romans 4,17, who speaks of God as the one "who gives life to the dead and calls into existence the things that do not exist" (NRSV). But Bonhoeffer goes a significant step further by actually deriving the belief in God the Creator from the Christian conviction of the resurrection of Jesus Christ:

Indeed it is because we know of the resurrection that we know of God's creation in the beginning, of God's creating out of nothing. The dead Jesus Christ of Good Friday and the resurrected *kýrios* of Easter Sunday – that is creation out of nothing, creation from the beginning. The fact that Christ was dead did not provide the possibility of his resurrection but its impossibility; it was nothing itself, the *nihil negativum*. There is absolutely no continuum between the dead Christ and the resurrected Christ, but the freedom of God that in the beginning created God's work out of nothing. [...] By his resurrection we know about the creation.[15]

So far Bonhoeffer only makes an epistemic assertion: the issue of knowing or not knowing stands in the foreground. But in the following sentence he again makes the leap from epistemology to ontology: "For had he not risen again, the Creator would be dead and would not be attested".[16] As far as I can see, this sentence is not without problems. For it is one thing to say that

---

13 DBW 3, 22. DBWE 3, 22.
14 DBW 3, 21. DBWE 3, 22.
15 DBW 3, 33f. DBWE 3, 35.
16 DBW 3, 34. DBWE 3, 35f.

God's power to create would not be "attested" without the resurrection of Jesus (itself a far-reaching statement), but it is quite another thing to say that God the Creator would be "dead" without the resurrection. This latter statement only makes sense if the sentence that "God would be dead" is a metaphor for not "making a difference" in the particular case of Jesus. But it hardly makes sense to say that God the Creator would not exist (or would die) without the particular resurrection of Jesus Christ. Probably for this very reason Bonhoeffer in the following sentence reverts to the more classic statement: "On the other hand we know from the act of creation about God's power to raise up again, because God remains Lord". However, if Bonhoeffer had taken this latter assertion more seriously, he could not have made his claim that a theology of creation stands and falls with the event of resurrection. Rather it would be the other way around: the belief in the resurrection *presupposes* the belief in God the Creator. This is, however, what Bonhoeffer does not say (but perhaps should have said).

This raises the more general question, whether Bonhoeffer undermines the critical role of philosophical reflection within Christian doctrine in a way that may also lead to blind spots in his own theological position. While interpreting Genesis 1,1, Bonhoeffer underlines that the *creatio ex nihilo* is to be understood as a reference to the unconditioned divine freedom: "Between Creator and creature there is simply nothing [das Nichts]".[17] Bonhoeffer is therefore quick to point out, how creation is *not* to be understood. Creation is *not* an outflow of divine creativity from the inner fecundity of divine nature in terms of a theory of emanation or of divine self-unfolding.[18] Likewise, creation is *not* just about the Word of God in-forming a chaotic matter.[19] In accordance with standard doctrinal tradition, Bonhoeffer points out that there is no inner divine necessity behind the beginning of creation, and no hidden potencies in a pre-existing matter. But Bonhoeffer goes on to claim that the Christian understanding of creation does not even allow us to ask for a plan in the mind of God prior to creation:

Thus it is impossible to ask why the world was created, what God's plan for the world was, or whether the creation was necessary. These questions are exposed as godless questions and finally disposed of by the statement: In the beginning God created heaven and earth. The statement declares not that in the beginning God had this or that idea about the purpose of the world, ideas that we must now try to discover, but that in the beginning God created. No question can go back behind the creating God, because one cannot go back behind the beginning.[20]

---

17 DBW 3, 31. DBWE 3, 32.
18 DBW 3, 38. DBWE 3, 40.
19 DBW 3, 32. DBWE 3, 34.
20 DBW 3, 30. DBWE 3, 31f.

Bonhoeffer is right that human beings are not in an epistemic position to inquire into the depths of divine knowledge. But can one legitimately say that there is no divine mind or self-conscious nature of God prior to, simultaneous with, and following upon the free divine decision of creation? Indeed this would be a difficult position to hold, since the freedom of God would then be indistinguishable from arbitrariness. One way to redeem Bonhoeffer's view would be to admit that Christian faith in fact presupposes a self-identical divine nature prior to creation, but that we, from our epistemic position, can only discern God's will and mind in the patterns of divine self-manifestation throughout history, a pattern of divine self-consistency revealed in a final form in the life, death and resurrection of Jesus Christ.[21] Or, one could argue that God's plan before the foundation of the world is in itself the result of a self-constituting act of divine love, in which God predestined Jesus Christ to be the chosen one, who is to carry the burden of sin for the human race, so that humanity be saved by divine grace.[22] But by expelling any metaphysical considerations Bonhoeffer, and his readers, are left with a divine *fiat* as "the beginning", a brute fact which is then explained by a reference to the unique event of the resurrection of Jesus.

The cost of this position is not only its lack of persuasiveness, seen from a common sense point of view. The problem is also theological in nature, in so far as he appeals to Christ outside of an expressed Trinitarian framework. Here a comparison with Karl Barth's solution in *Church Dogmatics* may be revealing. In *Church Dogmatics* II/1 § 28, Barth shows how the attributes of God's being, from the perspective of Christian faith, can be summarized as "the One who loves in freedom". Accordingly God's freedom is not a brute freedom, but the "freedom of love" expressed in the "acts" of creating a divine-human community. The eternal divine love between Father, Son, and Spirit constitutes itself as a community of love that in the eternal election decides to establish a community between God and humanity as "partners" (*Bundesgenossen*).[23] The freedom of God's act of creation, in other words, cannot be understood apart from the matrix of divine love, and the eternal divine love cannot be understood apart from God's self-determination to love the world in freedom.[24] Divine freedom and divine love cannot and should not be pitted against one another.

21　This is the solution offered by Wolfhart Pannenberg, see already Dogmatische Thesen, later refined in Systematische Theologie, Vol. 1, 207–282.

22　This is the solution of Karl Barth, Kirchliche Dogmatik, Vol. II/2, cf. the actualistic interpretation of Barth's theology of election in McCormack, Grace.

23　Barth, Kirchliche Dogmatik, Vol. III/2, 242–390. See Krötke, Gott.

24　This structure of Karl Barth's theology has been analyzed by Bent Flemming Nielsen, Rationaliät, esp. 127–145.

Also elsewhere in *Creation and Fall* Bonhoeffer is suspicious of philosophical reflection, and again this has theological repercussions. While interpreting Genesis 1,3 Bonhoeffer points to the *Tatwort* of divine creativity. But he is, for two reasons, worried about talking about a *Wirken Gottes*. The first is that one cannot call God's act of creation an "effecting", because this term "does not include within its meaning the character of creation as a demand".[25] This is an interesting observation, since Bonhoeffer points to the theological deficiencies in using a "thin" third-person language in the doctrine of creation. Rather, the indicative and the imperative are interwoven. Creation is not a neutral category, but presupposes a notion of a divine appeal. But, secondly, Bonhoeffer fears that by employing a general metaphysical scheme of "cause" and "effect", one paves the way for a natural theology that reconstructs God as a *causa mundi*. This also is a valid concern. But it seems to me that pointing to the inherent limits of the concept of divine *Wirken* and to the potential misuses of this concept does not preclude the possibility of its proper (though perhaps limited) use in theology. For one could ask the opposite question: What would happen if God's acts of creation had no effects? Either God would make no difference at all, or God's creative activity would be purely *ad hoc*, without affording any continuous structure within the world.

This, however, is not in line with Bonhoeffer's intentions stated elsewhere. In his interpretation of Genesis 1,1 he distances himself from the idea of a *creatio continua*: The idea of a "continual repetition of free acts" is mistaken, "because freedom does not allow itself to be repeated".[26] However, in the interpretation of Genesis 1,4a, he nonetheless introduces the classic distinction between *creatio* and *conservatio*:

Creation means wrestling out of nonbeing [Nichtsein]; *upholding* means affirming being. *Creation* is a real *beginning*, always 'before' my knowledge and *before* the upholding of what has been created. [...] Upholding is always *with reference to* creation, whereas creation is in itself.[27]

So there are continuous structures in the world, after all, though Bonhoeffer makes us aware of the fundamental mysteries of the beginning. In God's upholding, there is continuity. It is reasonable to assume that Bonhoeffer here wants to do justice to the possibility of scientific inquiries into the world's permanent mathematical structures. At least Bonhoeffer, throughout *Creation and Fall*, is keen to emphasize that no conflict exists between a scientific world view and the Christian doctrine of creation. "The beginning" is a theological statement about the uniqueness of divine creativity,

---

25　DBW 3, 40. DBWE 3, 42.
26　DBW 3, 31. DBWE 3, 33.
27　DBW 3, 44. DBWE 3, 47.

not a statement about temporal terms or dates of the beginning.[28] The creation of the human being as *imago dei* does not contradict an evolutionary understanding of the emergence of humanity in line with Genesis 2,7: "Even Darwin and Feuerbach could not use stronger language than is used here. Humankind is derived from a piece of earth. Its bond with the earth belongs to its essential being".[29] Human beings do not "have" bodies, but "are" bodies. And as is clear from his interpretation of *das Starre* or the "firmly fixed" in Genesis 1,6–10 and 14–19, there is a structure to the world, a divine *law* expressed in the regularities of nature: "As the firmament determines, days, years and epochs of time happen with complete regularity and without change. Here it is a number that rules with complete regularity and without change".[30] Accordingly Bonhoeffer sees scientific knowledge as expressing the human participation (*Teilnahme*) in the natural world of unchanging structures. Human beings know numbers and mathematical structures of the universe that apparently are unaffected by humankind's fall. But Bonhoeffer sees this knowledge as "the great temptation of human beings to seek comfort in the world of the unchanging, to flee to the world that is unaffected by their own existence".[31] On account of the fall, human beings do not recognize that the laws of nature are not self-contained or autonomous: "human beings no longer know that numbers too are upheld by God's word and command alone. Numbers are not the truth of God itself".[32]

The mathematical numbers and their expression in the stable structure of nature are creaturely, not divine. Thus the numbers have a beginning and they will have an end. But even so one might ask Bonhoeffer what the relation might be between the unchangeable structures of the world (that exist prior to human nature and the human fall) and the mind of the creator. Bonhoeffer seems to fear the spectre of natural theology to such an extent that he does not see the possibility of a theology of nature based on revelation. The alternative "to us in the middle" is either to take distance to the laws of nature, as opposed to human freedom, or to give into the temptation of boasting of nature's autonomy and "snatch its power away from the creator".[33] But is this the only alternative?

It is in this context that one cannot but notice the *contrastive thought patterns* that permeate Bonhoeffer's interpretation of creation. Just to mention a few of these contrast figures: "Not the created work, no, but the Creator

---

28 DBW 3, 31. DBWE 3, 32.
29 DBW 3, 71. DBWE 3, 76.
30 DBW 3, 48. DBWE 3, 52.
31 DBW 3, 49. DBWE 3, 52.
32 DBW 3, 49. DBWE 3, 53.
33 DBW 3, 51. DBWE 3, 54.

wills to be glorified".[34] But why would not God be glorified in and through the world of creation? "[I]t cannot be said that [...] God here espouses what God has created in order to make it fruitful, or that God becomes one with it".[35] But is not a unity of Creator and creature the only way to avoid an understanding of nature as radically self-contained? "God creates in complete freedom. Even in creating, God remains wholly free over against what is created. God is not bound to what is created, instead God binds it to God".[36] But does not the Word of God, understood in terms of an evangelical theology of promise, exactly bind God to the future fate of the universe and to the destiny of its human inhabitants in particular? In a sense, these are all questions that Bonhoeffer, as we shall see, was ready to affirm in the later period of *Ethics* and *Prison Letters*. But this view is not yet expressed in *Creation and Fall*. For sure, God is *in* the world in the form of the Word, which is utterly transcendent vis-à-vis the world. But the Word does not in any sense exist *as* world, or as the formative power of the world. Christ exists as the body of Christ, but not as nature. There is, as we saw above, no reflection on the inner relationship between the numbers or *logoi* of creation, and the Logos of God in Jesus Christ. It is therefore no wonder that the Augustinian choice of either turning to God or to the world is reiterated, in deferred form, in Bonhoeffer's principled distinctions between humanity and nature. Humans are called to be "free for" (*frei für*) other human beings, but are called to be "free from" (*frei von*) non-human nature by being the masters of nature, commissioned to this superior role by God.[37]

Now this contrastive thought pattern is one strand of thought in *Creation and Fall*. Another strand comes to the fore in Bonhoeffer's interpretation of God's creation of living beings in Genesis 1,11–13 and 1,20–25:

> The Creator wills that the creation should itself, in obedience, endorse and carry on the Creator's work – wills that creatures should live and should in turn themselves create life. That which is living differs from that which is dead in that it can itself create life. God gives to God's work that which makes God Lord, namely the ability to create.[38]

It is this strand of thought that may be said to be carried on in Bonhoeffer's later theology of God's blessing in the *Prison Letters*.[39] The contrastive thought pattern of God vs. world is here transformed into a picture of God unilaterally creating the world in order to facilitate a multilateral and mutual

---

34 DBW 3, 34. DBWE 3, 36.
35 DBW 3, 36. DBWE 3, 38.
36 DBW 3, 38. DBWE 3, 41.
37 DBW 3, 61. DBWE 3, 66.
38 DBW 3, 53. DBWE 3, 57.
39 LPP, 374. See further Scott, Christ, 416.

passing on of the fruits of creation in reproduction and growth. An even stronger affirmation of God's presence as creature is found in Bonhoeffer's interpretation of Genesis 2,7. Bonhoeffer here emphasizes that God breathed God's own Spirit into the body of the human beings, so that human beings have a special relation to God: "Other life is created through God's work, but in the case of human life God gives of God's own life, of God's own spirit".[40] The divine is *in* the spirit of human beings *as* divine Spirit. This may explain why God can be present in the world *as* the human being of Jesus Christ, whereas God elsewhere is only present *in* and *through* God's word, not *as* the world of creation. The incarnation, as we shall see in Bonhoeffer's *Christology* lectures, is not seen as a Kierkegaardian paradox or stumbling block, but is perceived as the free divine unfolding of the ubiquitous being of Logos *as* the love of Christ for human beings. One is here again reminded of Hegel's concept of genuine infinity (*das wahre Unendliche*): The infinite God must within Himself encompass the finitude of creation. "If God has the finite only over against himself, then he himself is finite and limited. Finitude must be posited in God himself, not as something unsurmountable, absolute, independent".[41] Otherwise God would posses only a "spurious infinitude", which would start on the other side of the finite world and from here go on indefinitely. But Hegel's point is that God hosts the finite while consciously distinguishing within himself the being of God and the being of the world. Bonhoeffer, one might say, re-applies this Hegelian thought-model to the relation between God and humanity (respectively Christ and community) while not following Hegel's universal vision of the God-world relation.

It seems, however, that Bonhoeffer has difficulty in explicating this concept of God's embracing infinity in *Creation and Fall*. Even the beautiful and much quoted sentence: "God, the brother [and sister], and the earth belong together",[42] does not entail a strong affirmation of the bond between God and creation. The unity of God and world is, according to *Creation and Fall*, only realizable as mediated by God's incarnation in Jesus Christ:

From the inception humankind's way to the earth has been possible only as God's way to humankind. Only where God and the brother [the sister] come to them can human beings find their way back to the earth.[43]

An unmediated nature mysticism is as far removed from Bonhoeffer's vision as are the various versions of a rationalized natural theology.

---

40 DBW 3, 73. DBWE 3, 78.
41 Hegel, Philosophy of Religion, Vol. III, 406.
42 DBW 3, 63. DBWE 3, 67.
43 DBW 3, 63. DBWE 3, 67.

4. The anthropology of center and limit in *Creation and Fall*

Bonhoeffer's theology of creation is not only conceptual, but likewise characterized by his vivid interpretation of the pictorial world of the creation stories. Bonhoeffer understands the anthropomorphic talk of God as more appropriate than generic concepts of God, since we cannot – and should not – speak of "God as such" apart from God's relation to human beings.[44] Accordingly, the being of God is condensed in God's proper name, used in personal address to human beings. "Jesus Christ – that is the name of God, at once utterly anthropomorphic and utterly to the point".[45]

Bonhoeffer is aware that the picture world of the paradise and fall stories should not be taken literally, but be translated into new pictorial ways of speaking for today. For "*we ourselves* are the ones who are affected, are intended, are addressed, accused, condemned, expelled".[46] This method is also used in his interpretation of the *two trees* that were standing in the midst of the paradise, the tree of life and the tree of the knowledge of good and evil. The "tree of life" refers in Bonhoeffer's interpretation to the unbroken human existence, in which human beings are immediately obedient, without even being required to be so by God. The tree of life "was in the center; that is all what is said about it. The life that comes from God is at the center; that is to say, God who gives life, is at the center".[47]

The tree of life is once *a given there*, standing in the middle of the garden: "es ist da"! But the tree is also a *gift* given for the disposal of human beings, for its fruits are to be reaped freely by Adam and Eve without any antecedent conditions. But, as Bonhoeffer observes, it is not the human beings themselves that are placed in the middle, but the tree of life which is (1) something given, (2) a gift from God, and therefore also (3) God *as* life-giver. This structure can be further elucidated: as a gift given for human use, the tree does not possess the human beings, but "Adam really possesses it". Yet by being placed there in the center,

Adam has life in the unity of the unbroken obedience to the Creator – has life just because Adam lives from the center of life, and is oriented toward the the center of life, without placing Adam's own life at the center. The distinctive characteristic of Adam's life is utterly and unbroken obedience, that is, Adam's innocence and ignorance of disobedience.[48]

---

44 DBW 3, 69. DBWE 3, 75.
45 DBW 3, 70. DBWE 3, 75.
46 DBW 3, 77. DBWE 3, 82.
47 DBW 3, 78. DBWE 3, 83.
48 DBW 3, 79. DBWE 3, 84.

In one sense, Adam is *more* than the tree of life (for he possesses it – as a gift handed over to him). Yet in another sense Adam is *less* than the tree of life, since the tree stands in the middle, not Adam who is bound to receive the gift of life (from God as life-giver).

To this excellent analysis Bonhoeffer adds his interpretation of the other tree, the tree of knowledge of good and evil. Also this tree is standing in the middle, but unlike the first tree, which was given for consumption, this second tree is surrounded by a divine prohibition: Don't eat from this tree, or you will die! Therefore this second tree in the middle, surrounded by the prohibitive command of God, signifies the limit of creaturely existence. Now the problem, of course, is that prior to the eating from the tree of knowledge of good and evil, how could Adam and Eve *know* that it was wrong to eat from it? And how could they know what death *means* before the knowledge of having to die? Bonhoeffer's answer is that both trees were given to Adam and Eve as human beings, not as brute animals. Simply by being *addressed* by God, Adam "knew" that he is at once a free creature, and yet a creature marked by limits. This pre-theoretical knowledge is given by human existence as an existence that is called to *respond* to the divine address:

The human being's limit is at the center of human existence, not on the margin; the limit or constraint that people look for on the margin of humankind is the limit of the human condition, the limit of technology, the limit of what is possible for humanity. The boundary that is at the center is the limit of human *reality*, of human *existence as such*.[49]

The story of the fall is not about external limits of certain things that human beings "can't do", but it is about the internal limits that emerge from the fact that Adam is addressed by God in his own humanity: *das Angeredetwerden Adams auf sein Menschsein*.[50] But more than that: since Adam knows God in his unbroken relation to God, Adam also perceives the prohibition, and even the threat of death, as yet another gift of God: "The limit is grace because it is the basis of creatureliness and freedom; the boundary is the center".[51]

So far the trees have an anthropological meaning. But they also have a theological significance: "*God is at once the boundary and the center of our existence*".[52] In this way, the concepts of center and limit serve both to clarify Bonhoeffer's concept of *imago dei* and to clarify how the divine warning and threat in Genesis 2 is not to be seen as an external law (*Gesetz*)

---

49 DBW 3, 81. DBWE 3, 86.
50 DBW 3, 80. DBWE 3, 85.
51 DBW 3, 80. DBWE 3, 85.
52 DBW 3, 81. DBWE 3, 86.

imposed by a foreign God on human beings. Rather it is an expression of God's protective grace that both involves a command (*Gebot*) and a prohibition (*Verbot*) that intends to shield the human beings. Not from God, but from themselves. For by eating the fruit of the tree of knowledge, Adam and Eve make themselves the center of the Garden, and they stand back as lonely individuals. Their immediate relation to God was broken, but so was the relation between Adam and Eve themselves. A breaking apart (*Entzweiung*) took place. The original world of sociality was replaced by a state of sin, where relations are broken and the urge for dissociation begins.[53]

There is no space here to lay out how Bonhoeffer in detail develops his concept of sin as emerging out of the mental distance of Adam to God, and as a consequent experience of a split (*Zwiespalt*) in human subjectivity and sociality.[54] From now on the human beings are left over to an ambiguity that only the revelation in Jesus Christ can overcome. We now turn to the theme of revelation in the context of Bonhoeffer's Christology.

5. Bonhoeffer's understanding of Christ as being *pro me* in his *Christology*

Also in his *Christology* lectures from 1933 Bonhoeffer takes his point of departure in the existential question: How is Christ present today – *pro me*. Accordingly his approach is personal and relational, but the importance of the *Christology* lectures is not least that Bonhoeffer here no longer avoids metaphysical expressions to describe the presence of Christ. The *How* of the presence of Christ can only be clarified in tandem with an exposition of *Who* Christ is and will be forever:

Christ is Christ, not just for himself, but in relation to me. His being Christ is his being for me, *pro me*. This being *pro me* is not to be understood as an effect emanating from him, nor as an accident; rather it is to be understood as the essence, the being of the person himself.[55]

---

53 DBW 3, 115–117. DBWE 3, 122–124. See the contribution of Christiane Tietz, The Mysteries of Knowledge, Sin, and Shame, in this volume.

54 See the illuminating monograph by Gottfried Claß, Zugriff. Claß also offers a balanced and convincing interpretation of the concepts of center and limit in *Creation and Fall*, DBWE 3, 83–98. A comprehensive interpretation of Bonhoeffer's concept is to be found in Busch Nielsen, Syndens.

55 DBW 12, 295; English translation in Bonhoeffer, Christology, 47. – It should be noted that the English translation (1981) was based on the reconstruction in the older German Bonhoeffer-edition in Gesammelte Schriften, Vol. 3 (1960), whereas a new German reconstruction has been laid out in the DBW 12 (1997). The two reconstructions sometimes differ significantly.

As usual, Bonhoeffer begins by making clear how things should *not* be understood. The presence is not to be equated with the historical influence of the historical figure of Jesus (as in Albrecht Ritschl), nor be seen as an inner psychological icon (as in Wilhelm Herrmann). Both these misunderstandings derive, according to Bonhoeffer, from Schleiermacher.[56] Christ is to be understood as a Person, not as a non-personal power. Bonhoeffer here refers to Luther's interpretation of the ascension: the risen Christ has ascended to heaven and is sitting at the right hand of the Father (that is, everywhere), so that Christ can be immediately present in the world of creation: "When he was on earth, he was far from us. Now that he is far, he is near to us".[57]

Bonhoeffer now explicates the ontological commitments of Chalcedonian Christology.[58] What is new in the *Christology* lectures is that not only humanity but also the space-time continuum is seen as the dwelling-place for Jesus Christ. The paradox and stumbling block is not the incarnation in itself, but the fact that Christ appeared veiled in sinful flesh:

The space-time continuum is not only the human definition of the God-Man, but also the divine definition. This space-time presence of the God-Man is hidden [verhüllt] 'in the likeness of sinful flesh' (Romans 8,3). The presence of Christ is a hidden presence. It is not that God is hidden in man, but rather this God-Man as a whole, and the principle of hiddenness is the 'likeness of sinful flesh'.[59]

What is characteristic for Bonhoeffer's position (but not new in relation to *Act and Being*) is also the emphasis that the pattern of Christ's ways of acting cannot be divorced from his being. One cannot speak of a presence of *Christ for us* without the prior assumption of Christ's simply *being there:* "the *for you* existence [*Dir*-Da-sein] and the *being there* for you [Dir-*Da-sein*] are joined together".[60]

This view also opens up for a new understanding that Christ himself has really bound himself in his freedom of his existence for the community. Freedom is here no longer referred to as a divine freedom prior to creation, but as the particular form of divine freedom exercised in God's presence for and with human beings. "That is, he is the community [Gemeinde]. He not only acts *for* it [für sie], he acts *as* it [als sie], when he goes to the cross, carries the sins and dies."[61] The meaning of freedom is now depicted in the

---

56   DBW 12, 292. Christology, 43.
57   Luther, Sermon am Himmelfahrtstage, WA 12, 562,25f, quoted DBW 12, 293. Christology, 44.
58   Bonhoeffer's own interpretation of the Chalcedonian Creed is presented in Part II of the *Christology* lectures, DBW 12, 315–340. Christology, 74–89.
59   DBW 12, 294f. Christology, 45f (translation corrected).
60   DBW 12, 296. Cf. Christology, 48.
61   DBW 12, 296. Christology, 48 (translation corrected).

image of divine love, as revealed in Jesus Christ. The idea of divine freedom is defined *a posteriori*, not prior to revelation.

In Bonhoeffer's doctrine of the three-fold form of Christ, Jesus Christ is now presented as Word, as Sacrament, and as Church. As *Word* Christ is not immediately present in the many words, thoughts and ideas of human beings, but in the Word that *addresses* human beings as forgiveness and command, as gospel and law. In so far as the Word addresses the world and the community, Jesus Christ stands over against the church, which, in Luther's terms, is itself a *creatura verbi*. But Bonhoeffer now goes further than that: "Christ is not only present in the Word of the Church, but also as Word of the Church, that means the spoken Word of preaching. *In* the Word, could be too little, because it could separate Christ from his Word".[62] Thus the whole presence of Jesus Christ in the preached Word is important.

As *Sacrament* the Word is embodied, for the sacrament is the form in which Logos reaches human beings in their natural conditions as bodies. In line with *Creation and Fall*, however, Jesus Christ is not embodied in all natural events in a self-revelatory way. After the fall, one no longer sees the Word in creation, since the world is no longer transparent [durchsichtig]: "The continuity of Word and nature is lost. The creation is not sacrament. There is sacrament only when God, by his special Word, in the midst of his created world, addresses, names and hallows an element".[63] Bonhoeffer is here presupposing Luther's distinction between God's reality and the divine reality *for us*, under our epistemic conditions. However, it is interesting that Bonhoeffer here criticizes a pan-sacramentalist view of nature by referring to human sin, and not by referring to a principled distance between the Word of God and world of creation, as we saw in *Creation and Fall*. Bonhoeffer is no doubt closer to Luther's doctrine of creation in the *Christology* lectures than he was the year before.[64] However, the sacraments do not mean that God becomes human or natural, but has to do with the humiliation of the God-Man in sinful flesh: "The primary question in Christology is not about the possibility of uniting deity and humanity, but rather about the concealment of the God-Man in his humiliation."[65]

The mystery and paradox, in other words, lies not in the incarnation (for incarnation is not foreign to God's nature), but is related to the presence of Christ in the world of sin, suffering and death. This is the stumbling block!

---

62 DBW 12, 299. Christology, 52.
63 DBW 12, 301. Christology, 53.
64 Gregersen, Grace.
65 DBW 12, 302. Christology, 54.

The section on the sacrament is one of the places where Bonhoeffer clarifies his relation to Luther.[66] He follows Luther closely in the question of the *genus majestatis*, in so far as "the transfigured body [of the human Jesus] is everywhere".[67] He also goes into some detail with Luther's view of the three ways, in which the body of Christ may be said to be present in the world, *localiter*, *diffinitive* and *repletive*. But Bonhoeffer does not want to choose between the theory of ubiquity (that Christ is everywhere) and the theory of an *ubivoli* presence (Christ is present only when and where he wishes to be).

> As metaphysical hypostases, both doctrines are impossible, for the first theory passes over the particular existence of Christ as person, while the second makes the presence of Christ merely accidental in relation to his being *per se*.[68]

For as earlier laid out, the being and the act of Jesus Christ cannot be separated, since it belongs to the essence of the embodied *Logos* to be there – for us.

Therefore, finally, the presence of Christ as *Church* must be asserted without restrictions. Jesus cannot be Christ without being there for his community. In this sense, "Christ is not only the head of the Church, but also the Church itself (see Corinthians 12 and Ephesians). Christ is head and also every member".[69] The concept of "Christ existing as community" from *Sanctorum communio* is still intact. The presence of Christ *as* Church is Bonhoeffer's own complement to the classic Lutheran doctrine. But as we have seen, this presence as community has already been reflected in Bonhoeffer's expositions of the presence of Christ in Word and sacrament. For as the Word is communicative, addressing the community, so the sacraments are communal, given for the community, which *is* the comprehensive reality of Christ as being both the head and the members of the church.[70]

---

66 See also in particular Part II of Christology, where he takes issue with the classic Christological problems, including the doctrine of *communicatio idiomatum* and the different versions of kenotic Christology in the Lutheran tradition (DBW 12, 330–336. Christology, 89–98). In particular, he fears that the kenotic theories presuppose an *Extra Calvinisticum*.
67 Bonhoeffer, Christology, 55.
68 Bonhoeffer, Christology, 56.
69 Bonhoeffer, Christology, 59.
70 As observed by Scott, Christ, 422: "[...] preaching and the sacraments do not merely happen *in* sociality; rather they are social events that, interpreted correctly, are acts *of* sociality", namely of the social nature of Jesus Christ.

6. The place of Christ as center and limit in the *Christology* lectures

After now having dealt with the question, *Who* is Christ?, Bonhoeffer has the courage to raise the question, *Where* is Christ? What is the place of Christ? It is in this context that Bonhoeffer reapplies the concepts of center and limit. Just as the tree of life was in the center of the garden, so the nature of person of Jesus Christ is to be in the center, both spatially and temporally:

> Where does he stand? He stands pro me. He stands there in my place (*Stelle*), where I should stand, but cannot. He stands on the boundary (*Grenze*) of my existence, yet for me. That brings out clearly that 'I' am separated from my 'I', which I should be, by a boundary that I am unable to cross. The boundary lies between me and me, the old and the new 'I'. It is in the encounter with this boundary that I shall be judged. At this place stands Christ, between me and me, the old and new existence. Thus Christ is at one and the same time, my boundary and my rediscovered centre. He is the centre, between 'I' and 'I', and between 'I' and God.[71]

Many theological topics are alluded to here. First of all we have the function of Christ as *Stellvertreter* or placeholder. Christ is standing in my place, not as a substitute, but more like Christ as the "forerunner of faith" in Hebrews 6,20. Christ is the one who is standing in and waiting for my transition into the form of Christ "beyond my existence". The term "boundary" (*Grenze*) is intentionally used in two different meanings. Anthropologically the boundary is the limit of sin that incapacitates the sinner from crossing over from the old self to the new self. But Christologically, the boundary is Christ as being both beyond my existence yet as existing for me in my place. As such the encounter with Christ is the judgment of my old self, but at the same time "the rediscovered center" facilitates my crossing over to the new self.

In the later German reconstruction from 1997 it is expressed more clearly: "Als die Grenze ist Christus zugleich mir wiedergefundene Mitte. Als Grenze kann die Grenze nur vom Jenseits der Grenze aus gesehen werden."[72] Two things are said here: First, only the boundary of Christ makes me understand my own limits; the ambiguities of sin are only unveiled in Jesus Christ. But second, Christ Himself is the re-discovered center. In short, *the revelation in Christ is the rediscovery of creation.*

Seen from the perspective of *Creation and Fall*, the tree of life planted in the center of the Garden of Eden *is* Christ. Thus, since primeval times Christ has always been standing there for me, *prior to* my transition from the old self to the new self. Christ is not only there *for* me. He is also there *before*

---

71 DBW 12, 306. Christology, 60.
72 DBW 12, 306.

me. Christ has always been standing there for me, before anybody ever noticed him or his community. By understanding re-velation as a re-discovery, the presence of Christ does not only unveil and remove the ambiguities of sin in the moment of revelation. Rather, Christ was also the hidden center in the life of the old self that did not re-cognize anything and did not understand anything. This is Bonhoeffer's ontology of Christ as the placeholder and forerunner of faith.

Because this is so, it is understandable that Bonhoeffer in his *Christology* lectures takes the step of extending the scope of his Christology into the worldly realms of creation. For Bonhoeffer can now assert that Christ is not only present in and for the community of Christians. "Christ is also our centre when he stands, in terms of our consciousness, on our periphery, also when Christian piety is displaced to the periphery of our being".[73] For Christ stands in the center, not our "I", not our consciousness, not our piety, not our church allegiance.

Therefore Bonhoeffer can also now say that Christ is "the center of history". Christ is not history, not identifiable with the failures, illusions and cruelties of history, but the Messiah, who is entering into the world of history to fulfil its promises. Likewise Christ the mediator is the "center between God and nature", because also nature (which does not need reconciliation, since it has no guilt) is in need of being freed from its dullness and lack of meaning. But in the sacraments, as means of communication, nature has meaning as mediating God and humanity. And so finally the church, the third form of Christ, is seen by Bonhoeffer as the hidden center of the state. For the church is defined as the community that responds to the address of Jesus Christ as the Word of God.[74]

7. The comprehensive Christology of *Ethics*: A Barthian solution to Bonhoeffer's problem?

The Christological position in *Christology* marks a first leap beyond the position in *Creation and Fall*. However, not until his unfinished *Ethics* did Bonhoeffer arrive at the point where he was finally able to affirm the presence of Christ in the world of creation without reservations. Christ is existing not only as community, as he had claimed in his *Sanctorum Communio*, but Christ is also existing in the world *as* the mediator between God and world. By implication, the world is never void of Christ, since Christ is the

---

73 Bonhoeffer, Christology, 60. Cf. DBW 12, 307.
74 DBW 12, 307–310. Christology, 60–64.

unity of the reality of God and the reality of creation. But this "one realm of the Christ-reality" (*Christuswirklichkeit*)[75] is not something that can be described from a neutral perspective, for the reality of Christ also involves an appeal to human participation in this reality:

> In Christ we are invited to participate in the reality of God and the reality of the world at the same time, the one not without the other. The reality of God is disclosed only as it places me completely into the reality of the world. But I find the world always already borne, accepted, and reconciled in the reality of God. That is the mystery of the revelation of God in the human being Jesus Christ. [...] What matters is *participating in the reality of God and the world in Jesus Christ today*, and doing so in such a way that I never experience the reality of God without the reality of the world, nor the reality of the world without the reality of God.[76]

Bonhoeffer is now using an imagery of intimacy, of God carrying the world (in creation and preservation), and of God accepting the world (in terms of justification) in order to be its final reconciler (in an eschatological perspective).

But again the interpreter will have to divine the exact theological meaning through an intertextual reading. The thesis I would like to propose is that Bonhoeffer here combines influences from Luther and Barth in a very telling manner. With Luther he affirms that one should never treat the human created nature of Jesus as just a cloak that is removed from Christ in ascension. This is the motif that we already noticed in *Christology*. But now Bonhoeffer also speaks of an acceptance and reconciliation of the world of creation "in the reality of God". What this means is not clear in the text itself, since it would require a Trinitarian framework in order to be worked out. Is Bonhoeffer implicitly informed by such a framework? Well one can only make a qualified guess. Between the *Christology* lectures from 1933 and the section on "Christ, Reality, and Good" from *Ethics*, written in 1940, Karl Barth's short but groundbreaking essay, *Gnadenwahl Gottes* (God's Gracious Election) had appeared in 1936.[77] Here Barth announced his new revolutionary interpretation of the doctrine of the divine election (*Erwählung*) and the covenant of grace (*Bund der Gnade*), which Barth laid out six years later, in 1942, in his opus magnum, *Church Dogmatics* II/2. It seems to me a reasonable hypothesis that Karl Barth's doctrine of election gave Bonhoeffer the courage to think of the world as already destined for creaturely fruition, for divine acceptance and for divine reconciliation (with respect to human sin) and redemption (with respect to the potentialities of nature). If this is the case, Christ as the Word of God is not only the free

---

75 DBW 6, 43. DBWE 6, 58.
76 DBW 6, 40f. DBWE 6, 55.
77 Barth, Gottes Gnadenwahl.

creator vis-à-vis the world, but also the bond of love that ontologically precedes participation in Christ of the individual believer.

In his *Ethics*, Bonhoeffer's focus is clearly on the human participation in the reality of Christ. Christ being both the center *and* the limit of Creation means that Christ is at once in the midst of worldly affairs, but is there as the self-identical One, who continues to call the creatures to attune themselves to the comprehensive reality of Christ. Construed in this way, Bonhoeffer's *Ethics* consistently transcends the contrastive thought pattern that we identified in several passages in *Creation and Fall*. Christ is not only different from the world by virtue of divine freedom, but is also different from the world by embracing the world in a self-communicating love. Accordingly, the power of Christ is no longer depicted as an overpowering of human nature, but as the empowering of human beings to become what they are destined to become: icons of Jesus Christ. In the section "Ethics as Formation" this new picture is spelled out:

God became human. That means that the form of Christ, though it certainly is and remains one and the same, intends to take form in real human beings, and thus in quite different ways. Christ does not abolish human reality in favour of an idea that demands to be realized against all that is real. Christ empowers reality, affirming it as the real human and thus the ground of all human reality.[78]

The boundaries of the church vis-à-vis the world is now only a penultimate matter, as one can see throughout the *Prison Letters*. The comprehensive reality of "Christ as community" no longer has walls, for the difference between Church and the wider society is a penultimate distinction. The Word of God continuously addresses the community of the church while constituting its limit, and the world from the outset stands under the promise of divine acceptance and reconciliation at its very center.

In this manner, the beginning and the end correspond to one another, as it was the case in *Creation and Fall*. But the beginning is no longer without a divine purpose of reconciliation, and the end is no longer the end of extermination. The new creation (*creatio nova*) is now seen as emerging out of the old creation (*creatio nova ex vetere*), for also the fallen creation is both preserved, accepted and reconciled in the comprehensive reality of Jesus Christ.

In the end of his own pilgrimage, Dietrich Bonhoeffer perhaps learned more from both Hegel and Barth than he was able to acknowledge himself. He applied the structure of Hegel's notion about the true infinity of God to his way of thinking about the universal significance of Jesus Christ. He also tacitly incorporated Karl Barth's doctrine of predestination, though under

---

78 DBW 6, 86. DBWE 6, 99.

the eschatological proviso that the world is not already fulfilled as it *is*, but as it *will be* in the end, and was *destined to be* from the beginning.[79]

Bibliography

Primary Sources

BARTH, K., *Gottes Gnadenwahl*, Theologische Existenz heute 47, München 1936.
–, *Kirchliche Dogmatik*, Vol. II/2, Zürich 1936.
–, *Kirchliche Dogmatik*, Vol. III/2, Zollikon-Zürich 1948.
BONHOEFFER, D., Sanctorum Communio. Eine dogmatische Untersuchung zur Soziologie der Kirche, Dietrich Bonhoeffer Werke, Vol. 1, ed. by J. von Soosten, München 1986 (= DBW 1).
–, Sanctorum Communio: A Theological Study of the Sociology of the Church, ed. by C.J. Green, Dietrich Bonhoeffer Works, Vol. 1, Minneapolis 1998 (= DBWE 1).
–, Schöpfung und Fall. Theologische Auslegung von Genesis 1–3, Dietrich Bonhoeffer Werke, Vol 3, ed. by M. Rüter/I. Tödt, München (1989) ²2002 (= DBW 3).
–, Creation and Fall: A Theological Exposition of Genesis 1–3, Dietrich Bonhoeffer Works, Vol. 3, ed. by John W. de Gruchy, Minneapolis 1997 (= DBWE 3).
–, Nachfolge, Dietrich Bonhoeffer Werke, Vol. 4, ed. by M. Kuske/I. Tödt, München 1989 (= DBW 4).
–, Discipleship, Dietrich Bonhoeffer Works, Vol. 4, ed. by G.B. Kelly/J.D. Godsey, Minneapolis 2001 (= DBWE 4).
–, Ethik, Dietrich Bonhoeffer Werke, Vol. 6, ed. by I. Tödt/H.E. Tödt/E. Feil/C.J.Green, München 1992 (= DBW 6).
–, Ethics, Dietrich Bonhoeffer Works, Vol. 6, ed. by C.J. Green, Minneapolis 2005 (= DBWE 6).
–, Vorlesung 'Christologie' (Nachschrift), in: Berlin 1932–1933, ed. by C. Nicolaisen/E.-A. Scharffenorth, Dietrich Bonhoeffer Werke, Vol. 12, München 1997 (= DBW 12), 279–348.
–, *Jesus Christ* and the Essence of Christianity, in: A Testament to Freedom, ed. by G.B. Kelly/F.B. Nelson, San Francisco 1990.
–, *Christologie*, in: Bonhoeffer, Gesammelte Schriften, Vol. 3, ed. by E. Bethge, München 1960, 166–242.
–, Lectures on *Christology*, transl. by Edwin Robertson, London 1981.
–, Letters and Papers from Prison, London 1971 (= LPP).
HEGEL, G.W.F., Lectures on the *Philosophy of Religion*. Volume III: The Consummate Religion [1827], ed. by P.C. Hogdson, Berkeley (1985) 1998.
LUTHER, M., *Sermon am Himmelfahrtstage*. 1523, WA 12, 552–565.

Secondary Sources

BETHGE, E., Dietrich *Bonhoeffer*. Theologe, Christ, Zeitgenosse, München (1967) ³1970.
CLASS, G., Der verzweifelte *Zugriff* auf das Leben. Dietrich Bonhoeffers Sündenverständnis in 'Schöpfung und Fall', Neukirchen-Vluyn 1994.

---

79 I wish to thank Kirsten Busch Nielsen, Peter Scott, and Christiane Tietz for helpful comments on earlier drafts of this chapter.

FEIL, E., Die *Theologie* Dietrich Bonhoeffers. Hermeneutik – Christologie – Weltverständnis, München/Mainz ²1971.

GREGERSEN, N.H., *Grace* in Nature and History. Luther's Doctrine of Creation Revisited, Dialog: A Journal of Theology 44, 2005, 19–29.

KRÖTKE, W., *Gott* und Mensch als 'Partner'. Zur Bedeutung einer zentralen Kategorie in Karl Barths Kirchlicher Dogmatik, ZThK.B 6, 1986, 158–175.

MCCORMACK, B., *Grace* and Being: The Role of God's Gracious Election in Karl Barth's Theological Ontology, in: The Cambridge Companion to Karl Barth, ed. by J. Webster, Cambridge 2000, 92–110.

NIELSEN, B.F., Die *Rationaliät* der Offenbarungstheologie. Die Struktur des Offenbarungsverständnisses von Karl Barth, Aarhus 1988.

NIELSEN, K.B., *Syndens* brudte magt. En undersøgelse af Dietrich Bonhoeffers syndsforståelse [The Broken Power of Sin: An Investigation of Dietrich Bonhoeffer's Concept of Sin] (forthcoming).

PANGRITZ, A., Karl *Barth* in the Theology of Dietrich Bonhoeffer, Grand Rapids 2000.

PANNENBERG, W., *Dogmatische Thesen* zur Lehre von der Offenbarung, in: Offenbarung als Geschichte, ed. by W. Pannenberg, Göttingen 1961, 91–114.

–, *Systematische Theologie*, Vol. 1, Göttingen 1988.

PRENTER, R., Dietrich *Bonhoeffer* and Karl Barth's Positivism of Revelation, in: World Come of Age, ed. by R.G. Smith, London 1967, 89–111.

RUMSCHEIDT, M., The *Formation* of Bonhoeffer's Theology, in: The Cambridge Companion to Dietrich Bonhoeffer, ed. by J.W. de Gruchy, Cambridge 1999, 50–70.

SCOTT, P., *Christ*, Nature, Sociality, SJTh 53, 2000, 413–430.

Christoph Schwöbel

"Religion" and "Religionlessness" in *Letters and Papers from Prison*

A Perspective for Religious Pluralism?

1. Ambiguities

The theme of "religion" and "religionlessness" has played a highly perplexing role in the discussion of Bonhoeffer's thought in theology and the churches. It was first widely discussed in connection with a reappraisal of the situation of secularism in the Western world. Bestsellers like John Robinson's *Honest to God*[1] and Paul van Buren's *The Secular Meaning of the Gospel*[2] introduced Bonhoeffer's reflection on the "non-religious interpretation" of Christianity in connection with a revisionist programme of exploring the transformations of Christian faith in a context that was seen as a situation of increasing secularity. Harvey Cox's *The Secular City*,[3] although not explicitly referring to Bonhoeffer, popularized many of the assumptions and perspectives related to Bonhoeffer's views on Christianity in a world come of age. Cox's main contention that God is just as present in the secular as in the religious realms of life reads almost like a summary of Bonhoeffer's thoughts. However, when the pendulum swung in the other direction, questioning many of the underlying assumptions concerning the irreversible trend of secularisation, Bonhoeffer also became the champion for the rediscovery of spirituality, of a new way of being religious in a world come of age. One may wonder whether the many uses of Bonhoeffer's poem "Powers of Good" in various contexts of more or less Christian spirituality could still be connected to the thoughts and reflections of the Christian theologian Dietrich Bonhoeffer. These ambiguities which could be described in far greater detail and which have occasioned a burst of interpretative energy by Bonhoeffer scholars provide a good reason for looking once again at Bonhoeffer's use of the terms "religion" and "religionless-

---

[1] 1963.
[2] 1963.
[3] 1965. The theological development of Harvey Cox mirrors the major stages of the religious history of the West in the second half of the 20th century. Cf. the succession of his works Turning; Religion; Mansions; Fire.

ness" and relating his views explicitly to our situation at the beginning of the 21st century which is described by many as a situation of religious pluralism.

2. The guiding question, the context and the method of Bonhoeffer's theological interpretation of "religion" and "religionlessness"

For anyone engaging with Bonhoeffer's theology its most characteristic feature is perhaps the fact that it is focussed on one guiding question, clearly identified in the Christology Lectures of 1933. In its classic wording from *Letters and Papers from Prison* it is the question: "Who is Jesus Christ, for us, today?" For Bonhoeffer this question summarizes the essence of Christianity and the heart of Christian theology. The whole development of Bonhoeffer's theology from *Sanctorum Communio* to the last fragments shortly before his execution may be understood as a passionate engagement with this question. The identity of Jesus Christ can be seen in this context as: the focus of Bonhoeffer's attempt at defining the nature of the Christian church, as the criterion for all statements on God's being and act, the matrix for shaping Christian life together, and as the point in which the reality of the world and the reality of God find unity in the reality of Christ. The question concerning the identity of Christ can, of course, only have this significance if it is conceived as a question concerning the personal being of Jesus Christ; that is, whatever can be said in response to the question "who?"; and if the relational structure of the "for us" can be understood as part of the ontological structure of the personal identity of Christ which also bridges and comprehends the "spaces" of time and eternity and the "realms" of God and the world. Constant attention to this question explains both the underlying continuity of Bonhoeffer's theology amid the many discontinuities and self-corrections in the elaboration of his theological thought. The changes become transparent once they are related to the guiding question which provides the integrative focus for Bonhoeffer's theology and his personal piety. Bonhoeffer's reflections on "religion" and "religionlessness" are also clearly focussed on the christological question. It is, for Bonhoeffer, a question about the identity and presence of Christ. Therefore it is highly significant that Bonhoeffer's reflections on religion are introduced by this christological question: "What is bothering me incessantly is the question what Christianity really is, or indeed who Christ really is, for us today."[4] A few lines further on in the same letter the question is phrased in

---

4   April 30, 1944. LPP, 279. Cf. DBW 8, 402. For the sake of accuracy I have not amended the non-inclusive language of the English translation.

this way: "How can Christ become the Lord of the religionless as well? Are there religionless Christians?"[5] A few months later Bonhoeffer summarizes his explorations under the heading: "[T]he claim of a world that has come of age by Jesus Christ".[6] Or again: "The question is: Christ and the world that has come of age."[7]

For Bonhoeffer this question is placed in the context of a general assessment and evaluation of the cultural development in the West since the thirteenth century. Bonhoeffer offers in many places in his letters a complex and multi-dimensional genealogy of the present as the stage in history where the world has come of age. The engagement with this topic seems to start with reading Adolf von Harnack's history of the Royal Prussian Academy of Science at the beginning of 1944 which provokes many observations of the changes in the understanding of humanity. It is continued with reading Wilhelm Dilthey's *Weltanschauung und Analyse des Menschen seit der Reformation* which becomes one of the key works for Bonhoeffer's inquiry into the factors that have shaped the situation of modernity. Whatever Bonhoeffer read during that time, whether historiography, history of art or novels, it was related to that topic. Carl Friedrich von Weizsäcker's book *Das Weltbild der Physik* completes the interpretation of this development from the perspective of the natural sciences. In all these different variations Bonhoeffer is concerned to understand the genealogy of the present and to identify the factors in various spheres of culture that have contributed to the situation of religionlessness. However, this is not just an engagement with the history of ideas and the social effects. For Bonhoeffer this investigation is part of the theologians's task to respond to the question "Who is Jesus Christ for us today?" The present is for him not merely a historical category but it is a theological, more precisely, a christological category. The present is the way in which God, in which the living Lord confronts us today. The historical genealogy is therefore the background for understanding what it means to say that Jesus Christ is the same for us – yesterday and today. Understanding the process of taking leave of God in the history of the West is part of the task of understanding the presence of God in Christ in a world that does not need to refer to God in order to interpret itself.

The theological criteria which Bonhoeffer applies for the diagnosis of the cultural situation are derived from a re-lecture of Scripture, especially of the Old Testament. Although Bonhoeffer was a systematic theologian by profession, albeit one who had contemplated starting his academic career in

---

5   LPP, 280. DBW 8, 404.
6   LPP, 342. DBW 8, 504.
7   June 8, 1944. LPP, 327. DBW 8, 479.

church history, he is very much a biblical theologian. At all turning points of the development of his theological thought referring back to the biblical text plays a crucial role. It is no accident that the attempt at diagnosing the ills of Christianity's religious response to the advent of modernity is accompanied by an intense re-reading of the Old Testament. The Old Testament becomes for Bonhoeffer a primary diagnostic tool. "Unlike the other oriental religions, the faith of the Old Testament isn't a religion of redemption", Bonhoeffer states.[8] He insists that redemption in the Old Testament has to be understood historically so that the people of Israel can live before God on earth. In this connection, Bonhoeffer rejects an understanding of the resurrection which is based on the myths of redemption and focusses on a life after death.

> The difference between the Christian hope of resurrection and the mythological hope is that the former sends a man back to his life on earth in a wholly new way which is even more sharply defined than it is in the Old Testament.[9]

The Old Testament appears as the hermeneutical key for an understanding of the New Testament which rejects all tendencies towards spiritualization. The Old Testament does not recognize a distinction between the internal life and the external life, it does not permit us to separate between the individual and the social, between bodily life and spiritual and in this way it forces us to take the Incarnation seriously.[10] From the perspective of such a hermeneutics, to interpret the biblical writings non-religiously means to interpret them holistically, both with regard to God's relationship to the whole of reality and with regard to the totality of human life, integrating all dimensions of life into a multi-dimensional whole.

3. A world come of age

In the course of his attempt at understanding the present situation by sketching its genealogy and analysing the factors that have come to fruition in it, Bonhoeffer presents the whole development in the West as a process which is directed towards realizing the "autonomy of man".[11] Bonhoeffer defines

---

8   June 27, 1944. LPP, 336. DBW 8, 500.
9   LPP, 336f. DBW 8, 500.
10 On May 5, 1944, Bonhoeffer can describe the agenda for interpretation in the following way: "I'm thinking about how we can interpret in a 'worldly' sense – in the sense of the Old Testament and of John 1,14 – concepts of repentance, faith, justification, rebirth, and sanctification" (LPP, 286f. DBW 8, 216).
11 June 8, 1944. LPP, 325. DBW 8, 476.

"autonomy" quite literally as "the discovery of the laws by which the world lives and deals with itself in science, social and political matters, art, ethics, and religion".[12] The overall result which has, according to Bonhoeffer, had an "undoubted completeness" in his time can be summarized as follows: "Man has learnt to deal with himself in all questions of importance without recourse to the 'working hypothesis' called 'God'". This is the cumulative effect of different but related developments which Bonhoeffer traces in different spheres of culture and which he therefore understands as "one great development that leads to the world's autonomy".[13] Taking most of his material from Dilthey's description of this process, Bonhoeffer refers to Herbert of Cherbury and his thesis that reason is a sufficient source of knowledge in matters of theology and cites Bodin and Montaigne as representatives of a view which replaces the commandments with "rules of life". The detachment of politics from morality, programmatically proposed by Machiavelli, is for him another indicator of this process. He finds a similar emphasis, though based on a different understanding of politics, in Hugo Grotius' maxim that the validity of natural law must be established "etsi deus non daretur". The net result of this process is reached according to Bonhoeffer in Descartes' deism which he interprets (historically hardly correct) as the mechanistic understanding of the world which functions without divine intervention and in Spinoza's pantheism which Bonhoeffer sees as proclaiming the identity of God and nature. Kant he sees as following the "deism" of Descartes, while Fichte and Hegel he interprets as pantheists. In the natural sciences he sees the development towards autonomy beginning with Nicolas Cusanus' and Giordano Bruno's thesis that world is infinite which – although it has again become questionable in modern physics as Bonhoeffer knew from his reading of Carl Friedrich v. Weizsäcker – indicates that the physical world has to be understood by its immanent regularities which do not accept any reference to God as causal factor in the network of worldly causes.[14]

This process which leads to the situation of a world come of age is, however, only the background for the theological point Bonhoeffer wants to make. Bonhoeffer does not believe in historical developments as having an inherent necessity. He therefore would have been sceptical about interpretations of secularisation as an irreversible process which has its own intrinsic inevitability. In an earlier letter he explicitly addresses the problem. In this

---

12 LPP, 325. DBW 8, 476.
13 July 16, 1944. LPP, 359. DBW 8, 530.
14 Weizsäcker, Weltbild. The German edition of *Widerstand und Ergebung* in DBW 8 (526–538) documents in footnotes Bonhoeffer's reliance on Dilthey's view of the development with regard to philosophy and the humanities and his dependence on Carl Friedrich von Weizsäcker's book on the "world-view" of physics.

connection he distinguishes the "worldliness" of the thirteenth century from the "emancipated" worldliness which establishes itself in the Renaissance. The worldliness which he perceives in the thirteenth century he sees as "not 'emancipated', but 'Christian', even if it is anticlerical".[15] In connection with these observations Bonhoeffer offers a number of interesting reflections on the understanding of history. He criticizes the view of a historical *continuum* based on the views of Leopold von Ranke and Hans Delbrück which he sees as rooted in Hegel's philosophy: "The idea of the historical *continuum* goes back to Hegel, who sees the whole course of history as culminating in 'modern times' – i.e. in his own system of philosophy."[16] In contrast to this view Bonhoeffer expresses some sympathy for Spengler's view of cultural phases as self-contained cycles, although he criticizes it for the biological character of this morphology. In contrast to the idealistic view of the continuum of history he refers to von Ranke's famous dictum that every age is "immediate to God" as an important corrective of developmental schemes: "that assertion *might* have supplied a corrective of the whole conception of the *continuum* of development, but it didn't do so".[17] Because of these doubts concerning an intrinsic logic of historical development, Bonhoeffer states as a preliminary rule for the interpretation of history: "Until we can see further into it, it will be as well to base our attitude to the past not on a general concept of history, but solely on *facts* and *achievements*."[18] This denial of an immanent continuum of history implied in a general concept of history paves the way for the theological interpretation of the situation of a world come of age. The situation of a world come of age is the situation in which God wants to be encountered by us.

[W]e cannot be honest unless we recognize that we have to live in the world *etsi deus non daretur*. And this is just what we do recognize – before God! God himself compels us to recognize it. So our coming of age leads us to a true recognition of our situation before God. God would have us know that we must live as men who manage our lives without him. The God who is with us is the God who forsakes us (Mark 15,34). The God who lets us live in the world without the working hypothesis of God is the God before whom we stand continually. Before God and with God we live without God. God lets himself be pushed out of the world on to the cross. He is weak and powerless in the world, and that is precisely the way, the only way, in which he is with us and helps us. Matt. 8,17 makes it quite clear that Christ helps us, not by virtue of his omnipotence, but by virtue of his weakness and suffering.[19]

---

15 March 9, 1944. LPP, 229. DBW 8, 353.
16 LPP, 230. DBW 8, 354.
17 LPP, 230. DBW 8, 354.
18 LPP, 230. DBW 8, 354.
19 July 16, 1944. LPP, 360f, DBW 8, 533f.

The situation of a world come of age is therefore according to Bonhoeffer only grasped correctly if it is interpreted theologically – and theologically means for Bonhoeffer christologically.

4. "Religion" – the critique of theological escape routes from our situation

Bonhoeffer's employment of the term "religion" has to be seen in the context of a description of a world come of age. For Bonhoeffer it is not a general concept which he would apply to the world's religions or to an intrinsic dimension of human nature. Rather, the term summarizes a contingent cluster of features which characterize the response of theology and the church to the situation of a world come of age. Bonhoeffer does not offer a definition of religion, rather he lists a number of aspects which, if interpreted theologically, display a certain Wittgensteinian family resemblance. This way of speaking of "religion" criticizes a phenomenon within Christian theology and the church and is only occasionally applied to other religions.[20]

The different features of Bonhoeffer's sketch of "religion" can be related to different aspects of the theological task. They can be summarized as follows:

a) In the "religious" understanding *faith* is a specialized act. "The 'religious act' is always something partial", Bonhoeffer writes and contrasts it in this way to the Christian understanding of faith.[21] Faith as understood in the religious sense becomes in this way a privileged, but only partial dimension of human life and of reality.

b) Epistemologically, religion places knowledge of God at the boundaries of our knowledge of the world. God is used "as a stop-gap for the incompleteness of our knowledge".[22] Bonhoeffer states the principle of "religious knowledge" with unambiguous clarity: "Religious people speak of

---

20   One of the surprising instances where Bonhoeffer writes about other religions is in the context of his reading of Walter F. Otto's *Die Götter Griechenlands* (1929) about which he reports on June 21, 1944: "I'm at present reading the quite outstanding book by W.F. Otto, the classics man from Königsberg, *The Gods of Greece*. To quote from his closing words, it's about 'this world of faith, which sprang from the wealth and depth of human existence, not from its cares and longings'. Can you understand my finding something very attractive in this theme and its treatment, and also – *horribile dictu* – my finding these gods, when they are so treated, less offensive than certain brands of Christianity? In fact, that I almost think I could claim these gods for Christ? The book is most helpful for my present theological reflections." (LPP, 333. DBW 8, 492).
21   July 18, 1944. LPP, 362. DBW 8, 537.
22   May 29, 1944. LPP, 311. DBW 8, 454.

God when human knowledge (perhaps simply because they are too lazy to think) has come to an end, or when human resources fail".[23] And even more pointedly, one can grasp his view of "religious" knowledge from the negative assertion: "God's 'beyond' is not the beyond of our cognitive faculties."[24] Religious knowledge is therefore placed at the boundaries of our ordinary worldly knowledge, and religious experiences are located in the limitations of human existence, most notably in connection with death.

c) Theologically, "religion" places God in the gaps of human knowledge of the world. It defends "an abstract belief in God, in his omnipotence etc." The religious relationship to God is, according to Bonhoeffer, "a relationship to the highest, most powerful and best Being imaginable"[25] who – for religious people – appears as *deus ex machina* from his other-worldly transcendence "either for the apparent solution of insoluble problem, or as strength in human failure".[26]

d) Anthropologically, "religion" focuses on the boundaries of the human condition, on human weakness and human failure in order to establish a basis for the "religious" dimension. Humans are "religiously" addressed as sinners when their weaknesses have been exposed and in this dimension of human interiority is the place where God can find his domain.[27]

e) Soteriologically, "religion" focuses on personal redemption and conceives of salvation individualistically. Salvation is in this view placed "on the far side of the boundary drawn by death".[28] "Redemption now means redemption from cares, distress, fears, and longings, from sin and death, in a world beyond the grave."[29]

f) Ecclesiologically, "religion" defines the role of the church as a specialized religious institution over against society and makes self-preservation the primary aim of the life of the church.[30]

We can see from this description that Bonhoeffer gives of "religion" in its different dimensions that "religion" is for Bonhoeffer a critical evaluative term for assessing the misguided response of theology and the church

---

23 May 30, 1944. LPP, 281. DBW 8, 407.
24 LPP, 282. DBW 8, 408.
25 Outline of a Book. LPP, 381. DBW 8, 558.
26 April 30, 1944. LPP, 281f. DBW 8, 407.
27 "First it is thought that a man can be addressed as a sinner only after his weakness and meanness have been spied out. Secondly, it is thought that Man's essential nature consists of his inmost and most intimate background; that is defined as his 'inner life', and it is precisely in those secret human places that God is to have his domain." (July 8, 1944. LPP, 345. DBW 8, 510f).
28 June 27, 1944. LPP, 336. DBW 8, 500.
29 LPP, 336. DBW 8, 500.
30 "Our church, which has been fighting in these years only for its self-preservation, as though that were an end in itself, is incapable of taking the word of reconciliation and redemption to mankind and the world." (Thoughts on the Day of the Baptism of D.W.R. Bethge, May 1944. LPP, 300. DBW 8, 345).

to the situation of increasing autonomy of human beings. For Bonhoeffer, the contrast of this "religious" form of crisis management with the biblical message, if one reads it christologically through the eyes of a hermeneutic gained from the engagement with the Old Testament, makes it clear that "religion" is not a name for a "religious apriori" which is given with human nature. Christianity can then not be understood as a specific difference of the general concept of religion. This is what the advent of the situation of a world come of age reveals: There is no religious a priori, and religion is not given with the essence of what it means to be human so that Christianity could be its contingent expression. Rather, it is the other way around: "Religion" is a transitory and contingent expression of the "essence" of Christianity which is nothing other: or rather nobody else than Jesus Christ himself. Bonhoeffer expresses his thesis in the form of a question:

> 'Christianity' has always been a form – perhaps the true form – of 'religion'. But if one day it becomes clear that this *a priori* does not exist at all, but was a historically conditioned and transient form of human self-expression, and if therefore man becomes radically religionless – and I think that that is already more or less the case – what does that mean for 'Christianity'?

This is exactly what the situation of the world come of age seems to indicate. With the full realization of human autonomy in all dimensions of life and spheres of reality the hypothesis of the religious apriori seems to have been falsified. For Christianity this raises the crucial question: "If religion is only a garment of Christianity – and even this garment has looked very different at different times – then what is religionless Christianity?"[31] Christianity – this is Bonhoeffer's assumption – has outgrown its "religious" garment when humanity came of age. This situation leaves no "religious" escape routes open.

5. "Religionlessness": description and programme

The term "religionlessness" which Bonhoeffer employs frequently in his letters has a two-fold function. On the one hand, it summarizes the cumulative effect of the tendencies towards autonomy in all spheres of culture in which religious interpretations and explanations have been replaced by the laws by which the world "lives and deals with itself".[32] In view of the radical nature of this development Bonhoeffer sees the responses of the theol-

---

31 April 30, 1944. LPP, 280. DBW 8, 403f.
32 June 8, 1944, LPP, 325. DBW 8, 476.

ogy of his time as deficient. In Bonhoeffer's view, Bultmann's strategy of demythologization "didn't go far enough": "You can't, as Bultmann supposes, separate God and miracle, but you must be able to interpret and proclaim both in a 'non-religious' sense."[33] Barth has for Bonhoeffer the distinction of understanding the criticism of religion as a theological task. However, in Bonhoeffer's view he replaces religion by a

> positivist doctrine of revelation which says, in effect, 'Like it or lump it': virgin birth, Trinity, or anything else; each is an equally significant and necessary part of the whole, which must simply be swallowed as a whole or not at all. That isn't biblical.[34]

Bonhoeffer's criticism of Barth seems to be that Barth sets up a dualistic strategy by positing the revelation over against the world, interpreting "revelation" as the sum of all Christian doctrines and confronting the world with the demand to accept it.

> The positivism of revelation makes it too easy for itself, by setting up, as it does in the last analysis, a law of faith, and so mutilates what is – by Christ's incarnation! – a gift for us. In the place of religion there now stands the church – that is in itself biblical – but the world is in some degrees made to depend on itself and left to its own devices and that's the mistake.[35]

This criticism has a number of connected aspects. First of all, the dualism of revelation and the world falsifies the unity of reality in Christ, in whom humanity and divinity, the world and God form a personal reality. To make the world depend on itself is, in effect, a denial of the Incarnation. It accepts the religionless self-interpretation of a world come of age as godlessness. This dualism furthermore includes that the way in which God relates to the world in Christ is replaced by a demand, obscuring the character of the Incarnation as a gratuitous gift. In this context Bonhoeffer makes the mysterious assertion: "There are degrees of knowledge and degrees of significance; that means that a secret discipline must be restored whereby the *mysteries* of the Christian faith are protected against profanation."[36] The profanation occurs where – against the truth of the Incarnation – Christian faith is posited against the world and where it is presented as a whole which must be accepted as a whole. That turns the gospel into law, and the gift into a demand. The mystery has become subject to profanation. The reference to degrees of knowledge and significance seems to point to the fact that the concepts of Christ faith must be grasped at the point and in the way in which the gift is given: in the presence of God in the incarnate Christ in

---

33 May 5, 1955. LPP, 285. DBW 8, 414.
34 LPP, 286. DBW 8, 415.
35 LPP, 286. DBW 8, 416.
36 LPP, 286. DBW 8, 415.

the midst of worldly reality. Therefore there is a way of faith, a pilgrimage, which retraces the steps God took to establish communion with the world in the incarnate Christ. This seems to be what Bonhoeffer means in the concluding sentence of this argument: "I'm thinking about how we can reinterpret in a 'worldly' sense – in the sense of the Old Testament and of John 1,14 – the concepts of repentance, faith, justification, and sanctification."[37] Here is the point where "religionlessness" is no longer a descriptive concept but becomes a programmatic concept for the reconceptualization of Christian faith in religionless, worldly terms.

6. "Religionless Christianity"

In *Letters and Papers from Prison* Bonhoeffer's analysis of the situation of his time as one of religionlessness is from the beginning accompanied by questions how the Christian gospel can be communicated in this situation:

What do a church, a community, a sermon, a liturgy, a Christian life mean in a religionless world? How do we speak of God – without religion, i.e. without the temporally conditioned presuppositions of metaphysics, inwardness, and so on?[38]

For Bonhoeffer this is a radical question, comparable only to the Pauline turn towards the missionizing of gentiles. Just as circumcision was no longer regarded as a condition for being justified, so for Bonhoeffer's time it has become clear that "religion" is no longer the condition for being justified. Religionless Christianity is therefore the life of faith that is lived in the "freedom from religion".[39]

We can try to set out the different dimensions of religionless Christianity in parallel to the different aspects of Bonhoeffer's understanding of "religion" which we have outlined above. If we take Bonhoeffer's guiding question "Who is Jesus Christ for us today?" seriously and try to follow his method of a retrieval of the core concepts of Christian faith from the interpretation of Scripture, then these dimensions must comprise both the modes of God's presence in Christ in a religionless world and the modes of response enabled and empowered by God's presence in Christ.

a) If the identity of Jesus Christ defines the identity of Christianity, the Christian faith must be understood as faith in Christ – also in the situation of religionlessness. Faith, for Bonhoeffer, is essentially metanoia, "not in

---

37 LPP, 286. DBW 8, 416.
38 April 30, 1944. LPP, 280. DBW 8, 405.
39 LPP, 281. DBW 8, 306.

the first place thinking about one's own needs, problems, sins, and fears, but allowing oneself to be caught up in the way of Jesus Christ, in the messianic event".[40] A little later in the same letter Bonhoeffer states the character of the messianic event more precisely. It is "being caught up into the messianic sufferings of God in Jesus Christ".[41] Bonhoeffer illustrates this with a wealth of material from the New Testament which supports his thesis that all the different examples he refers to have one thing in common: "The only thing that is common to all these is sharing in the suffering of God in Christ. That is their 'faith'."[42] However, the different biblical examples indicate that this faith, as being caught up in the suffering of God in Christ, is a comprehensive relationship, comprising all dimensions of life, both the worldly and the divine because they are one in Christ. In contrast to the religious act which is always partial: "'[F]aith' is something whole, involving the whole of one's life. Jesus calls men, not to a new religion, but to life."[43] This understanding of faith transcends the boundaries of the religious and the secular, having a participatory character as the conformitas Christi which is passively constituted, since Christ creates it in us.

To be a Christian does not mean to be religious in a particular way, to make something of oneself (a sinner, a penitent or a saint) on the basis of some method or other, but to be a man – not a type of man, but the man Christ creates in us. It is not the religious act that makes the Christian, but participation in the sufferings of God in the secular life.[44]

---

40 July 18, 1944. LPP, 361f. DBW 8, 536.
41 LPP, 362. DBW 8, 536.
42 LPP, 362. DBW 8, 537.
43 LPP, 362. DBW 8, 537.
44 LPP, 361. DBW 8, 535. This understanding of faith characterizes a significant change in Bonhoeffer's theology which he comments upon in the letter from July 21, 1944: "I remember a conversation that I had in America thirteen years ago with a young French pastor. We were asking ourselves quite simply what we wanted to do with our lives. He said he would like to become a saint (and I think it's quite likely that he did become one). At the time I was very impressed, but I disagreed with him, and said, in effect, that I should learn to have faith. For a long time I didn't realize the depth of the contrast. I thought I acquire faith by trying to live a holy life, or as something like it. I suppose I wrote *The Cost of Discipleship* as the end of that path. Today I can see the dangers of that book, though I still stand by what I wrote.

I discovered later, and I'm still discovering right up to this moment, that it is only by living completely in this world that one learns to have faith. One must abandon any attempt to make something of oneself, whether it be a saint, or a converted sinner, or a churchman (a so-called priestly type!), a righteous man or an unrighteous one, a sick man or a healthy one. By this-worldliness I mean living unreservedly in Life's duties, problems, successes and failures, experiences and perplexities. In so doing we throw ourselves completely into the arms of God, taking seriously, not our own sufferings, but those of God in the world – watching with Christ in Gethsemane. That, I think, is faith [...]" (LPP, 369f. DBW 8, 541f). It is interesting that this understanding of faith underlines Bonhoeffer's appreciation of Luther: "I think Luther lived a this-worldly life in this sense." (LPP, 369. DBW 8, 541).

b) Epistemologically, religionless Christianity is an attempt to locate knowledge of God not on the boundaries of human experience and knowledge but at the centre. This implies not attempting to link the knowledge of faith to situations of failure and weakness where humans experience their limitations but to establish experiences of success, of happiness as the point of contact of knowledge of God.

> I should like to speak of God not on the boundaries but at the centre; not in weaknesses but in strength; and therefore not in death and guilt but in man's life and goodness. As to the boundaries, it seems to me better to be silent and leave the insoluble unsolved. Belief in the resurrection is *not* the 'solution' of the problem of death [...] The transcendence of epistemological theory has nothing to do with the transcendence of God.[45]

c) This epistemological reorientation which is not focussed on the limiting conditions of human knowledge as the foundation for *knowledge of God* is based on a new perception of the "place" of God in relation to the world. God is located in the totality of life, including those experiences in the situation of religionlessness where God seems to be pushed out of the world. Bonhoeffer interprets this experience christologically as God's presence for the world in his suffering. The references to the suffering of God are therefore strictly christological references to the death of Christ on the cross which completes the incarnation. After the demise of the "religious" conception of the "other-worldly" transcendence of God, the "this-worldly" transcendence of God is disclosed. The new paradigm for transcendence which overcomes the "spatial" notion of God's transcendence is the transcendence of another person. God's transcendence is his unconditional being there for others as it is manifested in Christ.

> God lets himself be pushed out of the world on to the cross. He is weak and powerless in the world, and that is precisely the way, the only way, in which he is with us and helps us. Matt. 8,17 makes it quite clear that Christ helps us, not by virtue of his omnipotence [...] The Bible directs man to God's powerlessness and suffering; only the suffering God can help. To that extent we may say that the development towards the world's coming of age outlined above, which has done away with a false conception of God, opens up a way of seeing the God of the Bible, who wins power and space in the world by his weakness.[46]

The *Outline for a Book* expounds the revision in the understanding of God's transcendence most clearly in pointed catch-phrases:

> Who is God? Not in the first place an abstract belief in God, in his omnipotence etc. That is not a genuine experience of God, but a partial extension of the world. Encoun-

---

45 April 30, 1944. LPP, 282. DBW 8, 408.
46 July 18, 1944. LPP, 361. DBW 8, 534f.

ter with Jesus Christ. The experience of the transformation of all human life is given in the fact that 'Jesus is there only for others'. His 'being there for others' is the experience of transcendence. It is only this 'being there for others' maintained till death, that is the ground of his omnipotence, omniscience, and omnipresence. Faith is the participation in this being of Jesus (incarnation, cross, and resurrection). Our relation to God is not a 'religious' relationship to the highest, most powerful, and best Being imaginable – that is not authentic transcendence – but our relation to God is a new life in 'existence for others', through participation in the being of Jesus. The transcendence is not infinite and unattainable tasks, but the neighbour who is within reach in any given situation.[47]

"Being there for others" as the paradigm for God's transcendence which is disclosed in participation in Christ's life, death and resurrection implies that God is not only intermittently present like the *deus ex machina* who intervenes in extraordinary ways in a situation where he is not ordinarily present. Paradoxically, the situation of religionlessness, if it is interpreted theologically, as the situation of God being pushed out of the world on to the cross is the situation of God's continuous presence in the world. Similarly, God is not the solution to human problems or the strength in situations of failure and weakness, God's presence is gratuitous, not dependent on the failure of human life. If God's transcendence is disclosed in Christ's being-there-for-others it directs Christians to the "this-worldly" sphere as the place of the encounter with God.

d) Anthropologically, religionless Christianity therefore includes an appreciation of human life not in its weak moments and limitations but in the situations of strength and courage. The participation of God in human life which is the centre of Jesus' ontological and not just ethical "being-there-for-others" excludes a negative anthropology that is eager to exploit human weakness and failure. Religionless Christianity implies an affirmation of dignity of human life, also in its dimensions of worldliness. Since *propter Christum* God is present in the totality of life, human sin and weakness does not have to be theologically exploited. Bonhoeffer therefore castigates a theological apologetics that relates parasitically to human weakness and suffering and relentlessly exposes the "'clerical' sniffing-around-after people's-sins in order to catch them out", even in the forms of psychotherapy and existentialist philosophy.[48] This concentration on human weakness and its passion to expose the innermost perversion of humans contrasts for Bonhoeffer sharply with the Bible's engagement with the totality of human existence and with Jesus' relationship to people.

---

47   LPP, 381. DBW 8, 558.
48   July 8, 1944. LPP, 345. DBW 8, 510.

When Jesus blessed sinners, they were real sinners, but Jesus did not make everyone a sinner first. He called them away from their sin, not into their sin. It is true that encounter with Jesus meant the reversal of all human values. So it was in the conversion of Paul, though in his case the encounter with Jesus preceded the realization of sin [...] Never did he [Jesus] question a man's health, vigour, or happiness, regarded in themselves, or regard them as evil fruits; else why should he heal the sick and restore strength to the weak? Jesus claims for himself and the Kingdom of God the whole of human life in all its manifestations.[49]

e) Soteriologically, religionless Christianity is not focussed on the question of personal salvation which is intrinsically tied up with being "religious" in Bonhoeffer's sense. With the demise of "religion" the communal, historical, integrative dimensions of redemption can be rediscovered from the biblical sources. Salvation is no longer concerned but "with this world as created and preserved, subjected to laws, reconciled and restored".[50]

Hasn't the individualistic question about personal salvation almost completely left us all? Aren't we really under the impression that there are more important things than that question (perhaps not more important than the *matter* itself but more important than the *question*!)? I know it sounds pretty monstrous to say that. But fundamentally, isn't this in fact biblical?[51]

f) With regard to the *church* Bonhoeffer is concerned to show that religionless Christianity requires a new mode of existence for the church which allows it to be reshaped by the conformitas Christi, by his being-there-for-others as the core of its own existence. Here Bonhoeffer's proposals are perhaps the most radical, and – one has to say – the most unrealistic, perhaps even unworldly.

The church is the church only when it exists for others. To make a start, it should give away all its property to those in need. The clergy must live solely on the free-will offerings of their congregations, or possibly engage in some secular calling. The church must share in the secular problems of ordinary human life, not dominating but helping and serving. It must tell men of every calling what it means to live in Christ, to exist for others. In particular, our own church will have to take the field against the view of *hubris*, power-worship, envy and humbug, as the roots of all evil. It will have to speak of moderation, purity, trust, loyalty, constancy, patience, humility, contentment, and modesty. It must not under-estimate the importance of human example (which has its origin in the humanity of Jesus and is so important in Christ's teaching); it is not abstract argument, but example that gives its word emphasis and power.[52]

---

49 June 30, 1944. LPP, 341f. DBW 8, 504.
50 May 5, 1944. LPP, 286. DBW 8, 415.
51 LPP, 286. DBW 8, 415.
52 *Outline for a Book*. LPP, 382. DBW 8, 56. Even if this invites the criticism of clericalism I should like to take note of my disagreement with Bonhoeffer at this point. Although one has to admire the radical character of Bonhoeffer's suggestions, which may to some extent be fuelled by

Outlining the basic dimensions of "religionless Christianity" nevertheless still leaves open the question how the fundamental dimension of faith as participating in the pattern of Christ's existence is to be integrated with participating in the worldly dimensions of life. This task of integration which should also prevent a sectarian mode of existence for the church which would inhibit its calling of being-there-for-others in witness and service is by Bonhoeffer presented in the image of a polyphonic harmony of the different dimensions of life. Bonhoeffer raises the question with regard to the integration of what he calls a "strong, erotic love" into the pattern of the Christian's love of God.[53] He develops this theme of the "polyphony of life" in the following way:

> What I mean is that God wants us to love him eternally with our whole hearts – not in such a way as to injure or weaken our earthly love, but to provide a kind of *cantus firmus* to which the other melodies of life provide the counterpoint.[54]

After stressing the significance of the inclusion of the Song of Songs in the Bible – a recurrent theme in *Letters and Papers* – Bonhoeffer goes on to

---

his disappointment with the German churches during the time of the National Socialist régime and his discontentment with the theology and the church politics of the Confessing Church, it nevertheless seems questionable whether this programme for church reform is in accordance with the theological foundations that Bonhoeffer laid down in his reflections on the character of faith and Christian life in a religionless world. Would it not be necessary to emphasize that Bonhoeffer's view of faith as "allowing oneself to be caught up in the messianic suffering of God in Jesus Christ" (LPP, 362. DBW 8, 536) as *conformitas Christi* requires institutions of the proclamation of the Gospel in word and sacrament which have their core in the celebration of the ongoing community with Christ and the participation in his "being-there-for-others"? In view of the significance Bonhoeffer attaches to sacramental communion in his poem "Christians and Pagans" ("[...] Feeds body and spirit with his bread", LPP, 349. DBW 8, 516) the omission of the constitution of the church through the celebration of the presence of Christ in word and sacrament in his proposal for church reform is astonishing. Would such institutions not also require a community life whose modes of interaction correspond to the message this community proclaims? And furthermore, would the existence of the church in a world that has come of age not also require to maintain an institutional structure as modes of interaction with an institutionally organized society so that the church does not become a religiously specialized counter-culture pitted against the culture of the world? Would not stressing the function of a praxis of witness, also in communal and institutional structures, be more in keeping with Bonhoeffer's views than the rather individualistic example of personal virtues Bonhoeffer suggests? To put it quite sharply: Is Bonhoeffer not in danger of committing a similar mistake to the one he accused Barth of, i.e. positing a "law of faith", only that here the danger seems to be that of positing a "law of discipleship"? I put these questions so bluntly, because it seems to me that a purely ethical (mis)understanding of Bonhoeffer's formula of "being-there-for-others" cuts off the sources of discipleship and has done much to undermine the seriousness of Bonhoeffer's challenge to today's theology and the church.

53 May 20, 1944. LPP, 303. DBW 8, 440.
54 LPP, 303. DBW 8, 440. In the preceding sentence the English translation has a typographical error which obscures the meaning of the sentence. It should read: "There's always a danger in all strong, erotic love that one may lose [not: love] what I might call the polyphony of life." (LPP, 303).

extend this to the question of polyphonic integration of the life of faith by pointing to the christological paradigm of the Chalcedonian Definition:

> Where the *cantus firmus* is clear and plain, the counterpoint can be developed to its limits. The two are 'undivided yet distinct' in the words of the Chalcedonian Definition, like Christ in his divine and human natures. May not the attraction and importance of polyphony in music consist in its being a musical reflection of this Christological fact and therefore of our *vita christiana*?[55]

The importance of this musical analogy lies in the fact that the christological paradigm does not just underline the significance of the dimension of faith, of love of God, but serves as a model for the integration of all dimensions which have their "full independence" when they are related to the cantus firmus. The christological matrix thereby also becomes the matrix for Christian life in a religionless situation, for a life that can appreciate and participate in the worldly dimensions in their full independence and yet in their complete relation to the dimension of faith. The fuller the life of faith is developed, the fuller can all other dimensions of life be polyphonically integrated in their relative independence. This is the model for the *vita christiana* in a world come of age.

7. Religious pluralism – aspects of a perplexing phenomenon

We have so far tried to give a brief sketch of Bonhoeffer's use of the concept of "religion" and of the theological perspectives he develops under the heading of a religionless Christianity. Anyone reading Bonhoeffer's reflections on the rise of an age of religionlessness cannot miss the fact that in the last sixty years things have changed considerably. Bonhoeffer could not foresee that the situation of a world come of age has provided ideal conditions for a renaissance of the religious interests in a perplexing pluralism of phenomena. It is important to note that this resurgence of religious interests occurred against the background which Bonhoeffer described as the rise of the autonomy of humanity in the various spheres of culture. This development does not falsify Bonhoeffer's analysis. It seems to be the case that the developments which he reflected have had consequences and implications which he could not foresee but which are intrinsically connected to the rise of "religionlessness" as he described it. The revitalisation of religious sensibilities – that is an assumption shared by most interpreters of the situation – occurs against a background of strong tendencies towards secularisation in

---

55 LPP, 303. DBW 8, 331.

many societies. Therefore terms like the "return of religion" or the "renaissance of religious interests" or the "revitalisation of religious sensibilities" are only partially correct. Religion, religious interests and religious sensibilities do not return in a form they had in the past, they appear in new variations on the scene which cannot simply be understood as a revival of religion after it had been seemingly dead during a phase of consistent secularisation. However, the pluriform phenomena of post-secular religiosity show clearly that those forms of secularization theories which predicted that secularization would be a global, uniform and irreversible phenomenon involving all spheres of culture have been proved wrong.[56] A new assessment of the situation is required.

A theology that follows Bonhoeffer's inspirations in reading the "signs of the times" and in seeing the theological diagnosis of the religious situation as a central element of the theological task cannot simply repeat Bonhoeffer's diagnosis of *his* time and apply it to *our* time as if nothing had changed. Rather, it seems to be much more in keeping with the spirit of Bonhoeffer's theology to attempt a careful description of the phenomena and to try to assess them theologically. That this is a genuinely theological task which will nevertheless have to be carried out in conversation with historians, sociologists and other representatives from the humanities (and increasingly) from the sciences is an essential part of Bonhoeffer's legacy.

While Bonhoeffer could still detect a common effect of the various developments which he summarized in the metaphor of humanity "coming of age" and described as a process of achieving autonomy, the post-secular revival of religion cannot be seen as a unitary phenomenon. The resurgence of religious interests has an irreducibly pluralistic character. Understanding the religious situation of the times as a situation of religious and ideological pluralism seems to be the most appropriate description of the situation.[57] If one looks a little more carefully at the situation it seems that pluralism is to a large extent a result of secularization. If secularization is understood as the process whereby realms of life and spheres of culture which were formerly integrated within a religious system of meaning, represented by religious institutions and their representatives, are interpreted as secular this does not only imply that these realms of life and spheres of culture are now to be understood according to their own laws and regularities but also that the authority of interpretation is no longer represented by a religious institution. The drive towards autonomy does not only involve different spheres of culture but also affects the people who are involved in this process. Autonomy becomes both a social and a personal phenomenon. The ethos of

---

56 Cf. Berger, Desecularization.
57 Cf. Schwöbel, Pluralismus; Schwöbel, Glaube.

autonomy necessarily involves an element of choice. Consistent secularisation makes choice universal, and in this sense one can say: secularization pluralizes, more precisely: secularization pluralizes choices. This is the element which continues even after the process of secularization has lost its momentum. Even in a post-secular situation the element of choice, based on the notion of personal autonomy, remains. The return of religious interest is therefore not a return towards a situation in which social custom defines adherence to religious beliefs and communities but continues the element of choice. Even if people decide to follow religious movements which deny the notion of autonomy (like various forms of fundamentalism), they nevertheless decide for heteronomy on the basis of autonomous choices.

Post-secular forms of religion cannot be interpreted as a return to traditional religion. They presuppose a radical break in the continuity of tradition and a conscious, often selective re-connection with traditions. Therefore post-secular forms of religion are, by definition, post-traditional forms of religion, even if they are programmatically traditionalist. This also means that post-secular forms of religion lack the critical control of tradition. One characteristic feature of tradition, especially in the religions, consist in the fact that traditions contain a rich critical potential, by providing criteria of authenticity (like a canon of religious writings), by defining the status and scope of authority (like a religious hierarchy) and by containing a long history of maintaining continuity through situations of crisis and disruption. Post-secular (and therefore always post-traditional) forms of religion often lack the critical controls and criteria of tradition and therefore tend to be far more radical than traditional forms of religion or tend to have much more direct systems of authority than the balance of authorities in traditional religions.

Another feature that requires attention seems to be that post-secular religion changes the forms of institutionalization in the religions. Many sociologists distinguish between "hard institutions" and "soft institutions". "Hard institutions" are characterized by clearly defined criteria of belonging, statutory rules which define the rights and obligations of members of such an institution, and a fixed "creed" which declares to those inside and to those outside the institution what the institution stands for. "Soft institutions" have a low threshold of belonging, often implicit rules of association, a set of largely tacit attitudes shared by its members rather than an explicit creed and flexible rules of inclusion and exclusion. In many societies, especially in Western Europe, "hard institutions", whether they are churches, trade unions or political parties, seem to have been in decline for some time, not only with regard to their membership but also with regard to their influence in society. "Soft institutions", on the other hand, seem to be on the rise in various forms of voluntary associations, not least because they are much better adapted to flexible systems of supply and demand in a market society. These developments have had a significant influence on the situation of religious pluralism and explain some of the uncertainties of empirical research. Empirical data from surveys focussing on "hard institutions" may state a decline of religion, while at the same time surveys investigating religious attitudes apart from institutional settings may assert a rise of interest in religion. Since "soft institutions" may also develop within "hard institutions" – take, for instance, the numerous Taizé groups within institutionalized churches, which nevertheless have all the characteristics of "soft" institutions – even the distinction between "hard" and "soft" cannot be made precisely. All this belongs to the situation of religious pluralism and presents in itself a task for interpretation.

One further characteristic which is particularly relevant for some of Bonhoeffer's observations of the "religious" exploitation of the private realm is presented by the new constellation of "private" and "public" in the situation of religious pluralism. While the "privatization" of religious beliefs was an integral part of the Enlightenment project the resurgence of religious interest in the situation of religious pluralism has brought the re-entry of religious questions and answers in the public realm. This phenomenon is connected to a general reversal of "public" and "private" in societies dominated by the omnipresence of visual communication media. The inundation with "private" information in public and the staging of the "private" in public has become a persistent feature of a *Lebenswelt* in which nothing seems real unless it is present in the media. However, what no secularization theory could foresee: the religions and religious sensibilities have become part of public culture to such an extent that all areas of public life seem to be interspersed with religious elements.[58] No political problem can be adequately dealt with if one cannot deal with the religious factors shaping the political situation; and religious issues, often represented in symbolic forms, seem to be pervasive in all social situations. Religious pluralism is therefore also characterized by the pluralistic presence of religion in the private realm. One may wonder how the external public expression of religion relates to the internal, "private" engagement with religion.

Although the tendencies which we have briefly sketched here influence almost every aspect of the situation of religious and ideological pluralism we can nevertheless distinguish three distinctive types of pluralistic constellations:

– the *competitive pluralism* of historical religions which is characterized by the conflict of competing religious truth claims, all claiming to offer

---

58 Cf. Casanova, Religions.

comprehensive orientation for the lives of their believers, a situation which is particularly characteristic for the relationship of Christianity and Islam;

– the *combinatory pluralism* of religious *pastiches* which depend on the combination of different religious symbols, mythos, rituals and practices based on aesthetic patterns of inclusivity while suspending dogmatic or ethical claims to exclusivity – the hallmark of postmodern spirituality;[59]

– the pluralism of post-secular quasi-religions where a particular realm of life which achieved its autonomy by being emancipated from an integrative religious framework through being interpreted non-religiously is now interpreted on the analogy of a religious orientation in the world and now exists in the forms of *connective quasi-religions* (e.g. "healthism")[60] or *combative quasi-religions* (e.g. "scientism").[61]

8. Rephrasing Bonhoeffer's question: How can Christ become the Lord of the post-secular religious as well?

Bonhoeffer's question in his time was: "How can Christ become the Lord of the religionless as well?"[62] If the brief remarks that we have made to point to some of the features of the situation of religious and ideological pluralism are correct, our question in our time should be: How can Christ become the Lord of the post-secular religious as well? Can Bonhoeffer's reflections on Christian faith in the situation of religionlessness provide theological inspiration for us in the situation of religious pluralism? The very religious pluralism which followed Bonhoeffer's situation of religionlessness by building upon it in important respects.

If we attempt to take up some of Bonhoeffer's inspirations and develop them further in our situation we should heed his guiding question: "Who is Jesus Christ for us today?" If Bonhoeffer is correct that the claim of Christ is not bound to the situation he sees as characterized by "religion" since this

---

59 Cf. Heelas/Woodhead, Revolution.

60 I call a quasi-religious orientation like healthism a "connective" quasi-religion because it connects both to a realm that achieved its secular interpretation in modernity (the whole field of medicine and health care provision) and to the world of religious symbols, myths and rites so that a formerly secular field is then re-invested with religious significance by intensifying well-being into salvation.

61 "Scientism" is in my view a combative form of quasi-religion since by renewing the "warfare between religion and science" it attempts to criticize religion by replacing its orientational function. An interesting contemporary example is Dawkins, Delusion. Dawkins is also one of the main speakers of the Atheist Alliance International.

62 April 30, 1944. LPP, 280. DBW 8, 404.

is only a temporary garment of Christianity, it seems reasonable to suppose that "religionlessness" can also be seen as such a temporary garment, a transient phase in the history of Christian faith, at least in those aspects which refer to the self-interpretation of a world that has come of age. The claim of Christ also extends to a world that has come of age and has decided to interpret itself religiously again. If that is the case then we should take the situation of religious pluralism seriously as the situation in which God in Christ encounters us today. However, it seems that ours is not a situation where the displacement occurs through the dismissal of God as a "working-hypothesis" but rather through the displacement of God through the inundation of the public realm by diverse gods, goddesses and "quasi deities". Can God in Christ also be present in such a situation? Like Bonhoeffer, we should find our theological resources in a re-reading of Scripture which invites us to discover anew its concern for the identity of the true God in a world of deities and for the flourishing of human life that is liberated by God from the reign of idols.

It is perhaps most helpful to set out our reflections in parallel to the characteristics of "religion" and "religionless Christianity".

a) With regard to *faith* Bonhoeffer's insistence on the comprehensive and holistic character of Christian faith which is not a "something partial" can offer helpful insights into the way Christian faith should be practised in a situation of religious pluralism. The way in which many people in our post-secular age (inside and outside the church) are attracted to forms of spirituality and religious practice in other religions, whether it is in search of a deepening of their spiritual life through forms of meditation derived from other religious traditions or of a religious concern for their bodily health and well-being, calls into question whether Christian faith is indeed a comprehensive and holistic reality for Christian believers, comprising all spheres of life. The religious interest in health and healing in other religious traditions and forms of spirituality, for instance, serves as a clear indication that Christian faith has often lost the dimension of healing so central to the ministry of Jesus. This should not be understood as a plea for "faith healing". Rather, if Bonhoeffer's insistence on the comprehensive character of faith would seem to make it theologically necessary to point to the connections of Christian faith to the development of modern medicine and to reflect on the criteria how medical practice should be conducted if it is informed by the world-view of Christian faith. For Bonhoeffer, Christian faith receives its shape and content through Christ, through the one in whom God has united himself with humanity and the world and has borne the suffering and death of all humanity. The comprehensiveness of faith would therefore also include taking God's presence in Christ seriously in all realms of life and in dealing with all aspects of reality.

b) Concerning knowledge of God, Bonhoeffer's challenge would seem to consist in connecting belief in God not just to special old or new religious aspects of knowledge, but to the totality of our knowledge in all fields of the culture of knowledge. In a situation of religious and ideological pluralism this would mean to make the religious or ideological presuppositions explicit on which the search for knowledge rests. Following Bonhoeffer's hints we should not accept the value neutrality of science as something given and try to adapt our theological knowledge to it. Rather, we should ask which view of reality and which understanding of what it means to be human inform the scientific endeavours in the sciences. Which are the meta-scientific values and principles that inform theory and practise of science? Are they the values and principles that can be squared with the Christian view that humanity achieves its wholeness in being united to God in Christ? In what way would our scientific endeavours have to change if they were shaped not by the aim of perfectibility of humans and their world but by God's presence in the suffering of Christ? In this way we should speak of God not when "human knowledge [...] has come to an end",[63] but with regard to its beginning, the foundations and the framework within which the quest for knowledge is conducted.

c) Just as Bonhoeffer understood the rise of religionlessness not as an accident in the divine economy but as the situation in which God encounters believers in their specific circumstances, so we should see religious pluralism in our times as the situation in which God challenges us. Just as Bonhoeffer insisted that God's transcendence is not other-worldliness but that God wants to be encountered in the world – even where he is pushed out of the world – so we should ask ourselves how God can be encountered in the world of the religions. Just as for Bonhoeffer the situation in which the working-hypothesis God is denied is the situation in which God encounters us. "God lets himself be pushed out of the world on to the cross".[64] Perhaps the displacement of God today has another form. It does not consist in the denial of God but in conflating the reality of God with other gods and goddesses. However, Bonhoeffer wants us to understand this displacement not as God's absence but as the form of God's presence to the world. The presence of God is the suffering of God on the cross of Christ. Bonhoeffer sees at this point the decisive difference between Christianity and other religions:

Here is the decisive difference between Christianity and all other religions. Man's religiosity makes him look to the power of God: God is the deus ex machina. The Bible directs man to God's powerlessness and suffering; only the suffering God can help.[65]

---

63 April 30, 1944. LPP, 281. DBW 8, 407.
64 July 16, 1944. LPP, 360. DBW 8, 534.
65 LPP, 361. DBW 8, 534.

What would that mean for our situation of religious pluralism? If in Christ the world is taken up into communion with God so that the worldliness of the world can be a place for the presence of God, then the religions of the world also have to be understood as a place for the presence of God, although God's presence is mixed up with that of other gods, goddesses or religious ideals. When we encounter the religions of the world from the perspective of faith in Jesus Christ who "is no longer an object of religion, but something quite different, really the Lord of the world",[66] we do not encounter enemy territory but the hidden presence of God. God does not want to exercise his power like a *deus ex machina* from without, but by the transforming presence of the incarnate Lord from within. The suffering of God in the cross of Christ is not God's defeat but the victory of the transforming love of God. This means for the Christian witness to this God that it is called to participate in Christ's being-there-for-others, even for the others of other religions and other paths of religiosity, as the reality of God's transcendence. Being *against* others in trying to demonstrate the superiority of God's omnipotence would be the denial of the God who wants to be there *for* others in the transforming suffering on the cross. Today in the situation of religious pluralism, I suggest, a theology that takes up Bonhoeffer's inspirations should not be a theology of religionlessness but a Christian theology of religions.

d) If we try to adapt Bonhoeffer's insights in anthropology to our situation, his denial of exploiting the weaknesses and sorrows of human beings should inform our attitude to believers of other religions. We should therefore not denounce other religions as idolatry and attempt to make the most of the religious crises which believers of other religions may experience. Bonhoeffer's maxim: "[W]e shouldn't run man down in his worldliness, but confront him with God at his strongest point"[67] should read for us today: We should not run human beings down in their religiousness. Just as Bonhoeffer insisted that people do not have to become religious first so that they can then become Christians, we should not require believers of other religions to become religionless first so that they can then become Christians. The critique of religion outside Christianity and the critique of religion within Christianity is not a precondition for, but a consequence from the encounter with God in Christ. We should value and respect other religions and other forms of religiosity. But this respect necessarily includes witness to the truth of the Gospel of Christ because failure to communicate the truth that has become certain for myself by withholding it from others, perhaps motivated by a misunderstanding of the *disciplina arcana*, is a sure

---

66 April 30, 1944. LPP, 281. DBW 8, 405.
67 July 8, 1944. LPP, 346. DBW 8, 511.

sign of disrespect and a flagrant violation of the commandment of loving one's neighbour, even one's enemies. The relationship of Christians to other religions is an integral part of the witness of the truth of the Gospel. Bonhoeffer's challenge would seem to consist in conducting the Christian witness in such a way that it can participate in Christ's being-there-for-others without the rude tastelessness which Bonhoeffer castigates in many forms of so-called pastoral care.

e) Soteriologically, we should, following Bonhoeffer's insights, hold fast to the exclusive claims that salvation is exclusively God's work and comes through Christ alone, by grace alone and only through faith. Witnessing to the gift of salvation in this exclusiveness includes its comprehensive inclusiveness for the world – even for the world of religions, religiosities and quasi-religions. For Christians, this includes the liberating insight that the ultimate status of the deities of other religions, quasi-religions and of other spiritual paths to the ultimate goal is denied and they are firmly placed in the realm of the penultimate. In a world flooded by deities faith in the God of Jesus Christ is the liberation for worldliness. Before God in Christ the gods become world.[68] However, as Bonhoeffer consistently pointed out, because of Christ no part of the world, even those parts where God is denied or other gods are worshipped, can be entirely devoid of God. The message of salvation does not bring God to a place where he is not, but to a place where he is already present.

f) Ecclesiologically, the church in its attempt at participating in Christ's being-there-for-others must consistently find its orientation in its conformity with Christ. For the church this means "standing by God in his suffering", but knowing, perhaps more intensely in the situation of religious pluralism than ever before, that God's suffering is God's way of coming to all people, to Christians, to the religionless and to the religious, feeding their bodies and their souls, dying the death on the cross, forgiving them all. Perhaps Bonhoeffer's outline for a theology of religions in the situation of religious pluralism is already contained in the last stanza of his poem "Christians and Pagans":

> Gott geht zu allen Menschen in ihrer Not,
> sättigt den Leib und die Seele mit Seinem Brot,
> stirbt für Christen und Heiden den Kreuzestod
> und vergibt ihnen beiden.

---

68 For a theological interpretation of idolatry cf. Schwöbel, Götter.

Bibliography

Primary Sources

BONHOEFFER, D., Widerstand und Ergebung. Briefe und Aufzeichnungen aus der Haft, Dietrich Bonhoeffer Werke, Vol. 8, ed. by Ch. Gremmels/E. Bethge/R. Bethge/I. Tödt, Gütersloh 1998 (= DBW 8).
–, Letters and Papers from Prison. The Enlarged Edition, ed. by E. Bethge, transl. by R. Fuller/ F. Clark et al., New York et al. 1997 (= LPP).
DILTHEY, W., *Weltanschauung* und Analyse des Menschen, Gesammelte Schriften, Vol. 2, Stuttgart/ Göttingen ⁷1964.

Secondary Sources

BERGER, P.L. (Ed.), The *Desecularization* of the World. Resurgent Religion and World Politics, Grand Rapids 1999.
CASANOVA, J., Public *Religions* in the Modern World, Chicago 1994.
COX, H., The Secular City. Secularization and Urbanization in Theological Perspective (1965), 25th anniversary edition, New York 1990.
–, *Turning* East. Why Americans Look to the Orient for Spirituality – And What That Search Can Mean to the West, New York 1978.
–, *Religion* in the Secular City. Toward a Postmodern Theology, New York 1985.
–, Many *Mansions*. A Christian's Encounter with Other Faiths (1988), reprint Boston 1992.
–, *Fire* from Heaven: The Rise of Pentecostal Spirituality and the Re-shaping of Religion in the 21st Century (1994), reprint, publisher 2001.
DAWKINS, R., The God *Delusion*, London et al. 2006.
HEELAS, P./WOODHEAD, L., The Spiritual *Revolution*: Why Religion is Giving Way to Spirituality, Oxford 2005.
ROBINSON, J.T.A., Honest to God, London 1963.
SCHWÖBEL, CH., Art. *Pluralismus* II. Systematisch-theologisch, TRE 26, Berlin/New York 1996, 724–739.
–, Christlicher *Glaube* im Pluralismus. Studien zu einer Theologie der Kultur, Tübingen 2003.
–, *Wiederverzauberung* der Welt? Die Transzendenzen der Kultur und die Transzendenz Gottes, in: Ch. Gestrich/T. Wabel (Ed.), Gott in der Kultur. Moderne Transzendenzerfahrungen und die Theologie, Berlin 2006, 58–86.
–, Du sollst keine anderen Götter haben neben mir. Zur Aktualität des Problems des Götzendienstes in der postmodernen Gesellschaft, in: M. Welker/M. Volf (Ed.), Der lebendige Gott als Trinität. FS für Jürgen Moltmann zum 80. Geburtstag, Gütersloh 2006, 315–337.
VAN BUREN, P.M., The Secular Meaning of the Gospel. Based on an Analysis of Its Language, New York 1963.
WEIZSÄCKER, C.F. VON, Zum *Weltbild* der Physik, Leipzig 1943.

Contributors and Editors

PETER DABROCK. Born 1964. Prof. Dr. theol., MA, Junior-Professor for Socialethics and Bioethics at the Department of Protestant Theology at the University of Marburg. Main research areas: Social Implications of Biomedical Technologies, Theological Understanding of Justice and Meta-ethical Questions in a Perspective of Foundational Theology. Publications include: *Antwortender Glaube und Vernunft*, Stuttgart 2000, *Menschenwürde und Lebensschutz*, Gütersloh 2000, and *Therapeutisches Klonen als Herausforderung der Statusbestimmung menschlicher Embryonen*, Paderborn 2005.

NIELS HENRIK GREGERSEN. Born 1957. PhD, Professor, Department of Systematic Theology, University of Copenhagen. Main reseach areas: 20th Century theology, Constructive theology and Science & religion. Publications include: *The Human Person in Science and Theology*, Edinburgh 2000, *From Complexity to Life*, Oxford 2003, and *The Gift of Grace: The Future of Lutheran Theology*, Minneapolis 2005.

BARRY HARVEY. Born 1954. Professor of Theology, Honors College and the Graduate Program in Religion, Baylor University. Main research areas: Theological Hermeneutics, Dogmatic Theology and Moral Theology. Publications include: *Politics of the Theological: Beyond the Piety and Power of A World Come of Age*, Bern/Berlin/Bruxelles et al. 1995, *Another City: An Ecclesiological Primer for a Post-Christian World*, Harrisburg 1999, and *Prophesy to These Bones: Re-membering the Church as the Body of Christ* (forthcoming), Grand Rapids 2008.

KIRSTEN BUSCH NIELSEN. Born 1962. PhD, Ass. Prof., Department of Systematic Theology, University of Copenhagen. Main research areas: Theology of Dietrich Bonhoeffer, Theology of Sacraments, Ecclesiology. Publications include: *Teologi og omvendelse. Introduktion til Bernard Lonergan* (Theology and Conversion), Copenhagen 1996, *Dietrich Bonhoeffer*, Copenhagen 2000 (^{2}2004), and *Nadver and Folkekirke* (Eucharist and 'Folkchurch'), Copenhagen 2002.

ULRIK NISSEN. Born 1969. PhD, Ass. Prof., University of Aarhus. Main research areas: Christian Ethics, Social Ethics, Dietrich Bonhoeffer. Publications include: *The Christological Ontology of Reason*, in: NZSTh 48, 2006, 460–478, *Luther between Present and Past. Studies in Luther and Lutheranism*, ed. by Ulrik Nissen/Anna Vind/Bo Holm/Olli-Pekka Vainio, Helsinki 2004, and *The Sources of Public Morality – On the Ethics and*

Religion Debate, ed. by Ulrik Nissen/Svend Andersen/Lars Reuter, Münster/ Hamburg/Berlin et al. 2003.

ANDREAS PANGRITZ. Born 1954. Dr., Professor of Systematic Theology and Director of the Ecumenical Institute at the University of Bonn. Main research areas: Bonhoeffer studies, Aspects of the Jewish-Christian relationship and Friedrich-Wilhelm Marquardt's theological approach. Publications include: *Karl Barth in the Theology of Dietrich Bonhoeffer*, Grand Rapids 2000, *Polyphonie des Lebens. Über Dietrich Bonhoeffers "Theologie der Musik"*, Berlin ²2000, and *Vom Kleiner- und Unsichtbarwerden der Theologie. Ein Versuch über das Projekt einer "impliziten Theologie" bei Barth, Tillich, Bonhoeffer, Benjamin, Horkheimer und Adorno*, Tübingen 1996.

PETER MANLEY SCOTT. Born 1961. Dr., Senior Lecturer and Director of the Lincoln Theological Institute, the University of Manchester. Main research areas: Theological anthropology, Doctrine of creation and Political Theology. Publications include: *Theology, Ideology and Liberation*, Cambridge 1994, *A Political Theology of Nature*, Cambridge 2003, and *Blackwell Companion to Political Theology*, Malden, paperback edition 2006.

CHRISTOPH SCHWÖBEL. Born 1955. Dr., Professor for Systematic Theology and Director of the Institute for Hermeneutics and Dialogue of Cultures at the University of Tübingen. Main research areas: Key questions of Dogmatics, Ecumenics, Interreligious and Intercultural Dialogue. Publications include: *Martin Rade. Das Verhältnis von Geschichte, Religion und Moral als Grundproblem seiner Theologie*, Gütersloh 1980, *God: Action and Revelation*, Kampen 1992, *Gott in Beziehung. Studien zur Dogmatik*, Tübingen 2002, *Christlicher Glaube im Pluralismus. Studien zu einer Theologie der Kultur*, Tübingen 2003.

CHRISTIANE TIETZ. Born 1967. PD Dr., Heisenberg-scholarship holder of the Deutsche Forschungsgemeinschaft and Privatdozentin for Systematic Theology at the University of Tuebingen. Main research areas: Dietrich Bonhoeffer, Religion and Politics, and Interreligious Dialogue. Publications include: *Bonhoeffers Kritik der verkrümmten Vernunft. Eine erkenntnistheoretische Untersuchung*, Tübingen 1999, and *Freiheit zu sich selbst. Entfaltung eines christlichen Begriffs von Selbstannahme*, Göttingen 2005.